CHINESE FOOTPRINTS:

EXPLORING WOMEN'S HISTORY IN CHINA, HONG KONG AND MACAU

SUSANNA HOE

ROUNDHOUSE PUBLICATIONS (ASIA) LTD

Published in Hong Kong by:

Roundhouse Publications (Asia) Ltd

409 Yu Yuet Lai Building

43-55 Wyndham Street

Central, Hong Kong

© Susanna Hoe 1996

ISBN: 962-7992-03-8

Editor Robyn Flemming

Design George Ngan/New Strategy

Cover George Ngan/New Strategy

Layout Polly Yu Production Ltd

Cover: Snuff bottles from Canton depict Soong Ching Ling (right) and
an unknown European woman (left)

Printed and bound in Hong Kong.

This publication is supported by the Hong Kong Arts Development
Council; the opinions expressed do not necessarily represent their views.

Also by Susanna Hoe: *Lady in the Chamber* (Collins, 1971); *God Save the Tsar* (Michael
Joseph/St Martins Press, 1978); *The Man Who Gave His Company Away: A Biography of Ernest
Bader, Founder of the Scott Bader Commonwealth* (Heinemann, 1978); *The Private Life of Old Hong
Kong: Western Women in the British Colony 1841-1941* (Oxford University Press, 1991).

FOR DEREK
ALWAYS AND EVERYWHERE

AUTHOR'S NOTE

It is impossible to standardise the romanisation of Chinese names, particularly for historians. Throughout the book I have used the historical system of Wade-Giles, or international convention, or Hong Kong usage. Where appropriate, I have put the more modern Pinyin in brackets when it is used for the first time in the book. And two versions are then in the index and biographical notes. But brackets would be clumsy for the more informal pieces. There I have sometimes had to mix, depending on which name is generally better known. Peking is Beijing throughout; but Peking University insists on retaining that name in English. I have consistently used Soong Ching Ling for Mme Sun Yatsen/Song Qingling.

Scholars of the writer Xiao Hong (Hsiao Hung) now use Pinyin. In the four chapters about her, therefore, Pinyin is to the fore.

I apologise for all inconsistencies – a lot of effort has gone into making my transliterations reader-friendly.

Another issue that could lead to confusion is the variety of subjects, periods, places and characters I have introduced. I have therefore prepared biographical details to help make more easily recognisable those who are mentioned most frequently within a chapter or across chapters.

Notes and bibliographies – where they exist – are at the end of each chapter.

Differences in styles and tone are explained in the introduction.

Entries in the index, for example under history and research, show how themes have been developed.

ACKNOWLEDGEMENTS

As I venture into writing about Chinese women, my first thanks must be to those who have translated and interpreted for me. Without Simon Che Wai-kwan's generous translations, I could not have written about Xiao Hong; and without Yu Jing's interpreting I could not have interviewed Xiao Hong's husband, Duanmu Hongliang. Yu Jing also translated my letters to Duanmu into Chinese, and the relevant parts of four draft chapters. I thank Duanmu not only for twice seeing me but also for a long letter and much patience. Jora Ma took me to visit Koon Sau Chan, formerly of St Stephen's Girls College, and interpreted for me. Eva Hung interpreted when I first met Xiao Si (Lo Wai-luen). Xiao Si was too modest about her English, and the most generous scholar.

Zhao Yuhong paraphrased and translated material for me on Shi Liang. Again, I could not have written that chapter without her. She has also read the chapters on China, checking for transliteration and other infelicities. Others who gave me invaluable guidance and information about my Chinese characters were, in Beijing, Ruth Weiss (biographer of Lu Xun), Israel (Eppy) Epstein (biographer of Soong Ching Ling), Huang Wanbi and Xiao Qian. Professor Tao Jie (Peking University) prompted my work on Xiao Hong; she deserves my special thanks.

In the United States, the biographers Howard Goldblatt (Xiao Hong) and Steve Mackinnon (Agnes Smedley) have been most patient. I must particularly acknowledge Howard Goldblatt's inspiring translations of Xiao Hong's work. Dr Alison Conner brought Shi Liang to my attention and added important details and read the chapter. In Australia, Dr Lily Xiao Hong Lee directed me to works on Shi Liang in Chinese and later read the completed chapter.

I wish I could give individual details here of all the help I have received. Often, fellow researchers and other informants are thanked, implicitly or explicitly, in the text or notes; our relations are part of practising history. I thank, formally but warmly, the following (in alphabetical order); first, for help with the chapters about Xiao Hong: Dr Solomon Bard, Dr Kay Barker, the late Mary Baxter, Phillip Bruce, Sir Oswald Cheung, Sansan Ching, Florence Chiu, Hugh Chiverton, Joan Lebold Cohen, Amy Corney, Tom Cowlam, Geoffrey Emerson, Sir Kenneth Fung, Professor David Geggus, Louise Mary Gill (Billie Lee), Gerald Godfrey (and his staff), Emily Hahn, Cora Ho, Susan Kay, Anthony Lawrence, Dr Ellen Li, Professor Ma Meng, Judith Richardson, Lady Ride, Dr Mary Seed, Anne Selby (for use of her picture library), Margaret Watson Sloss, Dr Anthony Sweeting, Joseph Tam, Agnes Wong.

For help with other chapters: Helene Avissau, Lady Badenoch, Anthony Barton, Pat and Geoffrey Burnstone, Peggy Cheng, Dr Irene Cheng, Barbara Clarke, Lord and Lady de Clifford, Shann Davies, Baroness Dunn, Patrick Ensor, Father Ernest Even, Wilma Fairbank, Peter Ward Fay (whom, to my chagrin, I omitted from the acknowledgements of *The Private Life of Old Hong Kong*), (staff of) the Fung Ping Shan Library, University of Hong Kong, Valery Garrett, Olive Geddes (National Library of Scotland), Moya Germain, the late Jean Gittins, General Ho Shai Lai, Nan Hodges, Clare Hollingworth, Chris Holmes, Arthur Jacobs, Dr Linda Koo, Dr Clara Lau (who invited me to write about Clara and Margaret Ho Tung), Margaret Lee (Hongkong and Shanghai Bank), Liu Ru Ping, Lo Tak-shing, Vera Lo, Pat Loseby, Sujata Madhok (Women's Feature Service), Joan von Mehren, Mei Ling, Dr Suzanne Miers, Dr Norman Miners, Lord Minto, Morden College, Lilian Sartorius, Geeta Singh, Paul Tam (John Leung Studios), Alison Taylor (Wesleyan Chapel and Leysian Centre), Dr Joseph Ting (Hong Kong Museum of History, who took us to Whampoa), Dr Elsie Tu, Professor Wang Guiguo, Professor Wang Liming, Margaret Wang, Christina Ward, Frank Welsh, Professor Peter Wesley-Smith, Bradley Winterton, Alice Wong, Lorna Workman, Yip Shuk-ping, Judy Young (*South China Morning Post* library). Dr Elizabeth Sinn's door has always been open at the History Workshop of Hong Kong University.

Individuals and institutions have given me permissions, for which I thank them and for their help: the late Diana Shipton Drummond, the Fleming family, Han Suyin (and for her encouragement), *The Liverpool Daily Post and Echo*, Ella Maillart, Syndics of the University Library, Cambridge (Stella Benson's diaries).

Several friends have helped particularly with the introduction, 'Lighting the Corridors', the tone of which was not easy to get right. I would like to thank them specially: Miguel Azaola, Marianne Dever, Margaret Kitchen, Janet Salaff, Pat Elliott Shircore. And several friends have patiently and responsively read other chapters: Geoffrey Weatherill Bonsall, Patrick Conner (who gave substance to 'Who Was Clara Elliot?'), Staci Ford (who read the whole book), Dr Maria Jaschok (much involved with 'It Made Their Blood Boil'), Christopher Munn. The reaction of my mother, Joanna Hoe, has also been important. Carl T. Smith, as always, deserves special thanks for information, opinion and support. His name appears often in the chapters that follow.

One of those to whom my last book was dedicated, Sione Latukefu, died in 1995. His loss to the writing of the history of the South Pacific, and the loss of his friendship, are immeasurable.

At last I am able to dedicate a book just to my husband, Derek Roebuck. Our wedding anniversary this year, I have decided, should be marked by paper. The dedication is, therefore, more than ever appropriate. His help has also been intensely practical.

Four professionals have shown special faith in my work, for which I thank them: Stephanie Holmes (formerly of Holmes Literary Agency); Frances Bartlett and Debra Maynard of Roundhouse Publications (Asia) Ltd; and Robyn Flemming (editor). I also thank Polly Yu.

Finally, this publication is supported by the Hong Kong Arts Development Council; the opinions expressed do not necessarily represent their views. I thank them for their support.

Hong Kong, May 1996

CONTENTS

Some Biographical Details

BAYNES, Julia (née Smith) (1793-1881). Called by Harriett Low 'the prettiest woman in Macao'; also known as first to flout Chinese rule against Western women in Canton (1830). Husband William was then President of East India Company's Select Committee.

BENSON, Stella (1892-1933). Novelist and women's rights activist. Lived Hong Kong 1930-1932 and, with Gladys Forster, campaigned against licensed prostitution.

CH'EN Yuanyuan, also known as the 'Roundfaced Beauty'. Favourite concubine of General Wu San-kuei (Wu Sangui) (1612-1678). Said to have caused downfall of Ming Dynasty (1644).

CONNER, Patrick. Informant – see acknowledgements; author of *George Chinnery 1774-1852: Artist of India and the China Coast* (1993).

DANIELL, Harriet. Wife of Anthony Stewart, merchant. Arrived Macau 1834; probably lived Franciscan Green; George Chinnery sketched her (1838); left Macau 1839.

DANIELL, Jane (née LeGeyt). Wife of James Frederick Nugent (J.F.N.), Chief Agent, East India Company, until 1834. They married in Macau 1823; she left early 1836; described in warm terms by Clara Elliot.

DENG, Cora. Head of YWCA Labour Bureau, Shanghai (late 1920s); secretary of YWCA (1936); organised night schools for women factory workers.

Deng Yingzhao (see Teng Ying-chao)

Ding Ling (see Ting Ling)

EDEN, Emily (1797-1869). Writer of letters home from India where her brother Lord Auckland was Governor General and responsible for Britain's relations with China (1835-1842). First cousin of Captain Charles Elliot.

ELLIOT, Clara (née Windsor) (c.1806-1885). Wrote letters home to sister-in-law Emma Hislop from Macau (1834-1841); wife of Captain Charles Elliot (1801-1875), British Plenipotentiary at time of Hong Kong's cession to Britain by China (1841). Eldest child was Harriet Agnes (1829-1896), m. 1852 Edward Russell, later Lord de Clifford.

FORSTER, Gladys (née Jennings) (1894-1982). Teacher and women's rights activist. Lived Hong Kong 1918-1937; responsible, with Stella Benson, for campaign against licensed prostitution; ran school for prostitutes with Ruby Mow Fung.

FUNG, Ruby Mow (1894-1956). Christian activist. Ran To Kwong Girls School (for prostitutes), Miu Nam Street, Yaumatei, Hong Kong (c.1931-1936); helped Stella Benson and Gladys Forster with research.

HASELWOOD, Clara (née Taylor) (born c.1875). Instigated campaign against *mui tsai* system. She and husband Hugh took campaign to England when her activities caused his resignation; wrote *Child Slavery in Hong Kong: The Mui Tsai System* (1930).

HISLOP, Emma (Lady, née Elliot) (1794-1866). Recipient of letters from Charles, her brother, and Clara Elliot at Charlton Villa, southeast London. Looked after their children. Emma's daughter Nina (1824-1882) later married a cousin and became Countess of Minto, perhaps explaining how the letters came to be among the Minto papers.

HO Hsiang-ning (He Xiangning) (1876-1972). Women's and civil rights activist and painter. Born Hong Kong but active in China; Chair Women's Department, Wuhan (1927); member China League for the Protection of Civil Rights (1932-1933); joint-founder Shanghai Women's National Salvation Association (1936); honorary chair China Women's Federation (post-1949); known for revolutionary bobbed hair; widow of Liao Chung-kai (Liao Zhungkai) assassinated 1925.

HO TUNG, (Lady) Clara (Ho Cheung Ching-yung) (1875-1938). Buddhist philanthropist. Set up Po Ko Primary School for Girls, Hong Kong and Macau (1930) and Tung Lin Kok Yuen Buddhist Temple Complex (1933). Married Robert Ho Tung as second but 'level' wife (1881), 10 children.

HO TUNG, Margaret (Lady) (Mak Sau-ying) (1865-1944). Agriculturalist; first wife of Robert Ho Tung. On Ho Tung land near Sheung Shui, New Territories, Hong Kong, created farm, Tung Ying Hok P'o; experimented with rearing silkworms and growing smaller mulberry trees.

HODGES, Nan. Preparing journals of Harriett Low for publication; informant concerning Low journals.

HSIEH Ping-ying (Xie Bingying) (c.1903-). Writer and feminist. Took part in Northern Expedition 1926-1927; best known for *Autobiography of a Chinese Girl* (1943; written 1928).

KOO, Madame Wellington (Oei Hu-lan) (c.1887 or c.1899-1990). Socialite. Married, 1919, 3rd wife, diplomat V.K. Wellington Koo (Koo Wei-chun) (1887-1985); wrote *No Feast Lasts for Ever* (1975).

KUAN YIN, Chinese Goddess of Mercy (or Compassion). Popularly believed to have been a princess who became a nun over parental objection.

LATTIMORE, Eleanor Holgate (1894-1970). Teacher, historian and traveller. In 1927 travelled overland from Beijing to British India via Kashgar with new husband Owen (1900-1989); wrote *Turkestan Reunion* (1934).

LEI TSU (Lei Zu), also known as Lady Hsi Ling (fl.2602 BC). Legendary empress and goddess. Inventor or discoverer of silk; patron saint of silkworkers. Wife of Third, or Yellow, Emperor Huang Ti (Huang Di) (2698-2598 BC).

LI, Ellen, CBE, LLD, JP, also known as Mrs Ellen Li Shu-pui (m. 1936) (née Tsao Sau Kwan) (Saigon 1908-). Women's rights activist and legislator. First woman appointed to Legislative Council, Hong Kong (1966-1973); responsible for legislation abolishing legal status of concubines (1970-1971); founder/president/chair Chinese Women's Club (1938); founder/president Hong Kong Council of Women (1947).

LITTLE, Alicia (née Bewicke) (1845-1926). Women's rights activist. Joined husband Archibald in China (1887); founded Anti-Foot Binding Committee, Shanghai (1895) and campaigned widely in China and Hong Kong; vice-president Women's Conference Shanghai (1900). Best-known books, *Intimate China* (1899) and *In the Land of the Blue Gown* (1912).

LOW , Harriett (Harriet) (both spellings found, although current editor of journals uses Harriett) (1809-1877). Lived Macau (1829-1834) with uncle William, senior partner in American trading firm Russell and Company; kept journal, nine volumes of which are invaluable source material in various abridged, published and unpublished forms.

MA Ying-piu (née Fok Hing-tong) (1872-1957). Known as first Chinese woman in Hong Kong with a public position; only woman on Anti *Mui Tsai* Society organising committee (1922).

MACARTNEY, Catherine (née Borland) (c.1877-1949). In 1898 joined new husband George (1867-1945) in Kashgar where he had been posted since 1890 (Consul-General 1912); she stayed there 17 years and was responsible for house (Chinibagh, built 1913) praised by visitors; wrote *An English Lady in Chinese Turkestan* (1931).

MAILLART, Ella (Kini) (1903-) Sportswoman, traveller, writer. Olympic yachtswoman (1924); world-class skier for Switzerland (1931-1934); travelled to Soviet Central Asia (1932) and wrote *Turkestan Solo* (1934); travelled with Peter Fleming (1907-1971) from Beijing to British India (1935); wrote *Forbidden Journey* (1937).

NEVILLE-ROLFE, Sybil, OBE (née Burney) (c.1885-1955). General-secretary National Council for Combating Venereal Disease. Joint-author confidential report on Hong Kong for British Colonial Office (1921); on inquiry into re-introduction of state regulation of prostitution in Singapore (1925).

PITTS, Ada (b. c.1865). Missionary (Church Missionary Society) and social reformer. In Hong Kong c.1904-1922; worked with Lucy Eyre in Hong Kong Refuge for Chinese Women and Girls (prostitutes) (1904); spoke out against child labour (1918); leading to Child Labour Ordinance 1922; informant for anti *mui tsai,* venereal disease and licensed prostitution campaigns.

SHI Liang (1900-1985). Civil rights lawyer and activist, one of 'the Seven Gentlemen' (1936) and Minister for Justice (1949-1959). Engaged by China League for the Protection of Civil Rights (1932/1933); chair Shanghai Women's National Salvation Association (1935); executive committee All-China League National Salvation Association; founding member China Democratic League; involved in formulation and implementation of Marriage Law (1950).

SHIPTON, Diana (née Channer, later Drummond) (c.1917-1995). In 1946 joined mountaineer husband Eric in Kashgar where he was Consul-General (and 1940-1942); left 1948 (he died 1977); wrote *The Antique Land* (1950).

SHUCK, Henrietta (née Hall) (1817-1844). American Baptist missionary and teacher. Arrived Macau 1836; concerned with well-being and education of Chinese girls and women; died in childbirth early days of Hong Kong.

SMEDLEY, Agnes (1892-1950). Radical American journalist and activist. Arrived China 1928; one of only two Western members of China League for the Protection of Civil Rights. Best known for autobiographical novel *Daughter of Earth* (1929) and reportage *Battle Hymn of China* (1943).

SMITH, Carl T. Informant – see acknowledgements. Author of *Chinese Christians; Elites, Middlemen, and the Church in Hong Kong* (1985), and *A Sense of History: Studies in the Society and Urban History of Hong Kong* (1995).

SOONG Ching Ling (Soong Qingling) (Mme Sun Yat-sen – m. 1915) (Rosamunde – Western name) (1892-1981). Revolutionary and post-revolutionary icon and women's rights activist; founder China League for the Protection of Civil Rights (1932); executive committee All-China League National Salvation Association; vice-chair government, People's Republic of China; named honorary chair on her deathbed. (Her sister Soong Mei-ling married Chiang Kai-shek.)

STRONG, Anna Louise, PhD (1885-1970). Radical American journalist. Visited China first 1924; Chungking 1940; interviewed Mao Tse-tung, Yenan (1946); lived China from 1958; wrote, among other books on China, *China's Millions* (1928).

SYKES, Ella (c.1863-1939). Traveller and women's rights activist. Accompanied brother Percy to Kashgar 1915 when he temporarily relieved Sir George Macartney; wrote, with Percy, *Through Desert Oases of Central Asia* (1920); after similar experience, wrote *Through Persia on a Side Saddle* (1901).

TENG Ying-chao (Deng Yingzhao) (1903/1904-1992). Revolutionary and women's rights activist. Active in May Fourth Movement; joined Communist Party and married Chou En-lai (1925); vice-chair Women's Department, Wuhan (1927); took part in Long March (1934-1935); first vice-president All-China Federation of Democratic Women (1949).

TING Ling (Ding Ling) (1905/1907-1986). Communist and feminist writer. Kidnapped 1933; rescued by China League for the Protection of Civil Rights; joined Communist Party 1931 but in conflict with it 1942 and 1955; best known for *The Diary of Miss Sophie* (1928) and *The Sun Shines Over the Sangkan River* (1951).

WEISS, Ruth (1908-). Writer. Arrived Shanghai from Austria 1933; joined circle of progressive Westerners, e.g. Agnes Smedley; settled in China 1951; wrote *Lu Xun: A Writer For All Times* (1955); her autobiography in English and German in preparation; informant – see acknowledgements and notes.

XIAO Hong (Hsiao Hung; pen-name of Chang Nai-ying) (1911-1942). Autobiographical writer. Born Hulan, Heilongjiang, died Hong Kong. Protegée of writer Lu Xun (1881-1936); m. Xiao Jun 1932, Duanmu Hongliang 1938 (both pen-names), patron in Hong Kong literary editor Zhou Jingwen (*Shidai Piping*). Best known for *The Field of Life and Death* (1935) and *Tales of Hulan River* (1941).

XIAO Si (pen-name of Lo Wai-luen), Hong Kong scholar (Chinese University) and newspaper columnist. My informant on Xiao Hong – see acknowledgements.

YU Jing, graduate, Law School, Peking University; now postgraduate student City University, Hong Kong. Informant and interpreter, Beijing – see acknowledgements.

PHOTOGRAPHS

CHAPTER I

LIGHTING
THE CORRIDORS
Introduction

When strangers find out that I write women's history, their first question is nearly always, 'How do you do your research?' Or, 'Where do you get your material?' They suspect that material and information are not as readily available about women as about men. How do you answer such a question in one sentence, or even a paragraph? You need a book. This is it.

I have gone a little further. There are at least four aspects to the re-creation of history: deciding what or who to write about, and why; seeking the facts; your relationship with your characters; and how you present the result. The book attempts to cover all these aspects.

The chapters are set in China, Hong Kong and Macau. Their order started as a convenience but ended by emphasising the underlying link within a region the component parts of which have been somewhat separated by recent history – a transient separation. The encylopaedia entry on Clara Ho Tung, who moved easily between the three places, symbolises this relationship – one given an added twist by the fact that she was both Chinese and European.

Sometimes, too, an event or social condition is referred to in more than one chapter and is cross-referenced; and some characters straddle more than one story. Nevertheless, the pieces are often distinct, not necessarily or overtly connected by a character or period, a place or a series of events. The structure is episodic. The unifying theme is the author's exploration of the re-creation of history. And, because it is my search, it is personal.

For an introduction to anthropology course some years ago, I read Laura Bohannan's *Return to Laughter* (1954). As a respected anthropologist, she had taken the risk of exposing – apparently in the form of a novel (and under a pseudonym) – the underbelly of her discipline. She had written not a scholarly study of the West African people among whom she worked, but a personal account of how she lived with them. I was much taken by her daring in so revealing herself and the reality of her anthropologist's trade, and I have been influenced by that experiment.

The intensity with which Bohannan became involved with her villagers is the same as that I feel for my historical characters. The relations between me (the re-creator) and the women whose lives I am exploring exist in their own right, beyond the writing of conventional history.

I go to meet my characters whenever possible in their place. Many historians, particularly biographers, do the same. And I am not the first to write about the travelling side of historical writing. When I was writing about Fanny Osbourne, Robert Louis Stevenson's wife, I panted up the hill above Vailima in Western Samoa where they are both buried. And, at the same time, I bought Richard Holmes's *Footsteps: Adventures of a Romantic Biographer* (1985), because part of it was about Stevenson's own travels in France and how Holmes tracked him. Holmes's book is much more autobiographical than mine, and we are not necessarily exploring the same ideas, but his book has remained on my shelves, beaming certain waves at me.

I started travelling in the footsteps of my characters, tracing their footprints, long before that. In 1975, I took a train from Moscow to Odessa specially so that I could travel through the Steppes as Nicholas and Alexandra did in my historical novel *God Save the Tsar* (1978). The journey was not entirely rewarding. Most of it took place at night, and what daylight there was revealed poplar trees growing right up against the track on either side. Those were the days when it was easy to assume a sinister purpose; further travels have taught me that poplars act as an essential windbreak in many parts of the world.

In Odessa I had hoped to see a bit of the town as the imperial family might have seen it. But by then the 'flu that had been building up during the journey had laid me too low to do anything but hope I would somehow make the boat to Istanbul. That unsuccessful exercise failed to cool my continuing passion for sniffing out the 'spirit of place' and seeing embedded in that place my historical character. It also taught me the advantages of showing, as I do here, the processes and prejudices by which facts are established.

Often I do not choose what to write about: sometimes I am approached to write about a particular character; sometimes the character herself intrudes; or a contemporary issue that seems burning to me may introduce relevant historical characters. In *The Private Life of Old Hong Kong* (1991), a history of Western women in the colony, I explained that it would have been presumptuous of me to write about Chinese women. Since then, I have worked hard at learning not only about Hong Kong women past and present, but also about women in China itself, and over a longer period. In the next chapter, 'Sisters of the Mulberry Leaf', I illustrate how I have tried to extend my knowledge and understanding of Chinese women through the process of writing about them.

In later chapters, I write both about individual Chinese women and about the interaction between Chinese and Western women. In doing so, I raise or explore issues such as ethnocentricity, different perceptions of women and feminism in the West and in China, human rights, colonialism and universality.

Since I use the words 'feminist' and 'feminism' from time to time, and across time and cultures, I should explain what I mean. A woman is a feminist when she is conscious of her gender and strives to extend the rights of herself and other women. This search for equality may be as an activist or through her writing. It is not enough simply to get ahead oneself as if there were no inequality.

In the chapter on travel through Chinese Central Asia, the Western accounts of a woman and a man who travelled together are compared, raising different gender issues, as well as the perceptions of the biographer compared with those of her subject.

While most of the chapters are about different characters, two Chinese women and one Westerner are treated at greater length than others. One is Soong Ching Ling (sometimes better known as Mme Sun Yat-sen). She flits in and out of six chapters. This was unplanned and, in suggesting something about her as a historical character, it also gives a flavour of the book. The characters are yeast rather than pawns. (My informants behave similarly.)

The radical American Agnes Smedley is also mentioned quite frequently. The last four chapters are about the North East Chinese writer Xiao Hong; in the longest of these, her life and writing are compared with Smedley's.

As for 'the Seventh Gentleman', Shi Liang is a woman. In the revolutionary pantheon of 1936 – which includes Soong Ching Ling and Agnes Smedley – her gender was subsumed in that of her male collaborators, known as 'the Seven Gentlemen'. As the chapter on Shi Liang shows, she was very much a person, and a woman, in her own right. And yet, even where her identity has been explicit, she has merited barely a footnote in China's history. My most obvious purpose in that chapter is to redress the balance, to give Shi Liang her due.

But chapters such as that hint at another strand to my methodology of exploring, re-creating and writing history. History does not stop when my character dies. It rolls on and on until finally it reaches the present. I, too, am part of the evolving story, and not only as an observer standing physically where my characters have stood.

My direct descent emerges most clearly from the chapter 'It Made Their Blood Boil: The British Feminist Campaign Against Licensed Prostitution in Hong Kong, 1931'. There I see myself quite clearly as a link in a historical chain. One woman passes on the torch to another and, if you choose to take it, then you have a responsibility to carry on their work, in this case Stella Benson and Gladys Forster's efforts on behalf of women in Hong Kong. The last section of that chapter – 'Western Feminists in Hong Kong Today' – rather obliquely explores that phenomenon, together with that of 'interference' by Western women in Chinese society.

By no means all the chapters and episodes carry this heavy message. And the others are not written with the same consciously analytical intent, recasting material from earlier more descriptive work. Sometimes I spell out inferences that can be drawn; sometimes I refrain from doing so. The writer should do all the work for the reader in terms of style and accessibility; but I also believe that the writer should provide the spark to a silent inner conversation – that the reader should be left the pleasure of dotting some of the intellectual I's and crossing the T's. That space may be particularly useful to teachers.

The chapters deliberately suggest not just the versatility of research material and means of engaging the reader, but also a variety of styles of historical writing and presentation. Sometimes there is the full scholarly apparatus of notes and a bibliography; sometimes there is just a bibliography. One or two pieces were written as newspaper columns or articles; others make use of my diaries or letters. Some are accounts of my experience, perception or adventure while tracking footprints left by historical characters. In one chapter I follow several Western women who lived in the same place – Kashgar – over time. These chapters can also be used simply as a women's travel guide.

Some pieces chronicle the convolutions of researching. Those about Clara Elliot show how compulsive and intricate research can become. There may even be tips for students not yet familiar with the ropes, for the first was originally a guest lecture to a women's studies history class at the University of Hong Kong; indeed, I have purposely retained the oral style and cadences of an informal lecture.

In the chapter on International Women's Day, I demonstrate my belief that (women's) history should be functional at the most practical level. I wrote the chapter primarily because, although we celebrate Women's Day in Hong Kong with gusto, the details of its long and inspirational history have been obscure. But, in ending the chapter with the position of women in Hong Kong at that moment in their history, 1995, I intended that part to stimulate action. To that extent I sent it to the (international) Women's Feature Service, and to the local radio station, asking to appear to discuss the issues. It should be said that the

Women's Feature Service thwarted me by asking for a more 'international' ending; I have kept both endings in the chapter. We have since won the campaign for women's voting rights in Hong Kong's New Territories. The chapter 'The New Concubines' is even more specific about setting the search for solutions within the context of the past.

The same functional imperative, though without the social aim, was behind the broadcast I made about the progress of my research into Xiao Hong's life and death in Hong Kong. I was seeking further information, illustrating a stage of research and demonstrating a possible research tool. I was also putting down a marker for this book!

In presenting women's history in this idiosyncratic way, I have consciously sacrificed the theoretical aspects to the practical. In exploring it as a tool to be used constructively – in practising women's history – I am haunted by the image conjured up by Virginia Woolf: 'Those unlit corridors of history where the figures of generations of women are so dimly, so fitfully lit.'

CHAPTER 2

SISTERS OF THE MULBERRY LEAF
Women, Silk and History

Moon thin as water
And candlelight
Shine upon China
A sleeping silkworm
Exhaling a long long thread of silk
On a nine-hundred and sixty thousand square miles
Mulberry leaf.

Li Xiaoyu (1951-)
'The Silk Dream', *Women of the Red Plain*

When you are trying to gain access to the women of another culture through their history, and you do not speak or read the language, a metaphor may be helpful. And you may come across it by serendipity, as I did.

In a second-hand book shop, I bought a rather tatty copy of volume LXVI (1935) of the journal of the North China Branch of the Royal Asiatic Society. In it was an article called 'The Worship of Lei Tsu, Patron Saint of Silkworkers'. Lei Tsu (Lei Zu) caught my imagination, particularly when I read that there was an altar to her in a suburb of Beijing. With my passion for visiting sites connected with women wherever I travel, thus to distil and imbibe the 'spirit of place' most pleasurably, I started planning.

Soon I realised that mulberry trees, silkworms, silk and the making of it say a lot about the women of China from earliest times. The irony is that silk has shrouded women in luxury and in poverty, and has brought them both freedom and exploitation. And, because silk from China has appealed to women elsewhere for nearly a thousand years, it becomes a link between women across time and space.

If silk itself is a metaphor for Chinese women, the mulberry leaf, as the above poem by a woman shows, is a metaphor for China. The great landmass (960,000 square miles) is shaped like a mulberry leaf, with its tip reaching into the heart of Central Asia, home of the Silk Road along which the invaluable commodity was taken to Europe. There, too, in the caves of Tun-huang (Dunhuang), was found the Diamond Sutra, the world's oldest known printed document, over a thousand years after its creation in AD 868. The paper on which it was printed was probably made from mulberry bark.

This chapter, then, is a non-academic, Western-oriented effort to explore the metaphor of silk through a series of historical sketches. In the writing of them, I have learned more about Chinese women and

Feeding Silkworms, and Sorting the Cocoons;
engraving by T. Allom and A. Willmore

their history than reading through histories of China in which women seldom appear. Their history has, indeed, become 'a long long thread of silk'. And, because in the end I found the altar of Lei Tsu, this chapter says something too about my method of research and writing, and my relationship with the characters I write about.

It was a woman, an empress, a goddess, who 'discovered' silk back in the mists of time. And, because it is legendary, you can choose which story to accept. The one I prefer is of how Lady Hsi Ling was wandering in her garden in 2602 BC when she came across an 'ugly worm' chewing the leaves of a mulberry tree. She stopped herself killing it when she realised that the 'daughter of Heaven' would not notice such a thing without reason. This worm was a reincarnated ancestor. Day by day she watched as the cocoon spun by the worm gave way to a spool of natural silk.[1]

Until then, people had dressed in skins. Hsi Ling discovered how to care for silkworms and nurtured the rise of silk weaving and the production of textiles which were not only to clothe but also to indicate the status of officials thereafter. Thus she became deified as Lei Tsu.

Historically, she is known variously as Lady Hsi Ling, wife of the Third Emperor, or Yellow Emperor Huang Ti (Huang Di) (2698-2598 BC); Lei Tsu, 'patron of the silkworkers' or 'Goddess of Silk'; or Hsien T'san, meaning 'the inventor of silk'.[2]

Whatever the truth in the legend, there is archaeological evidence of sericulture in China — pottery distaffs and other weaving tools, and silkworm designs on ivory cups — dating from nearly 5,000 years ago.[3]

The worship of Lei Tsu as a goddess can only be traced back to the Chou (Zhou) dynasty (1122-256 BC). Then, at the mid-month of spring, the empress would lead ladies of rank to the altar to make a sacrifice to 'the first maker of silk'. The importance of the ceremony, as it evolved, to women's history is not only that the first maker of silk was a woman, but also that it 'seems to have been the only public function for whose observance, indeed, women were made imperial officers'.[4]

By the later Han dynasty (AD 25-221) the ceremony, from the point of view of show, could be compared to those today for International

Women's Day (see Chapter 18). Edward T. Williams writes:

> It was in the Fourth Moon that the Empress led the wives of the dukes, ministers and feudal lords in the worship of the Goddess of Silk. She rode under a canopy of blue (or green) plumes, in a carriage drawn by four horses. She had a dragon banner with a border of nine scallops. The wife of the Master of Horse drove the forward chariot with its bells and flags. It had a leathern hood, had scythes on its wheels and was armed with halberds.
>
> From Lo-yang [the Han capital] they led thousands of carriages and tens of thousands of horsemen to participate in this celebration. Since the official carriages were being occupied by the women, special provision had to be made for the officers themselves from the imperial supply. Five camps of guards protected the city.
>
> The wives of the provincial officers of Honan, imitating the court ladies, took their husbands' carriages with the symbols of their authority and, accompanied by their husbands' attendants, joined the imperial party. It was a gay cavalcade with its sounding gongs, its jingling bells, its fluttering banners and its brilliantly dressed women. … the Goddess of Silk was worshipped with the sacrifice of a sheep.[5]

Throughout the centuries, the empress would symbolically perform some of the activities that were normally the task of peasant women engaged in sericulture. For example, 'In the Spring, when the mulberry leaves were putting forth their leaves, the Empress went in person into the park to pluck mulberry leaves to take to the silkworm house to feed worms.'[6]

But the empress was among those who habitually wore silk, rather than produced it. The lives of the wearer and the producer were rather different. If you can picture the empress plucking mulberry leaves in the above paragraph, then look at this more explicit image, an exercise in transference by a male poet, of the peasant woman:

> When I lift my head, the mulberry branch catches my hair
> and lips;
> When I turn my body, the mulberry branch hooks and tears
> my skirt.
> Hard it is working at silkworms and mulberries.[7]

Male poets pitied the peasant woman for the hardness of her life. The empress was of the class of women which included courtesans, who might be, as Yi-tsi Feuerwerker puts it, 'objects of desire'. Unlike in Western culture, however, 'Woman is never seen in Chinese literature as an unattainable ideal with the power to transform and ennoble her worshiper.'[8] She is seen as 'material object'; to allude to her silk jacket is to evoke sensuality:

> On the bedscreen's folding panels, gold glimmers and fades.
> Clouds of hair verge upon the fragrant snow of cheeks.
> Languorous she rises, pencils the moth-eyebrows,
> Dawdles over her toilet, slowly washing, combing.
> Mirror front and back reflect her flowers;
> Face and blossoms illumine one the other.
> Upon her new-embroidered silken jacket
> Pairs and pairs of partridges in gold.[9]

For the peasant woman for whom the silk she has woven is essential as income, contemporary poetry conveys implications just as evocative, but worlds apart:

> It is not that her body does not love clothes of silk gauze.
> When the moon is bright through frost and cold, she never
> leaves the loom.
> Even when it is woven into gauze, she does not wear it.
> She sells it for cash to buy silk yarn to take back.[10]

But as Patricia Buckley Ebrey points out in her history of women in the Sung (Song) dynasty (960-1279), money earned meant, in the first instance, tax to the government:

> From the seven days that the silkworms are on the trays,
> We get one hundred *chin* of cocoons.
> After ten days of reeling, we get two skeins of silk threads.
> Then, strand by strand, we weave it into gauze.
> A hundred people labouring hard is not enough to clothe
> one person.[11]

And that poem ends:

> She lifted her head and noticed the yellow tips of the mul-
> berry leaves.
> She lowered her head and shed tears out of shame for her
> plain cloth skirt.

Ebrey ends her chapter 'Women's Work Making Cloth: 'In these poems, we might note, women's hardships are blamed on government tax collectors, not gender inequalities or anything to do with the family system.'[12]

The use of traditional Chinese poetry as social comment conveys much but not all, for those poems were written by men critical of the government. There was, alongside that, a division of labour that under-wrote gender inequality. On the whole, 'men ploughed, and women wove'.[13] Women involved in sericulture were mostly confined to the home, and the man of the house took the decisions about their economic activity. A woman's ability to perform in the cash economy did not grant her any sort of autonomy, for her earnings were part of the family's.

By the nineteenth century that lack of independence, at least in the Pearl River Delta of Southern China, seems to have given way to a system that has proved endlessly attractive to researchers. There, where there were six broods of silkworms a year rather than one, unmarried women chose to be autonomous rather than the victims of patriarchy.

Agnes Smedley, who appears several times in this book as a Western supporter of Chinese women, visited the Canton (Guangzhou) area from Shanghai as an investigative journalist in 1930. By then, silk production in China was in one of its periodic declines. What is more, silk production by hand in the home was almost over, and rather as in the Industrial Revolution in Europe, the craft system was being replaced by factories, or filatures.

Smedley writes of the Chinese silk industry in 1930 that it was 'rapidly losing its American markets to Japanese magnates'.[14] That is why she travelled to the Shuntak (Shunde) region where 'the millionaires of the South Seas' had erected many large filatures. Those spinning the silk from cocoons in them were all young women.

She found on her journey an aspect of sericulture which she had not expected:

> My young escort was awed by these [magnates], but when he spoke of the silk peasants or the girl filature workers, hostility and contempt crept into his voice. His particular hatred seemed to be for the thousands of women spinners, and only with difficulty could I learn why. He told me that the women were notorious throughout China as Lesbians. They refused to marry, and if their families forced them, they merely bribed their husbands with part of their wages and induced them to take concubines. The most such a married girl would do was bear one son; then she would return to the factory, refusing to live with her husband any longer. The Government had just issued a decree forbidding women to escape from marriage by bribery, but the women ignored it.
>
> 'They're too rich – that's the root of the trouble!' my young escort explained. 'They earn as much as eleven dollars a month, and become proud and contemptuous.' He

added that on this money they also supported parents, brothers and sisters, and grandparents. 'They squander their money,' he cried. 'I have never gone to a picture theater without seeing groups of them sitting together, holding hands.'[15]

Then Smedley visited a factory and wrote:

> The hatred of my escort for these girls became more marked when we visited the filatures. . . . lines of them, clad in glossy black jackets and trousers, sat before boiling vats of cocoons, their parboiled fingers twinkling among the spinning filaments. Sometimes a remark passed along their lines set a whole mill laughing. The face of my escort would grow livid.[16]

One evening, Smedley met a group of these young women and, in spite of both her escort and the language barriers, she found the rapport almost tangible:

> Girls crowded the benches and others stood banked behind them. Using my few words of Mandarin and many gestures, I learned that some of them earned eight or nine dollars a month, a few eleven. They worked ten hours a day – not eight as my escort had said. Once they had worked fourteen.
>
> My language broke down, so I supplemented it with crude pictures in my notebook. How did they win the ten-hour day? I drew a sketch of a filature with a big fat man standing on top laughing, then a second picture of the same with the fat man weeping because a row of girls stood holding hands all around the mill. They chattered over these drawings, then a girl shouted two words and all of them began to demonstrate a strike. They crossed their arms, as though refusing to work, while some rested their elbows on the table and lowered their heads, as though refusing to move.

They laughed, began to link hands, and drew me into this
circle. We all stood holding hands in an unbroken line laughing. Yes, that was how they got the ten-hour day![17]

No one has written about the 'sisterhood' in the Pearl River Delta
more vividly than Smedley, but many, mostly anthropologists, have since
written in greater depth and more scientifically. Of Western women,
Marjorie Topley went through the material and visited the area in the
1950s. In 'Marriage Resistance in Rural Kwangtung', she examined the
sisterhoods — the 'women who dress their own hair' and the 'women
who do not go down to the family' — as far as she was able historically
and from the rump that remained.[18]

She looked at the geography of the area and its society, seeking
explanations. She found that in Kwangtung (Guangdong) Province,
women did not have bound feet, and in the silk area there reports of
female infanticide were rare.[19] Because of her labour potential, a daughter was relatively more welcome in the family; she was not 'goods on
which one loses'.[20]

Topley observed a millenarian religion that stressed sexual equality
and, indeed, one local sect that was run entirely by women. She learned
of temples and monastic establishments to which the girls were free to
travel. They sold literature to women who could, thus, read.

Stories of model women were written in ballad form. One of
them was about Kuan Yin, the Goddess of Mercy, who, as Topley explains, 'is popularly believed to have been a princess who became a nun
over her parents' objections'. The story points out that 'she had no
husband to claim her devotion, no mother-in-law to control her, and
no children to hamper her movements'.[21]

Women were further induced to remain single because local married women who lived with their husbands were of less economic worth;
after the establishment of filatures their value as home spinners declined, and their status with it.

Topley's chapter in Wolf and Witke's *Women in Chinese Society* (1975)
was followed in 1989 by a monograph by Janice E. Stockard, *Daughters*

of the Canton Delta: Marriage Patterns and Economic Strategies in South China, 1860-1930, which described what Stockard calls 'delayed transfer marriage'. This was a system, hinted at in Smedley's account, by which wage-earning brides, often silkworkers, chose not to live with the husband arranged for them. Instead, they contributed from their wages enough money to buy a concubine to take their place. The children of the union regarded the wife, not the concubine, as their *daai ma*, or mother (see also Chapter 17, 'The New Concubines'). Economic independence was thus retained, and the earner's status in the afterlife secured by access to her husband's ancestral cult.

In 1994, Rubie S. Watson published her findings as 'Girls' Houses and Working Women: Expressive Culture in the Pearl River Delta, 1900-41', in *Women and Chinese Patriarchy: Submission, Servitude and Escape*.

My own very small original research into silk in the delta area pre-dates my interest in it as a metaphor. I was asked to write an entry on Margaret Ho Tung for an encyclopaedia of Chinese women. By chance, a major preoccupation of Ho Tung was technical improvements in the production of silk in the New Territories of Hong Kong, and in this she was helped by silkworkers from Shuntak.

Margaret Ho Tung (1865-1944) was the wife of the Hong Kong magnate Robert Ho Tung; she thus became *daai ma* of his ten children by Clara Ho Tung – a 'level' wife, rather than a concubine (see Chapters 16 and 17). But the children usually lived with Clara in her establishment and Margaret was able, therefore, to turn her energies and creativity to other matters.

On Ho Tung land near Sheung Shui in the New Territories, Margaret created a farm – Tung Ying Hok P'o. The New Territories was then in customary terms still part of China; it had been leased by Britain from China as part of the Colony of Hong Kong as recently as 1898.

Initially, the Ho Tung children walked through the paddy fields, while Margaret was carried in a chair, to Kam Tsin village where they stayed in the village ancestral home. Then a farmhouse in characteristic Chinese style was built for family weekends and outings. After the railway was completed in 1910, agriculture played an increasingly

Silkworkers at the Ho Tung farm,
New Territories, Hong Kong

important part. Crops included peanuts, rice, sugar-cane, tobacco and tea; there was also pig keeping, fish farming and a varied orchard, particularly lichee.

Margaret's main interest, however, became an experiment in the rearing of silkworms and the growing of small-sized mulberry trees, the leaves of which could be plucked standing on the ground. Traditionally, peasant families had needed ladders, an added expense. Traditionally, too, the production of the right kind of mulberry leaves was a science, and that was man's work.

Now, Margaret Ho Tung supervised experts brought from the Shuntak district. When the silkworms reached their important adult stage, she was usually at the farm. Tending the silkworms had always been women's work. The worms were notoriously temperamental, and women, as Patricia Buckley Ebrey explains it, 'invested both physical and emotional energy into trying to keep the worms happy'.[22]

In 1924, when Robert Ho Tung was commissioner of the Hong Kong section at the Wembley Exhibition, outside London, Margaret took a group of her silkworkers, at the request of the Hong Kong government, to demonstrate the industry. The demonstration was immensely popular and was visited by the Queen. The workers, who returned to demonstrate at Wembley in 1925, mainly came from the same native village as Kui P'aw who attended Margaret during visits to the farm. Kui P'aw also advised Margaret, who had a Scottish father but a Chinese mother, on traditional Chinese customary practices, particularly those of Shuntak.[23]

The emphasis in the above accounts and analyses of the Pearl River Delta is on autonomy and escape from the traditional system of Chinese patriarchy. But even Smedley's account is tinged with the less advantageous changes that industrialisation brought. It is in Shanghai, however, that these were to have the most devastating effect on women.

Shanghai in the 1930s, as has so often been said, was a city of extremes. Enid Saunders Candlin grew up in the city where her father was a tea merchant and wrote of those years in *The Breach in the Wall: A Memoir of Old China* (1974). For Westerners, the connotations of silk were more prosaic than the evocation of sensuality so much a feature of Chinese poetry. Nevertheless, Candlin's description of the finished product provides a useful contrast to descriptions of its production in factories. And she does capture the essence of silk's allure when she describes the silk shops on Nanking (Nanjing) Road in Shanghai. They were the best silk shops in the world!

> On their wide high shelves lay bolts of crêpe de Chine, luscious satin, thick silk, silk gauze, brocade, chiffon, in pure white, ivory, rose, robin's egg blue, Nile green, Moslem green, turquoise, russet, salmon, nut brown, palest fawn, and black so lustrous you could see reflections in it. There were striped silks, silks interwoven with the country's emblems and symbols, like the everlasting knot, the double-cash, the lotus; there were taffetas; there was silk shot with irridescent

colours, pink and mauve; there was pongee and Shantung silk; there was every range of gold – gold satin, gold gauze, after the old tribute gauze, a harking back to the imperial colours.

All these were as strong as iron and would last for years. Silk for men's shirts used to be something like thirty Chinese cents a yard, pongee was cheaper, even satin was only a couple of dollars – seldom more than four. Taffeta was so cheap you could have your French windows curtained with it. People made presents of bolts of crêpe de Chine – a handsome present, but not uncommon. Except for the very poorest, silk was worn by almost everyone – even the people on the ragged edge of poverty could manage to wear it on special occasions even if it meant hiring a silk gown.[24]

It is not surprising that bolts of silk should be regarded as a valuable present then. The character for a 'piece of silk' (*pi*) could still be used to mean 'money'.[25] In Sung times, the government needed silk for officials' salaries and payments.[26] What is more, as far back as the fall of the Han dynasty, there are records such as that quoted by Patricia Buckley Ebrey in her chapter 'Shifts in Marriage Finance' in *Marriage and Inequality in Chinese Society* which she edited with Rubie Watson: 'In the present age, when marriages are arranged, some people sell their daughters for the betrothal gift or buy a wife by making a payment of silk.'[27] Ebrey goes on to suggest that the highest officials could afford to give 140 pieces of plain silk, while the lowest gave 34.

Wives of officials, as opposed to the peasant women who 'made' silk, used it to do exquisite embroideries. Alicia Little, who, more than any one person, was responsible for the abolition of footbinding in China, writes in *Intimate China* (1898) of the 'ladies working at home, and putting all the fancy of a life-time into a *portière*, or bed-hanging'.[28] And then, omitting to mention the looting indulged in by the British when they entered Beijing in 1860, razing the Summer Palace as they did so, she adds:

One of the most fairylike pieces of embroidery I have ever seen was mosquito-curtains worked all over with clusters of wistaria for either the Emperor or Empress, and somehow or other brought, before being used, out of the Imperial Palace by a European collector. The rich yet delicate work upon the very fine silky material made these mosquito-curtains a thing to haunt the dreams of all one's after-life.

Women of rank had their worth counted in bales of silk, and, confined to the home, their creative energies were largely directed towards fine silk embroideries. Florence Ayscough, in *Chinese Women: Yesterday and Today* (1938), describes this process in the sort of lovely detail that Candlin did for silk itself:

> She sat for many hours before her frame creating flowers, birds, and butterflies in exquisite threads on glimmering silks and satins. Deftly her delicate fingers executed the different stitches: the 'enwrapping', which we call 'satin' stitch, both long and short; the 'struck or grass-seed' stitch, in our nomenclature French knots; the 'oblique' stitch, for stems of plants; the 'enveloping' or 'couching' stitch; the 'chain', the 'split', and the 'man-character' stitches; all these and more were in her repertory.[29]

But what of the life of the women who produced the silk in the factories in Shanghai?

Emily Honig in *Sisters and Strangers: Women in the Shanghai Cotton Mills, 1919-1949* (1986) explains how Shanghai's geographic and economic position provided a firm base on which the silk industry could flourish. Its first mechanised silk filature or silk reeling factory was built in 1862, and by 1894 there were 5,000 workers in the nine factories, four of them Japanese, five Chinese. In the first half of the twentieth century, Shanghai's silk industry became the city's second-largest employer of women workers.[30]

Honig quotes the first-hand account of Fan Xiaofeng in 1932 to illustrate how the changes in the traditional industry had affected life in the countryside:

> I came from Wujin Xian, in Jiangsu, near Wuxi. In that area we raised silkworms. Every year, in the season around the Spring Festival, we would raise silkworms. That way we could supplement our peasant income. We did this in my house. Everyone would take part. Later, when silk imports started, it destroyed our market, and we could not get any money for selling our silkworms. Without that money we didn't have enough to get by. So my parents tried to think of ways to send us children to work.[31]

Fan went to Shanghai to work in a cotton mill, and in the late 1940s became a well-known union activist.

Other women ended up in the silk filatures. Cora Deng, head of the YWCA Labour Bureau in the late 1920s, noted what life was like for them when she researched the workers from Subei Province and their apparently inferior position:

> Just as we got to the middle of this passageway we came to a door on the right hand side leading to the skeining department. ... the workers in this department look much better off than those in the other departments. They wear very good clothes and look like girls from more refined homes. They work only six or seven hours a day, while getting seventy cents per day, the highest wage in the factory. I learned from other girls that most of them are relatives and friends of the staff or of the management. Here you see in action the Chinese family idea of caring for its own members first!
>
> Then we came to the peeling and selecting departments. The two departments share one room with a partition of lattice work in the middle. The room looked dark and smelled

filthy. The windows could give them better light if they only cleaned them. ... According to what I learned from the head of the department most of the workers in these departments come from country places north of the Yangtze River. ... The work in these departments does not require much skill, and wages are comparatively lower than others – the highest being fifty cents, and only twenty cents for beginners – so naturally the places are filled with these northerners [Subei women] ... who are willing to accept lower wages

The head said to us, 'These northern women are rude, dirty and have no ambition to do better work.'[32]

Cora Deng was part of a research and support system for women workers in Shanghai; she reported as objectively as she could. For a more subjective account, one which sets the filature within the local landscape, Han Suyin's experience in the summer of 1934 tells it all. She wrote in *A Mortal Flower*, volume 2 of her autobiographical history:

With slogans of the New Life pasted all over the cities of China, I walked the Chinese section of Shanghai, Yangtsepoo, oozy with ruins and filthy with misery, saw the policemen openly accepting bribes from pimps in the squalor of back streets. Broken-down prostitutes looked at me; hideous women, crackling with laughter as I looked away. I walked in a trance, sweating, but not understanding.

'Go and see a bit of life,' said Hers. 'Stuck in your university, you think everything can be done by slogans. You will see that the Chinese are worse to their own people than Europeans.'

A small rat-like man with glasses took me to a silk filature in Chapei or Yangtsepoo, quite a way from the International Settlement. It was an area impossibly squalid, a slum of sagging huts, stinking unpaved alleyways. A barn-like structure, with a small courtyard in front, was the filature. Inside, great vats of boiling water, furnaces and children looking about six but who the rat-faced man told me were all of fourteen, standing round the vats. It was hardly possible to see what they were doing with the steam rising from the vats, and it was suffocatingly hot; but they were plunging silk cocoons in bundles wrapped in fine webs of gauze into the vats. The children's eyes were peculiar, bright red with trachoma, their arms were covered with scalds, and they worked almost naked; the temperature outside was ninety-eight degrees; inside it was one hundred and three or perhaps more. The smell was bad, and I could not stand it and no one wanted me to stay very long.

'These are refugees … we give them work, otherwise they would die of hunger. …' The rat-faced man told me how kind his manager was to give employment to these children, one hundred and twenty of them. Quickly we went out again. The car of the manager who had arranged this instructive trip for me because Hers had asked him to do so, was waiting beyond the mud lanes, as these were impassable; it whisked me away, back to civilization, in the French Concession. … 'Now you have seen the problem,' said Hers. 'Too many poor people in China.' Later I found out the silk filature belonged to a Japanese concern.[33]

Han Suyin's account hints at the changes that had taken place by 1934 in the lives of some women – such as those able to go to university – since the Revolution of 1911. These changes, and how the women concerned were able to support the women textile workers in Shanghai, will be further explored in Chapter 8, 'The Seventh Gentleman'.

By 1935, the silk slump in China had taken its full economic toll, and many filatures were closing down. In the Canton area, many women who were young enough became domestic servants in the city and in Hong Kong. Edward T. Williams, whose 'The Worship of Lei Tsu, Patron Saint of Silkworkers' set me on this trail, now brings the story full circle with the news with which he started his 1935 piece:

> In the summer of 1934 the *Shun Po* of Shanghai published a
> communication from Nanking to the effect that the Soci-
> ety for the Improvement of the Silk Industry had received a
> request that the Government be asked to designate the sev-
> enth day of the seventh month as a day for the celebration
> of the birth of Lei Tsu, the woman who is said by legend to
> have been the first to teach the Chinese the making of silk.
> The Government replied very promptly that history knew
> nothing of the birthday of Lei Tsu and that moreover the
> erection of temples in her honour could not aid the silk
> industry.
>
> In this the Chinese Government showed that it was un-
> willing to encourage the Chinese people in superstition.[34]

The Manchu (Qing) dynasty had fallen in 1911, giving way eventually, after 1927, to the Kuomintang (Guomindang), or KMT, government of Chiang Kai-shek (Jiang Jieshi) with its New Life Movement of
clean living. That in its turn would be overtaken by Liberation in 1949,
and government through the Communist Party. But it was under the
Manchus that the cult of Lei Tsu reached its apogee through Emperor
Chien-lung (1711-1799), described by Williams as 'an antiquarian and
a stickler for adherence to the ancient forms'.[35] He set up a shrine in
Beihai Park, a little to the west of the back gate of the Forbidden City in
Beijing. That was where I was headed. But did the altar still exist?

Williams's description of the area is less manageable than that of
L.C. Arlington in *In Search of Old Peking* (1935):

> Through the triple gateway immediately in front of us we
> enter the enclosure of the Altar of Silkworms (*Ts'an T'an*)
> with two stone terraces standing in the midst of a beautiful
> grove of mulberry trees. ... on the western [side] the mul-
> berry leaves were examined before being given to the silk-

worms. North of the eastern terrace is another enclosure, the *Ch'in Ts'an Tien* (Hall of Imperial Silkworms) in which sacrifices were offered up to the Goddess of Silkworms by the Empress or her deputies on a lucky (*chi*) day during the 3rd Moon of each year. Along the east wall of the main enclosure runs a row of dilapidated buildings, in which the silkworms were reared, and in front of them the *Hao P'u Chien* the water of which was used for washing the cocoons.[36]

Both Williams and Arlington are rather misleading, for, according to Juliet Bredon, that was no longer the scene in 1935 when they published their accounts. In *Peking*, which she brought up to date in 1931, she wrote:

> Here is the Temple of Silkworms dedicated to the Empress who taught Sericulture to the Chinese people 4,500 years ago, yonder a picturesque shrine encircled by a miniature city wall. It has, alas, been turned into a tea-shop.[37]

Don Cohn and Zhang Jingqing in *Beijing Walks* (1992) have more up-to-date news: 'The Altar of Silkworkers in Behai Park is a nursery school for the pupae of bigwigs in the Party and Government.'[38]

It sounded as if a tourist, even one with a serious historical intent, could not just walk in there, even assuming that it was identifiable. But usually on my trips to Beijing, I am able to benefit from my husband's status as an academic; often he is teaching or attending a conference which includes the generous services of an interpreter. Thus it was that I came to meet Yu Jing, a most special young woman who fell in love with the characters I was researching at that time: the Manchurian writer Xiao Hong (see Chapters 19-22) and Lei Tsu. Yu Jing arranged, by marvellous perseverance, for me to talk to Xiao Hong's second husband, and interpreted for me.

And quickly Xiao Hong became relevant to my exploration of silk, for she confirmed for me that silk is deeply embedded in the literary life of China, not just in the traditional poems from which I have quoted, but also in modern writing. She starts the autobiographical novel *Tales of Hulan River* (1941; 1988), by which she is best known, with a minute description of her home town, street by street. This includes the following subtly satirical and memorable image:

> The school located in the Dragon King Temple is for the study of raising silkworms, and is called the Agricultural School, while the one in the Temple of the Patriarch is just a regular elementary school with one advanced section added, and is called the Higher Elementary School.
>
> Although the names of these two schools vary, the only real difference between them is that in the one they call the Agricultural School the silkworm pupae are fried in oil in the autumn, and the teachers there enjoy several sumptuous meals.[39]

In Xiao Hong's first novel, *The Field of Life and Death* (1935; 1979), she uses silk as a simile, the way an English writer might have used the sea, on the first page when she describes the saliva on the whiskers of a goat gnawing at an elm tree: 'When these threads of saliva were caught up by the wind they looked like soap lather, or like sluggishly floating strands of silk.'[40]

Finally, Yu Jing also tracked down the state-run Beihai Nursery School and went with me to visit it. I wrote this when I got home that evening:

> We were five minutes late. Teacher Liu, chairperson of the school, was waiting just inside the main entrance for us. Past ponds overhung with willows we stepped through a moon gate set in the oxblood stone wall so typical of Beijing. As we appeared round the corner, a phalanx of six year olds, the oldest class, greeted us, 'Nihau, nihau.' Then, under the instruction of a tall, slim, long-haired, unsmiling teacher they spread out and started their calesthenics.

The school was founded in 1949; teacher Liu has been there since 1960. There are 500 infants between the age of three to five; from here they go to proper school. I could only gently press about whether or not it was for the privileged class; it is apparently open to anyone in the catchment area of Beijing. But I saw one mother come to get her child; she was in all ways in the height of fashion, including a leather skirt cut by a designer and very well cut hair and expensive makeup. Twenty years ago she would have been in a Mao suit. Most telling of all, those who stay for the week bring their own bedroll; these are of the very finest silk, competing with each other in colour and design.

Whether or not the children come from a privileged background, they are obviously privileged to be in this school – the old altar to the patron saint of silkworkers, where the empress and her court would come to obtain blessings for the silkworms. But nothing is left of the silk altar, not even a memory in teacher Liu's consciousness. Where it must have been, in the complex of buildings that still stands, are dormitories full of mini-beds with their silken bed rolls. In one of the two courtyards either side of the main building are large wire fish sculptures; in the other a hopscotch pitch where Yu Jing and I did some tentative jumps.

In the side rooms off the courtyards are classrooms. Peeping through the window of one we saw the music corner with tambourines and ukuleles on shelves, and costumes pinned to the walls. There is also a language corner. In another classroom, a still life class was in progress with baskets of fruit. In front of each child was a holder full of coloured marker pens. One child had drawn a huge yellow lemon with red worms, another a green apple with a purple segment and another segment munched away – perhaps by a silkworm. I'm told by a friend who, as a child, kept

silkworms in a box as pets, that the sound of their munch-
ing on mulberry leaves is quite striking.

If the Behai Nursery School is now for the privileged – and Yu Jing
has since checked that it is for the children of parents who work in the
'central government organisation' – at least the altar of Lei Tsu is put to
good use. And at least the granddaughters of Shanghai silkworkers of
the 1930s might be pupils there. And no doubt the ghost of Lei Tsu
feels comfortable among the silken bed rolls of her tiny acolytes.

> At all events,
> Your transparent dwellings
> Are neither dormitories
> Nor much less tombs,
> Life pulsates inside,
> In the water's turbulence you exchange death
> For the continuity of silver threads in time and space.

> Zheng Min (1920-)
> 'Silkworms', *Women of the Red Plain*

Written March 1995.

NOTES

1. Germaine Merlange, 'Silk in the Orient' (1939), p. 65.
2. Edward T. Williams, 'The Worship of Lei Tsu' (1935), p. 1.
3. China Pictorial, *The Silk Road on Land and Sea* (1989), p. 15.
4. Williams, 'The Worship of Lei Tsu', p. 2.
5. Williams, 'The Worship of Lei Tsu', p. 3.
6. Williams, 'The Worship of Lei Tsu', p. 3.
7. Patricia Buckley Ebrey, *The Inner Quarters* (1993), p. 139.
8. Yi-tsi Feuerwerker, 'Women as Writers in the 1920's and 1930's (1978), p. 148.
9. Feuerwerker, 'Women as Writers', p. 148.
10. Ebrey, *The Inner Quarters*, p. 150.
11. Ebrey, *The Inner Quarters*, p. 150.
12. Ebrey, *The Inner Quarters*, p. 151.
13. Ebrey, *The Inner Quarters*, p. 132.
14. Agnes Smedley, *Portraits of Chinese Women in Revolution* (1976), p. 104.
15. Smedley, *Portraits of Chinese Women in Revolution*, p. 105.
16. Smedley, *Portraits of Chinese Women in Revolution*, p. 107.
17. Smedley, *Portraits of Chinese Women in Revolution*, p. 109.
18. Marjorie Topley, 'Marriage Resistance in Rural Kwangtung' (1978), p. 67.
19. Topley, 'Marriage Resistance in Rural Kwangtung', p. 70.
20. Topley, 'Marriage Resistance in Rural Kwangtung', p. 78.
21. Topley, 'Marriage Resistance in Rural Kwangtung', p. 75.
22. Ebrey, *The Inner Quarters*, p. 141.
23. Much of the material on Margaret Ho Tung was given to me by General Ho Shai Lai (Robbie).
24. Enid Saunders Candlin, *The Breach in the Wall* (1974), p. 86.
25. Williams, 'The Worship of Lei Tsu', p. 14.
26. Ebrey, *The Inner Quarters*, p. 145.
27. Patricia Buckley Ebrey, 'Shifts in Marriage Finance' (1991), p. 98.
28. Mrs Archibald Little, *Intimate China* (1898), p. 305.
29. Florence, Ayscough, *Chinese Women: Yesterday and Today* (1938), p. 87.
30. Emily Honig, *Sisters and Strangers* (1986), p. 87. *The Thistle and the Jade*, the story of Jardine Matheson, claims that a French firm set up a 'European-style silk filature' in 1860 (p. 80).
31. Honig, *Sisters and Strangers*, pp. 62-63.
32. Honig, *Sisters and Strangers*, pp. 71-72.
33. Han Suyin, *A Mortal Flower* (1972), pp. 261-62.
34. Williams, 'The Worship of Lei Tsu', p. 1.
35. Williams, 'The Worship of Lei Tsu', p. 5.
36. L.C. Arlington, *In Search of Old Peking* (1935), pp. 87-88.
37. Juliet Bredon, *Peking* (1931), p. 151.
38. Don Cohn, *Beijing Walks* (1992), p. 164.
39. Xiao Hong, *Tales of Hulan River* (1988), p. 6.
40. Xiao Hong, *The Field of Life and Death* (1976), p. 6.

BIBLIOGRAPHY

Arlington, L.C. and Lewisohn, William, *In Search of Old Peking* (Hong Kong, Oxford University Press, 1987; 1st published 1935).

Ayscough, Florence, *Chinese Women: Yesterday and Today* (London, Jonathan Cape, 1938).

Bredon, Juliet, *Peking* (Hong Kong, Oxford University Press, 1982; 1st published 1931).

Candlin, Enid Saunders, *The Breach in the Wall: A Memoir of Old China* (London, Cassell, 1974).

China Pictorial (ed.), *The Silk Road on Land and Sea* (Beijing, China Pictorial Publishing Co., 1989).

Cohn, Don and Zhang Jingqing, *Beijing Walks* (Hong Kong, Odyssey, 1992).

Cormack, Mrs J.G., *Everyday Customs in China* (Edinburgh, Moray Press, 1935).

Ebrey, Patricia Buckley, 'Shifts in Marriage Finance', in Rubie S. Watson and Patricia Buckley Ebrey (eds), *Marriage and Inequality in Chinese Society* (Berkeley, University of California Press, 1991).

Ebrey, Patricia Buckley, *The Inner Quarters: Marriage and the Lives of Chinese Women in the Sung Period* (Berkeley, University of California Press, 1993).

Feuerwerker, Yi-tsi, 'Women as Writers in the 1920's and 1930's', in M. Wolf and R. Witke (eds), *Women in Chinese Society* (Berkeley, University of California Press, 1991).

Han Suyin, *A Mortal Flower* (London, Panther, 1972; 1st published 1966).

Honig, Emily, *Sisters and Strangers: Women in the Shanghai Cotton Mills, 1919-1949* (Stanford, Stanford University Press, 1986).

Hopkirk, Peter, *Foreign Devils on the Silk Road: The Search for the Lost Cities and Treasures of Chinese Central Asia* (London, John Murray, 1980).

Jaschok, Maria and Miers, Suzanne (eds), *Women and Chinese Patriarchy: Submission, Servitude and Escape* (London, Zed Books, 1994).

Keswick, Maggie (ed.) *The Thistle and the Jade: A Celebration of 150 Year's of Jardine, Matheson & Co* (London, Octopus, 1982).

Lam Siu Chan, 'History of Sericulture' in *Hong Kong University Journal of Law and Commerce*, No. 2, (Hong Kong, 1929).

Lin, Julia C. (trans.), *Women of the Red Plain: An Anthology of Contemporary Chinese Women's Poetry* (London, Penguin, 1992).

Little, Mrs Archibald, *Intimate China: The Chinese As I Have Seen Them* (London, Hutchinson, 1898).

Merlange, Germaine, 'Silk in the Orient', in *Journal of the Royal Central Asian Society*, vol. XXVI, part I (London, January 1939).

Smedley, Agnes, *Portraits of Chinese Women in Revolution* (New York, The Feminist Press, 1976; 1st published in *Battle Hymn of China*, 1943).

Stockard, Janice E., *Daughters of the Canton Delta: Marriage Patterns and Economic Strategies in South China, 1860-1930* (Hong Kong, Hong Kong University Press, 1989).

Topley, Marjorie, 'Marriage Resistance in Rural Kwangtung', in M. Wolf and R. Witke (eds), *Women in Chinese Society*.

Watson, Rubie S. 'Girls' Houses and Working Women: Expressive Culture in the Pearl River Delta, 1900-41', in Maria Jaschok and Suzanne Miers (eds), *Women and Chinese Patriarchy: Submission, Servitude and Escape*.

Watson, Rubie S. and Ebrey, Patricia Buckley (eds), *Marriage and Inequality in Chinese Society* (Berkeley, University of California Press, 1991).

Williams, Edward T., 'The Worship of Lei Tsu, Patron Saint of Silkworkers', in *North China Branch, Royal Asiatic Society*, vol. LXVI (Shanghai, Kelly & Walsh, 1935).

Wolf, M. and Witke, R. (eds), *Women in Chinese Society* (Stanford, Stanford University Press, 1978; 1st published 1975).

Xiao Hong (Hsiao Hung), *The Field of Life and Death*, trans. Howard Goldblatt and Ellen Yeung (Bloomington, Indiana University Press, 1979).

Xiao Hong, *Tales of Hulan River*, trans. Howard Goldblatt (Hong Kong, Joint Publishing Co., 1988).

MACAU

CHAPTER 3

WHO WAS
CLARA ELLIOT?
A Talk

Y ou need a deadline if you are ever to draw research to a conclusion. Otherwise, the chase becomes an end in itself. Thus it has been for me with Charles and Clara Elliot, but particularly with Clara.

My headlong descent into the joys of this research has been augmented by the fact that Clara is mine. Captain Charles Elliot everyone knew about: he was responsible for the taking of Hong Kong in January 1841. But of Clara there were just a couple of traces.

The first tells of May 1841 when Charles Elliot was, apparently, 'so eager to demonstrate to all his faith that the Chinese would honour their undertakings that he more than once brought his wife [from Macau] to the scene of his activities [in Canton], and unintentionally exposed her to the hazards of war'. The second incident took place in July when Charles was caught in a typhoon between Macau and Hong Kong and was rescued, rather than murdered for a reward. As one of his colleagues put it, 'What must have been the state of poor Mrs E, who must have given her husband up for lost.'

From these titbits, I was determined to track Clara down. Not only that; I got it firmly into my head that she must have written letters home. Those letters I must find, for they would form the springboard for the history of Western women in Hong Kong upon which I was then embarking.

Soon thereafter, I was on holiday in France with a couple of books I had recently bought in London. One was Pat Jalland's *Women, Marriage, and Politics 1860-1914* (1988). Flicking through the bibliography first, I came across the entry 'Minto Mss, National Library of Scotland, Edinburgh (Elliot-Murray-Kynynmound papers).' I suddenly realised that this was Charles Elliot's family – his father, Hugh, was the brother of the first Earl of Minto. I tried not to get too excited, for had not Peter Ward Fay, author of one of the best books on the taking of Hong Kong, *The Opium War 1840-1842* (1975), regretted that '[Elliot] left no diary, no private papers, and never set down his reminiscences, nor did his wife though she survived him'?

I wrote to the National Library of Scotland asking if they had any letters or diaries written by Clara Elliot. It was a long shot and I did not sit waiting for a reply. Olive Geddes, Research Assistant, wrote barely a week later: 'This library does indeed hold the papers of the Earls of Minto which include manuscripts of Lady Clara's husband Sir Charles Elliot. … While most of the manuscripts relate to Sir Charles's official business, there are some family letters which may be of interest to you. Ms13137 letters of Lady Clara to Emma Hislop, 1832-60, includes a few letters from 1836-41 …'

I suppose, of all the replies to research letters that I have ever received, that was the most explosive. Within weeks, Olive had sent me photocopies of Clara's letters, and then of Charles's, written at the same time from the China Coast (mainly Macau) to his sister, Emma Hislop, in England. Olive Geddes became the symbol of librarian virtue which no other librarian has ever begun to surpass. I have been to the National Library since, and it is like entering hallowed portals. To read the letters in the original manuscript is, in a way, to touch Clara and Charles Elliot.

I transcribed the Elliot letters, did a fair amount of research on the couple, and based the first three chapters of *The Private Life of Old Hong Kong: Western Women in the British Colony 1841-1941* (1991) quite heavily on the results. But, of course, Clara had to compete with a myriad other characters. It became clearer to me, as soon as I had finished that history, that the Elliot papers deserved a fuller life of their own and I started to prepare them for publication.

Clara and Charles's writing was the first obstacle. The rudimentary transcript I had originally made would by no means suffice. Happily, my husband, Derek Roebuck, apart from being a legal historian and, therefore, as passionate as I about the historical source material these letters would release into the public domain, has other talents. He has experience of reading medieval manuscripts in Latin and Law French, as well as 30 years under the yoke of students' handwriting. No student's writing, however, has ever been as bad as Clara and Charles Elliot's. Our only consolation was that they had not written both ways across the paper.

Then, with a serviceable manuscript to work with, I turned to annotation – most importantly and intriguingly, the background of Clara and Charles. He was easy enough. He had a public life of over 50 years and came from the distinguished and extended Minto family. Reference books were full of the ramifications of the Elliot-Murray-Kynynmounds, and even their close relationship with Lord Auckland, Governor General of India while Charles was 'taking Hong Kong'.

But Clara. She was a different matter. And there was Emma Hislop, too, the recipient of the letters. As women, their backgrounds were much more sketchy. Emma was Charles's sister, so there was more of a purchase, and she had married General Sir Thomas Hislop who was well enough known in his time. But it was almost impossible to gain a foothold on Clara's provenance. This then is the story of how I began to run Clara Elliot to earth.

I had started with a Minto/Elliot family tree which I built up over weeks, months and years, drawing first on obvious reference books such as *Burke*'s and *Debrett*'s. Thus I could see all Charles's ancestors, uncles, aunts and cousins, and then his siblings, including Emma Elliot Hislop, and his children.

Of Charles Elliot's wife, however, *Burke* remarks only, 'm. 1828 Clara Genevieve (d. 1885), dau[ghter] of Robert Harley Windsor'. In St Catherine's House, London, among the births, deaths and marriages records, there is no mention of Robert Harley Windsor's marriage (his birth is too early for those records) and no record of Clara's birth, nor of her marriage to Charles.

Early on, I had approached the current Earl of Minto, not only to seek permission to prepare the letters for publication but also to see if he knew anything I did not. He could not help with Clara's background. Nor could Lord de Clifford, descended from the marriage of Clara's eldest daughter, Harriet, though Lady de Clifford sent me a charming photograph of a portrait of Harriet which suggested something of Clara's looks.

From her letters to Emma, it seems that Clara's parents were dead by 1834, the date of her first letter from Macau; she does not mention them, even by implication. Every search for a suitable Windsor in *Burke* and *Debrett* draws a blank — for example, her father might have been a member of the Earl of Plymouth's family, whose name was Windsor before it was Clive-Windsor. There are plenty of Robert Windsors over the centuries, but no Robert Harley. He was doubtless named after the statesman Robert Harley, but that leads nowhere.

But Clara does mention her aunt, Miss Windsor. And then there is Emma Hislop's engagement diary for the years 1833-1843. In January 1841 she mentions going to Turnham Green where Miss Windsor was desperately ill; and on 12 February, she mentions her funeral.

It was a start. One day, when we were on leave in England, we decided to drive from our home in Oxford along the Southern Circular Road — the bottom curve of outer London. We would try to find the graveyard where Miss Windsor was buried; failing that, perhaps the parish records in the church would provide a lead. From there, we planned to drive eastward to Charlton where Emma Hislop lived.

Finding where Emma lived had been a stroke of luck. The sole address on the outside of Clara and Charles's letters was 'Charlton'. It could have been anywhere in England. I always look in the most obvious place first — in this case the *London A-Z*. There, quite clearly, in SE7 was Charlton Park and, too, quite unexpectedly marked, Charlton House.

We found Turnham Green quickly enough, and obviously the church where Miss Windsor was buried — Christ Church. But there was no graveyard and the church was locked. There were, however, names of wardens and the rector printed up, with their telephone numbers.

The churchwarden I rang told me that his church was celebrating its 150th anniversary that year (1993), so Miss Windsor could not have been buried there 152 years earlier. I should try St Nicholas, Chiswick Village, he suggested. It took me many months to establish by post that there was no record of Miss Windsor's burial there, either.

The drive from Turnham Green to Charlton that morning was long and tedious. And when we arrived, although Charlton House was easily identifiable, it was large and ugly, quite unlike where I had imagined Emma Hislop living.

We did it inside and out, taking photographs. Then we ventured upstairs and found an office where a helpful administrator explained that it had been a community centre since the war and gave me a history which included the residents going back to the nineteenth century. The Hislops did not seem to be among them. I was rather relieved, but also somewhat at a loss. However, we came away with the address of the Greenwich Local History Centre.

I wrote to them from Hong Kong and, on another visit to England, went to see them. There I learned that Charlton House was one place, and Charlton Villa, which the Hislops had rented in the 1830s and until 1843 when Sir Thomas died, was another. The villa was no longer extant, though some archaeological work had established its foundations. More important, there was an engraving at the History Centre of Charlton Villa, and some water-colours. The paintings were done by Emma's daughter, Nina (eventually the third Countess Minto), who features quite largely in the letters as she was much loved by Charles and a close cousin of Clara and Charles's burgeoning family, several of whom spent long years with the Hislops instead of in Macau.

These pictures were a find indeed. It was not possible to visit Charlton Villa, but I could prop photographs of the contemporary reproductions up in front of me as I read and wrote. And I did not have to picture Emma and Nina, and the Elliot children at Charlton House.

And it was no wonder that neither Christ Church nor St Nicholas had a record of Miss Windsor's burial because on a later visit I went to find the details of her will in the Public Record Office in Chancery Lane (because she died before 1838) and arranged to have a copy of the will sent to me here. Mary Windsor was not buried in Turnham Green. Her will specified clearly that she wished to be buried 'in the same grave with my father, mother and sisters in the burial ground of the City Road Chapel, belonging to the late John Wesley'.

From Hong Kong, I had a momentary disorientation about the City Road Chapel. The most obvious place to look was the London telephone directory which, like the *A-Z*, I keep in Hong Kong for just such eventualities. It was there, and soon a most helpful administrator was sending me details of the Windsor family's death records in the City Road Chapel.

Thus a day of physical searching which had seemed so disappointing, frustrating even, laid the seeds for later more successful visits to other sources. These were not quite the same as standing in a quiet graveyard, or in the echoing rooms of the fine mansion I had envisaged, but better than nothing.

Many of the Windsors were buried at the City Road Chapel, and Robert Harley's great-uncle had been a close friend and colleague of John Wesley; it was safe to assume that the family was Methodist, and that information might be useful later. But of Robert Harley and Clara's mother – still with no name – there was nothing to go on.

In the meantime, Carl Smith had introduced me to the Mormons' genealogical computer service which has a Hong Kong branch. From that I managed to find Robert Harley Windsor's baptism place and the date, 1777. With the death information from the City Chapel, and the details of his siblings' baptisms at the Holy Trinity, the Minories, I not only managed to cobble together a family tree for Clara's father, but also to muse that there might be a City of London – that is, a merchant – connection to his disappearance from England.

I now also knew, from St Catherine's records and from her will at Somerset House, where Clara had died (in England), how old she was then and therefore when she was born – 1806. But the mystery of her parentage, and even of the place of her marriage to Charles Elliot, continued to nag. And then I had the strangest break, one which even now I find it difficult to come to terms with.

When you write letters off into the blue to the descendant of a historical character, you have to be aware that you may not only be invading the privacy of the family but that you may be bothering a busy person. Every reply to a letter takes time, particularly if they have to look up papers or consult family members. The researcher may have to write dozens, if not hundreds, of letters, but you should always realise that you are asking a favour. Letters should be kept relatively brief, but they should be comprehensive enough to whet the appetite of a descendant who may not previously have realised how interesting their ancestor is.

It is less inhibiting when you communicate within a network of like-minded researchers; then you can swap information or leads, and not feel that you are sending glorified junk mail. Requests from other researchers tend to come when you are up to your ears, but at least you can smile a little when you receive them, for sometimes the titbit you are offered in return can be dynamite.

So it was when I received a letter from Patrick Conner who was working on a new biography of the artist George Chinnery (published in 1993 as *George Chinnery 1774-1852: Artist of India and the China Coast*). Chinnery lived in Macau at the same time as the Elliots (1834-1841), so Patrick wrote asking if, in the unpublished documents I had been through concerning my women, I had come across any references to Chinnery. He asked, too, if he should go to the trouble of following up the leads in my book, and he specified women characters in whom he was particularly interested.

As a subtle and tactful quid pro quo, he finished off his letter, 'Incidentally, what do you make of the reference in vol 3 of Vaillant's *Voyage Autour du Monde* ... (1852) pp 157-8, in which the French travellers are entertained (in Jan. 1837) by *"le vice-consul anglais M. Elliot"* and report that *"Mme Elliot etait une creole de Saint-Domingue c'est-a-dire presque une Francaise."*?' [Mrs Elliot was a creole of Saint-Domingue, that is to say, almost a Frenchwoman.]

I was stupefied by this new piece of information. I did not know of Captain Vaillant's book, and the suggestion that Clara Elliot was a creole from Saint-Domingue struck no chord with anything I knew. It was much more likely that Vaillant had been confused by the Elliots' sojourn in British Guiana in 1830-1833, when Charles was appointed Protector of Slaves there. But the more I thought about it, the more the information could not be ignored; after all, it might just be the reason why I had been able to find nothing about Clara's background.

As is so often the way, Vaillant's book was not available to me until my subsequent visit to England, but I could not wait until then. I began, therefore, to explore this new possibility. But where on earth do you start on such an apparently wild goose chase?

First I had to establish that what was Saint-Domingue is now Haiti and I got hold of as many books about Haiti as were available in the Hong Kong University library. Beginning to understand its history in the early nineteenth century gave some clues as to what Clara's background could have been.

Then I had to come to grips with the word 'creole', which was giving me trouble because nowhere was there any suggestion in Charles and Clara's letters that Clara was anything but European. In English, the usual meaning of 'creole' is a person of mixed race, white and black. But Vaillant had written in French and in that language the word can mean a person of white race born in a French overseas territory, or colony. Haiti was a prosperous French colony until 1798 when Toussaint l'Ouverture, a former slave, led a successful revolt.

Thus I began to form a picture of Clara's father, Robert Harley Windsor, going out to Saint-Domingue and marrying a Frenchwoman, accounting for Clara's second name, Genevieve. Given Haiti's history from 1798 to 1825, it seemed quite possible for Windsor to have been a British merchant or teacher there.

From a biography of Toussaint l'Ouverture bought many years ago and carted round the world with the rest of my library, I found an acknowledgement of help from a Catholic seminary in Port au Prince. I cobbled together an address, enclosed some US dollars to pay for photocopying, and asked if they could help me track down Robert Harley Windsor or Charles Elliot there. Clara and Charles had not married in England; perhaps the wedding had taken place in the West Indies.

I had a most touching letter back from Port au Prince with some photocopies that were not quite relevant and the return of most of the money. But now I had really got my teeth into Clara and Haiti, and this determination was reinforced a hundredfold when I finally read Captain Auguste Vaillant's full description of his onshore meeting with the Elliots in Macau; he had seen enough of them not to have mistaken who exactly he had met and what they had told him.

I went back to the details of Charles Elliot's career in W.R. O'Byrne's *Naval Biographical Dictionary* (1849). I tracked his every move in the years when he might have met Clara in Haiti. I found that in 1823, as a young lieutenant in the Royal Navy, he was appointed to the Jamaica station. By 1826, he was an acting-commander based at Port Royale. On 28 August 1828, the year of his marriage, he attained the rank of captain and was put on half-pay, but in the year before that he was on the *Harlequin* on the same West Indian station.

I had Charles in the West Indies at the right time; it was a good start. In the Guildhall Library in the City of London I ploughed through a compilation of the *Jamaican Gazette*'s births, deaths and marriages notices looking for the wedding of Charles Elliot and Clara Windsor; Jamaica, not far across the water, was surely the most suitable location in 1828. There was nothing.

In the Bodleian Library in Oxford I sniffed out every available travel account of Haiti for the period. They were few and far between; it was a country in turmoil in the early nineteenth century. And then I came across the first British Consul's *Notes on Haiti: Made During a Residence in the Republic* (1830). Such books have no index, of course, and it was not the first such volume that I had skimmed through without success during that week.

Then, of 1 March 1827, Charles Mackenzie wrote, as if it were the most casual incident in the world,

There being nothing of particular interest on the road from Port au Prince to St Mark's by way of Arcahai, and it being described as deep & sandy, I determined to avoid it, especially as I had so recently suffered from exposure to the sun; and accordingly despatching my guide and animals to St Mark's, I embarked on His Majesty's Ship Harlequin, in which my friend Charles Elliot had, with his usual attention, offered to convey me to that city. (vol. I, p. 126)

I wonder if you can imagine what I felt at that moment. My excitement was as intense as any such feeling can be, though it made not a ripple beyond my chair in that centuries-old, rather serious-minded reading room.

I had found Charles Elliot in Haiti in March 1827, the year before *Burke* tells me he married Clara Genevieve, daughter of Robert Harley Windsor (in a ceremony not entered in United Kingdom records).

I am still trying to find young Clara in Haiti. In Charles Mackenzie's account he writes a few lines later, 'We were on shore early in the afternoon of the 16th [March] at Gonaives, where we were hospitably received, and lodged at the house of two English merchants established there.' I knew in my heart when I read those lines that one of the merchants was Clara's father, that on that evening 21-year-old Clara and 27-year-old Charles met. But I cannot yet prove it.

I have been working on trying to prove that Robert Harley Windsor was a merchant. It was not enough that his siblings were baptised in the City of London, that his parents obviously lived there. From the records at the City Road Chapel, I discovered that when Robert's father Thomas died, his body was brought for burial from Morden College. Going back to the London telephone directory, I found an address and wrote to the secretary, having no idea what Morden College was.

Back came a letter and enclosures from the college archivist telling me that Sir John Morden founded his charity in 1695 to provide for 'Poor Merchants ... and such as have lost their estates by accidents, dangers and perrills of the seas or by any other acccidents ways or means in their honest endeavours to get their living by means of Merchandising.' Enclosed, too, was Thomas Windsor's petition of 1805: 'That your petitioner hath for many years been a Merchant ... shipped on his account to Jamaica. ...'

Robert Harley Windsor's father was a merchant trading with the West Indies, but there is still more work to be done. I have recently written again to my friend Father Ernest Even in Haiti. For years I have worried every time I open a newspaper, but I have felt able now to ask him to do research which previously might have put him in danger. He may decide to go to Gonaives (where the English merchants lived), 167 kilometres north of Port au Prince, for Mackenzie also wrote, 'I was fortunate enough to get possession of a copy of the registers of births, deaths and marriages during the years 1825 and 1826 in the Commune of Gonaives' (p. 117). And a few pages later he added, 'All persons, without reference to their religious faith, are allowed to be buried in the public cemetery' (p. 131). Father Even may find the graves or records of death of Clara's mother – named Genevieve, perhaps – and father. And perhaps the record of Clara's birth in 1806.

Just before I wrote to Father Even in December, I wrote to some friends not far from Bordeaux. I have asked them if they can do some research for me there. This summer I went back to Edinburgh, back to the engagement book of Charles Elliot's sister, Emma Hislop. There had to be some clue there of Charles's marriage, of Clara's background.

I found an entry on 11 June 1828, the year of their marriage, which I cannot clearly read but which says something like, 'In search for *du mariage la jeune femme Clara*.' Emma's use of French suggests, and thus confirms, Clara's French background. But it only takes me a small step further. However, in 1831, the year Charles and Clara left for British Guiana, there are three entries from which I have managed to gain something because, in that year, by a process of deduction, their second child, Hugh Hislop, was born.

On 5 February, Emma writes: 'Charles arrives from Bordeaux.' On 5 March: 'Charles appointed to Demerara [British Guiana].' 10 March: 'Charley to Bordeaux.' 31 March: 'Charles and Clara to England.'

22 April: 'To Gravesend with Charles and Clara [to see them off to Demerara].'

My reading of that is that by this time Robert Harley Windsor had died in Haiti. His wife had returned to her original family place, Bordeaux, and her daughter, Clara, had gone there to have her child. There is no record of that birth in England.

It is possible too, since there is no record of Charles and Clara's marriage in England, that they were married there. There is a gap in Charles's biographical details, apart from his marriage and being promoted to captain, between 1827 when he was on the West Indian station in the *Harlequin* and 1831 when he sailed for British Guiana as Protector of Slaves. It seems he was working for the Colonial Office, but the details are obscure. Clara may have spent some time in Bordeaux and, indeed, her first child, Harriet Agnes, may also have been born there in 1829.

The French connection is given added impetus by Vaillant. After his first meeting with Clara in Macau, when he learned that she was a '*creole de Saint-Domingue*', he met her again at a party and wrote:

> It was a most pleasant dinner and the evening itself was even better because of the beautiful women who adorned it, because they danced and made music and because of Mme Elliot … who showed by her talent, her pretty voice, her amiability and her witty conversation (in French) that she could easily have graced the most elegant salon in Paris.

There is more to Vaillant's appreciation of Clara than a simple confirmation of her Frenchness: he adds another dimension to the question, 'Who was Clara Elliot?'

In my original reading of her personality in *The Private Life of Old Hong Kong*, I suggested that from her letters to Emma she revealed herself as reserved, unsure of herself, and anxious about her health and appearance. She writes of Macau on 16 March 1836, 'nice people here … are very scarce', suggesting that people have not welcomed her, that she may even have been slighted.

It seems too that her confidence waxed and waned. Eighteen months earlier, after a few months in Macau, she wrote:

> I cannot tell you how happy we are for now that my health has improved, I have resumed confidence in my own self and become quite a different being. [Charley] has purchased a nice square piano for me and I am now rejoiced to say my voice has quite returned. Why, dearest Emma, was I in such a delapidated state when last in England. You would *really* be pleased to hear me sing now. . . . The nose too is nearly well!!!

But Charles wrote only six months later, 'For the last few days we have been worried about poor Clarey's nose. At one time we thought it was partly manageable, but in the course of the last week, her inflamation has returned.' And a historian, unfortunately not giving a source, talks of her 'red nose', so it was obviously noticeable, and that bothered her.

That she often lacked confidence is confirmed by her letter to her sister-in-law in August 1840 when she was on her way to stay with Charles's cousins Lord Auckland and Emily Eden at Government House in Calcutta:

> One thing only I hope that idiotical feeling which you must have observed tho' you were too kind to notice it will not seize upon me as on former occasions when I wished most to appear to advantage.

At that party described by Vaillant on 20 January 1837, a month after Charles had been appointed Britain's senior representative in Macau, Clara seemed to be at her best. From her letters, she spoke English as if it were her first language; but was she perhaps more herself as a Frenchwoman?

Clara had a red nose; so did most of the Western women in the portraits of George Chinnery. But there is no known portrait by him of

Is this Clara Elliot?
George Chinnery portrait, c 1830s

Clara Elliot. Lastly, therefore, in trying to discover who she was, I presume to question the art historians.

In Patrick Conner's fine and beautifully illustrated biography of Chinnery, he shows a portrait (colour plate 91) with the caption 'A woman seated at a piano, said to be Mrs Baynes'. In his text, however (p. 218), Patrick writes:

> The identification of the piano playing sitter as Mrs Baynes
> is far from certain ... Pianos were in short supply in Macau,
> and it is possible that the sitter is Mrs Daniell who (as Harriet
> Low records) had a piano in her house, and lent it to the
> Lows when they held a party on 11 April 1832.

Elsewhere, it is supposed that the subject is Caroline Shillaber College, Harriet Low's girlhood friend, so the ascription is wide open.

What is more, there was, as I have already shown, another piano owner – Clara Elliot. Look at the piano in the portrait in question (reproduced here); it appears to be square (technically, oblong, boxlike in shape, horizontally strung). Clara tells us that hers was square. At that stage, I decided that the portrait was as likely to be of Clara Elliot as anyone else.

Even regarding pianos, however, you have to be careful: I have since discovered – in Harriett Low's Journals – four other piano owners in Macau in the early 1830s (including Mrs Baynes). And while square pianos were being replaced in Britain by uprights between 1820 and 1850, they remained popular in the United States; they were not generally uncommon.

As it happens, there is now more evidence than a piano that the adult sitter could be Mrs Daniell. And thus, some time after I thought I had completed this chapter, unfolds a lesson in how scrupulously honest and meticulous the researcher must be in drawing conclusions.

If in the end, though, I am going to have to decide that the portrait is not, after all, Clara Elliot but Mrs Daniell, which Mrs Daniell? There has been some confusion in the past about the Daniells; I have had to sort them out for this exploration.

In 1823, Jane LeGeyt (pronounced Legatt) married J.F.N. (James) Daniell of the East India Company in Macau. Clara Elliot met her when she arrived in Macau in July 1834. James Daniell was, by then, Chief Agent for the East India Company. When the Daniells left Macau in January 1836, Clara described Jane as her dear and perhaps only real friend there. Jane was the Mrs Daniell, I am now certain, who lent Harriett Low her piano in 1832.

Jane's sister-in-law, Harriet, wife of Anthony Stewart Daniell, merchant, arrived in Macau in September 1834 (soon after the Elliots). And I think it is Harriet – the latecomer – who is the Mrs Daniell in the sketch also reproduced here. Where does the sketch come from? Once I started promoting the oil portrait as Clara Elliot, Patrick Conner, in the pursuit of scholarship and with his usual generosity, went back to his Chinnery research slides looking for clues that had previously been missed, found this and transcribed Chinnery's shorthand.

Mrs Daniell at Mrs Vachell's,
George Chinnery sketch, 31 March, 1838

As you will see, the sketch is not enough like the oil portrait to provide definitive proof that the one is preparation for the other, though at least the sketch is named and dated (1838), unlike the portrait. Harriet Daniell is not sitting by a square piano in the sketch, but it was apparently drawn in the house of the pastor's wife Mrs Vachell; Harriet may have inherited her sister-in-law's piano and it could have been added when the portrait was painted. Interestingly, Chinnery was not entirely satisfied with the sketch; he marked an X against it and added, 'Something of the sentiment but not quite right.'

For reasons which will become clear, I also need to establish where the oil portrait is set. By 1837, both the Elliots and the Anthony Daniells appear to have been living on Franciscan Green. In the next chapter I detail how I found out where the Elliots lived. According to the 1830 *Macao Directory*, a Mr Daniell had a house on Franciscan Green (while another Mr Daniell, presumably James, lived in a grand East India Company house with 16 pillars opposite S. Lourenço Church). The house was, perhaps, on a long lease to the Daniell family and was lived in then by another brother, Matthew.

The circumstantial evidence for Anthony and Harriet Daniell taking over that house when they arrived in 1834 is an article in the local press dated 25 October 1836:

> Notice. This is to notify all vagabonds who are in the habit of bathing in a stage of nudity in front of the house of Mr A. Daniell, that in the future they may be liable to suffer from broken glass if they persist in such indecorous and indecent behaviour.

Although Clara Elliot does not mention her departed friend's sister-in-law as a neighbour in her letters, not all her letters have survived and she was, anyway, by her own admission, an infrequent correspondent. And her letters tended to be of immediate family concerns and of Charles's work problems.

I am making it clear that Harriet Daniell probably lived in the same area of Macau as Clara Elliot because it is against the interests of my pet theory that she did so. (By 1839, a panoramic map shows that a Mr Daniell lived over the other side of the bay, also on the waterfront, where there might have been nude bathers, in the same house as Mr Innes. But I don't think that was Anthony; I think James, the older brother, returned to Macau without his wife Jane and shared that house; a newspaper report has James leaving Macau by himself in 1839.)

What remains, then, of my evidence that the portrait in question might be of Clara Elliot?

It is strange that there is no known portrait of her by Chinnery; I feel sure that he must have painted her, if only because of her husband's position. And, because of Charles Elliot's status from December 1836, the size of the portrait – much larger than many of them – should be taken into account. While Jane Daniell's husband held an important position until the ending of the East India Company's monopoly in 1834, Harriet Daniell's was only a merchant.

But there is more to it than that and, once again, it is Captain August Vaillant who provides support. When he first met Charles Elliot, Vaillant was sketching in the courtyard of S. Francisco; Elliot engaged him in conversation and 'talked of drawing like a real connoisseur'. He invited Vaillant home 'to see several pictures by a local artist'. They were, of course, by Chinnery. The Elliots and Chinnery were obviously friends, for Charles Elliot pronounced to Vaillant of Chinnery, 'He would be delighted to meet you. Would you like me to introduce you to him?' That evening, therefore, in the company of the Elliots, the French captain met the artist and was, as he wrote, 'received with open arms'.

If you look at the picture on the wall behind the portrait I hope is of Clara, you will see a painting by Chinnery of a view that the Elliots would have seen from their house – looking across the bay from S. Francisco to the Penha Hill. Did the Daniells have the same view? (That picture, variations of which Chinnery often drew and painted, is reproduced in the next chapter, p. 59.)

The Hon. Mrs Russell (nee Harriet Agnes Elliot)
Artist and date unknown

Finally, I reproduce a portrait of Clara's daughter Harriet Agnes Elliot as a young married woman (in the possession of her descendants). The portraits are rather small and in black and white but, still, look at them closely, I shall refrain from itemising the similarities I noted with growing excitement when I first saw them together. But I must draw attention to the pearl and garnet pendant or brooch worn by both women.

Replying originally to my Elliot–Chinnery theory, Patrick Conner wrote, 'I can only say you *may* be right!' In my letter, I had remarked, rather reprehensibly, on the looks of the sitter. Harriett Low described Julia Baynes as 'the prettiest woman in Macau. She is a real beauty'. I did not think the woman in the portrait would qualify, however much fashions of beauty change and whatever the artist's idiosyncrasies. Patrick Conner then added, to warm my heart, 'I certainly don't have any faith in the Julia Baynes identity – on the other hand, that painting is by no means my favourite Chinnery portrait, and for that very subjective and trivial reason I'm not particularly keen to believe that the sitter is Clara.'

Now, some months later, after we have explored further, and the Daniell sketch has intruded, Patrick keeps quiet; he does not say that the sketch proves that 'my Clara portrait' is Mrs Daniell, however hard I provoke him to do so. But he will say, 'It is seldom possible to link (with any certainty) Chinnery's portrait sketches to his portrait oils' (13 May 1996). And he has sent me another unnamed Chinnery oil that looks more like the sketch than does 'my Clara' oil.

For me, for the moment, therefore, that Chinnery oil portrait is of Clara Elliot.

There is one final problem, though. In the middle of all this, I went to the Hongkong and Shanghai Bank to see the original portrait in their skyscraping conference room. I went then to try and decipher the name on the sitter's piano so that I could write to the manufacturers. The portrait was grander than I expected and faces a magnificent harbour view – Hong Kong, not Macau. So unexpectedly impressed was I that now I am not sure that the sitter is not Mrs Baynes, 'the prettiest woman in Macau'!

History is the marriage of facts and imagination. No bits of the puzzle can be forced to fit. But without the leaps of imagination, there is often no way forward to the far bank of the river over the stepping stones of facts.

When I come to write the introduction to the letters from China Waters of Charles and Clara Elliot, the research underpinning this chapters may well merit only a couple of sentences: 'Clara Elliot (née Windsor) may have been born in Haiti in 1806 and brought up there. It seems likely that she and Charles Elliot met there in 1827'. A footnote will refer readers to this chapter.

Delivered as a lecture, autumn 1993, women's studies class, History Department, University of Hong Kong; elaborated on for a seminar talk, Centre of Asian Studies, January 1995.

FURTHER RESEARCH

A-Z London Atlas and Street Index.

Bodleian Library, Broad Street, Oxford.

British Library, Great Russell Street, London WC1.

Burford, Robert, *Description of a View of Macao in China* (London, 1840).

Burke's Genealogical Peerage, Baronage and Knightage and Heraldic History of the Landed Gentry (105th edn), P. Townsend (ed.) London, 1970).

Byrne, W.R., *A Naval Biographical Dictionary* (London, 1849).

Byrne, W.R., *A Naval Biographical Dictionary: A New and Enlarged Edition* (London, 1859).

Debrett's Peerage and Baronetage, Patrick Montague-Smith (ed.) (London, 1980).

Dictionary of National Biography (Oxford, Oxford University Press).

Family Record Centre of Utah Genealogical Society, 7 Lower Castle Road, Central, Hong Kong.

Greater London Record Office, 40 Northampton Road, London EC1 0HB.

Guildhall Library, Aldermanbury, London EC2P 2EJ.

London Telephone Directory.

Low, Harriett, Journal of, Low-Mills papers, Library of Congress, Washington D.C.

Macao Directory, 1830 (British Library).

Minto Mss, Department of Manuscripts, National Library of Scotland, George IV Bridge, Edinburgh E11 1EW; Clara Elliot, MS 13137 ff 4-37; Admiral Sir Charles Elliot, MSS 13135-6.

National Army Museum, Royal Hospital Road, London SW3 4HT.

Public Record Office, Chancery Lane, London WC2A 1FR.

Public Record Office, Ruskin Avenue, Kew, Richmond, Surrey TW9 4DU.

(Somerset House) The Principal Probate Registry (Wills and Letters of Administration), Somerset House, Strand, London WC2 1LP.

(St Catherine's House), General Register Office (Births, Marriages and Deaths), St Catherine's House, 10 Kingsway, London WC2.

CHAPTER 4

WHERE DID SHE LIVE?
A Near Failure in Macau

'Be prepared!' That is not only the Boy Scouts' solemn creed; it should be that of the historical researcher. If ever I was not prepared, and paid for it, it was on a visit to Macau in May 1994 in search of Clara and Charles Elliot.

Nan Hodges, preparing Harriett Low's 1829-1834 Journal for publication, had visited Macau for the first time earlier in the year. During a prolonged and enthusiastic telephone conversation just before she finally left Hong Kong, she drew my attention to the Guia fort and lighthouse. I got it firmly into my head that the complex atop its hill dominating the Macau skyline had some connection with the Elliots.

Derek and I left for Macau that May morning in a flurry. I took nothing with me but a guidebook; I did no preparation. I knew we must go to the Guia and was sure the guidebook would tell me why, and then that the stones of the Guia itself would elaborate. It had something, I was sure, to do with the Sao Francisco Monastery where Charles Elliot met the Frenchman whose account revealed to me that Clara was a creole from Saint-Domingue (Haiti).

'While we were busy with our sketching,' Auguste Vaillant started his account of that meeting, 'a good looking young man who, from his features and manners we guessed to be an Englishman, but who spoke French well enough to make us wonder if we were right, interrupted us very politely and engaged us without reticence in conversation.' The monastery was, thus, a key location for the researcher anxious to breathe as one with the 'spirit of place'.

On the slightly out-of-date map, I could see how easy it was to go from our hotel to the Guia and, as if to confirm my delusions, the road upwards that we should take was the Estrada de S. Francisco. It was 6.30 in the evening; the sun was sleepy and it would be a perfect time to climb to the Guia and watch Macau turning pink and gold. We would almost believe we were back in the nineteenth century as the opalescent light veiled the ravages of the developer and the town planner.

But the dimensions of so-called progress are not only aesthetic; they are also of concrete and tar. A new superhighway now links the centre of Macau to the new ferry terminal. It was beside that that we found ourselves trudging. Our lungs bursting with exhaust fumes, we tried to devise ways to ascend the hill to our left. It was impossible. There was no side road and its flanks, bald even a hundred years ago, were impenetrably and luxuriantly wooded. It was also very hot, in spite of the time of day, and we got increasingly flushed and bothered.

Eventually, more than a mile later, we climbed into a taxi and asked to be taken up the hill. Dropped at the pedestrian path there in the gloaming, our spirits revived. We turned to the right and started walking, and we walked and walked. It soon became apparent that we were walking in a circle. A few joggers and one or two walkers were going in the opposite direction, clockwise, the way the Chinese prefer.

It got darker. Frogs leapt in the ditches full of dry leaves alongside the path. An hour and a half later, we arrived back near where we had started out. Two steps to the left from where we had turned purposefully right was the drive leading up to the Guia.

There was no one about now; the recreational area was deserted for the night. But we had the bit between our teeth. We strode upwards and there was the remains of the fort and the lighthouse brightly lit and guarded by a pack of wild dogs. They stood on the ramparts with gleaming eyes. We prowled round outside the locked gates and felt mildly triumphant. We had found nothing to do with the Elliots. We did not even know what we were looking for. But we had got there.

If you give up at that stage of your researches, you might as well never start. The following morning we set off again by taxi. We saw all that the Guia has to offer: the little chapel, the cannons, the view of Macau harbour being further reclaimed, the Praia Grande being increasingly desecrated.

By this time, I had gone back to the guidebook and read more carefully. The Guia had nothing to do with the Sao Francisco Monastery, but on the site of the monastery, at the opposite end of the Estrada de S. Francisco from the Guia, is the startlingly pink Military Barracks erected in 1867, and the Military Club adjoining it.

The guidebook explained that the best view of this complex, which in my mind now reeked of the spirit of Charles and Clara Elliot, was from the restaurant of the Lisboa Hotel. I did not dare suggest we walk down the historic Estrada de S. Francisco to get to it. We took a taxi. The view when we got there was obscured by part of the flyover system that had thwarted us the previous evening.

Downstairs, we crossed over to the Military Club with which the Foreign Correspondents' Club in Hong Kong reciprocates; we would do much better there. It was closed for renovation. Beside the club, a driveway led up into the barracks where there is also a military museum. We should go up there. Sweat gathered behind our knees. We saw a taxi and hailed it. We headed away to where there was air-conditioning and a cold, cold drink.

Back in my office in Hong Kong, I started to do the research I should have done before I left for Macau. I even found photographs of how the water had once reached the walls of the Sao Francisco Monastery, now the Military Club and barracks. I also wrote to Nan Hodges asking her why I should have gone to the Guia.

She had gone there, she explained, because Harriett used to climb up there and Nan had, at the same time, followed the road down to what had been the Sao Francisco Monastery, where Harriett was wont to sit in the garden. There was the tenuous connection which I had misheard and misinterpreted.

But in that letter Nan also told me about a panoramic map of Macau that she had recently been given by Patrick Conner, George Chinnery's biographer. On it was marked Captain Elliot's house. Did I know about it? No!

Last week, on a gentle autumn day, we set out for Macau again. In the usual flurry I made a spare photocopy of the panorama. In even more of a flurry I rang Carl Smith to whom I had given a copy some weeks earlier. Had he managed to work out where the site of Clara and Charles's house was? He gave me directions.

We took a taxi straight from the Macau ferry terminal to the Military Club. It had been completely gutted. But this time we walked up the driveway to the side and so came out into what is, even today, the Sao Francisco Garden. I had not known of its existence.

It is not as it was 150 years ago. I know that because some lines from the poet Camões are inscribed in a wall under the date 1883. But there is a banyan tree overlooking it that seems much older. In this garden we wandered under the caressing sun and I quite clearly saw Charles Elliot interrupt the Frenchman quietly sketching.

In memory of that, I approached a Chinese family playing with their dog, Chao Yi, a cross between a dalmatian and a whippet. 'Chao Yi means grass,' explained the woman.

'Why is she called Grass?'

'Her mother was called Flower.'

George Chinnery watercolour [on paper] of Macau's
Praia Grande Bay, c1833, as depicted in his
'Clara Elliot' oil

Nearby is a pink and white folly which two plaques indicate was used at one time by a veterans' association and which commemorates the war dead of 1914-1918. Surely that at least dates from the Elliots' time – it is too bizarre to have been built by the military!

Now I mulled over the October 1833 extract from Harriett Low's diary that Nan had sent me:

> Then C [Caroline Colledge] and I walked out, went to the Franciscan Church yard. A lovely spot it is too, and of such an evening. We sat ourselves down under the protection of a great cross erected upon a tomb, and the evening bells were just ringing, which are always pleasing. The sun had just gone but left every thing tinged with its parting smiles, look-ing bright and beautiful. The water was still and smooth as glass, or moved only in a ripple. Not a discordant sound was heard, we were away from the busy world, and it was *lovely*. We sat there an hour and then went home lest the padres should seize us. For begging their pardon, I would not trust myself to their tender mercies more than to any *layman*. (Journal VII, 31 October, 1833.)

Harriett left Macau in November 1833 and in July 1834 the Elliots arrived. The following year, because of anti-Catholic sentiment in Por-tugal, religious orders were suppressed there and overseas, including Macau, and monastery buildings were sequestered by the government. (Incidentally, that is the year St Paul's Church burned down; today only the intriguing façade is left.) But it is obvious from Harriett's diary that the public was allowed into the grounds of the Sao Francisco Monas-tery before then and Harriett's account shows that it was not only Charles Elliot who enjoyed them. Although the spot is completely different now – and Macau is even more so – it is, remarkably, still peaceful and has a similar allure.

I had imagined that Charles came some distance to this secluded place; now I found, thanks to the panoramic plan, that it was only a step away from the house he probably moved into when he became Britain's senior representative in China at the end of 1836. Carl Smith had worked out, using the panorama and his records, that the Elliots then lived at the junction of Rua do Campo and Rua de Santa Clara.

Arriving there, I was delighted to see it was the site of the Chinese public library. This small round building on an island between two busy roads, with its red painted window frames, had attracted us before. Inside, it is just one room and that only big enough for a few readers; most of them were absorbed in newspapers. On the wall facing the door are two portraits of women whom the custodian was unable to identify on a previous occasion. Now, we got no further because he could not understand our question. But a fey passerby who heard us talking wanted us to take some advertisements for his Chinese medical services back to Hong Kong. In exchange, he told us that the library was erected by Ho Yin, in memory of his mother.

For me, that tiny, strange and rather splendid library dwarfed by ugly high-rise buildings was Clara and Charles Elliot's house. But when I got back to Hong Kong, Carl would have nothing of it. 'No, not there,' he said. 'Not on the [traffic] island. That would have been in the water. On the other side of the Rua de Santa Clara.'

He had been doing some more reading and thinking. He had found reference in the 1820s to two houses owned by the Santa Clara Order – one occupied by the Mendes family, the other by a Mr Rangel. One of those he felt had been the Elliots' house.

Back I went to Macau on New Year's Eve, back to the Rua de Santa Clara. There are the unobtrusive metal gates Carl told me about. If I stand on tiptoe, through the top I can see wide, low-slung stone steps leading up to a fading house with what has been an elegant Portuguese wrought iron balcony and beside it a church – buildings which I discover can only be seen from here; the back is a high, blank wall on the parallel road. At that time, I thought the wall was concrete; later, Shann Davies, an authority on Macau, explained that it was chunambo (crushed sea shells, lime, earth and straw, tightly pressed between wood) and impenetrable to cannon fire. It is the only remains of the old city wall.

This is the Santa Rosa di Lima, a school and church erected in the 1960s by Eric Ho Tung on the site of the old Santa Clara convent buildings, almost adjacent to the grounds of the Sao Francisco monastery. In 1824, the original convent (founded in 1634) was burned to the ground, killing a 90-year-old nun. It was rebuilt in 1827 and it was next door to that new building that Clara and Charles lived in the late 1830s. The Santa Clara were respected and the nuns who remained were allowed to live in the convent until the last of them died in 1875.

Charles and Clara Elliot's house (right)
by George Chinnery, Macau, 5 July 1836

The house where the Elliots had lived was still among the records of property that the Order finally submitted to the government in 1876.

Today, my revised site for that house is the Cinetheatre de Macau abutting the Santa Rosa di Lima gates, an odd, angular green building festooned on this visit with holy Christmas decorations. I prod my mind as I write, for it is in the act of writing and arranging the material that I have squirrelled away in my mental computer or on scraps of paper scrawled on while I talk to Carl on the telephone, that the imagination works best. Until recently, I could visualise Charles and Clara's

house quite clearly, with its wide verandah looking out over the gracious curve of the Praia Grande to the right, the Guia hill back and to the left, and the water, lively and stained by estuary mud, lapping against the shore below. Now, as this book is undergoing publication, in May 1996, Patrick Conner discovers for me an 1836 Chinnery sketch of the Elliot's house. It is not exactly as I imagined it! I have to re-arrange my thoughts, which is unsettling but exciting.

In February 1996, Carl Smith and I found ourselves in Macau at the same time. We resolved to trace the footsteps of Charles and Clara Elliot that evening in 1837 when they took the French naval captain Auguste Vaillant to meet the artist George Chinnery. And, if I am right that Chinnery painted Clara, it is probably in that house that she had some sittings for her portrait.

The most startling realisation as you make your way past the recently, and successfully, revamped Military Club that was the Sao Francisco Monastery, is that the Praia Grande ended there as recently as 1900. Photographs of 1930 show an area of reclamation extending past the headland, as yet without any development. Today, not only are such landmarks as the Lisboa Hotel on that expanse of reclamation, but much further work has been done, and continues to be done there.

But on these occasions you separate your mind and your soul from the evidence of your eyes and we trotted along, with the Avenida Almeida Ribeiro flowing north on our right, and the Solmar restaurant in the former shallows of the outer harbour on our left. I was bothered about Clara's long skirt; how did she keep it from trailing on the ground and getting dirty?

We passed the crushed raspberry Governor's Palace on our right and turned up Travessa de Padre Narciso. At the top used to be the House of Sixteen Pillars, where East India Company nobs lived and, opposite that site, dominating the square is Sao Lourenço Church. Clara and Charles would have skirted that, and you must ignore the road that now calls itself George Chinnery Street; he didn't live there. Turn instead down Rua Ignacio Baptista, named after a member of the powerful Portuguese Cortella family. Where the road bends, on your right, is an unassuming, unhappily modern, two-storey house with a metal blind – number 12 (formerly number 8). That is where Chinnery lived.

Reliving that evening of 1837 was the final act of establishing where Clara and Charles Elliot had their being in the 1830s, and what started as a false trail and a lesson against unpreparedness nearly two years ago has ended in a feeling of warm satisfaction.

Main draft written November 1994. See also 'Further Research' from previous chapter.

CHAPTER 5

TO DIE IN MACAU
The Protestant Cemetery

How often have we done this journey since I started my historical researches on Macau and Hong Kong? We take the jet foil from Shun Tak, Hong Kong. Fifty minutes later, the Praia Grande hoves into sight. It is not quite as it was 150 years ago, but you can conjure up the scene well enough if you try.

Going through immigration, we always choose the slowest queue; but never mind, the warm moist air that greets you outside heightens the senses and the lighthouse on the hill above gives you a historical *frisson*.

The taxi driver never understands the address – The Protestant cemetery, or the Camões Museum. I point at the map, trying not to seem impatient and, grudgingly, he sets off through streets entirely unlike those of Hong Kong.

The taxi stops outside the iron gates to the museum, which is rarely open. Slightly to your left is the entrance to the public gardens and the grotto where Camões is said to have written his *Os Lusiadas*. On your right is the archway leading to the cemetery. I pass the little chapel on the left and then the cemetery opens out before me, green and marble, shaded by trees, impeccably kept.

Barbara, who was born in China and brought up in Hong Kong, tells me that it was not always thus. She used to play in the cemetery before it was made orderly – the graves and the ghosts they contain respected – by Sir Lindsay and Lady Ride. She remembers it as overgrown and unkempt, the tombstones somewhat higgledy-piggledy – a secret garden for the carefree. My mind's eye does a quick double take, then I get down to the business in hand. Macau's Western history is waiting for me there, asleep – quiet as the grave. I get out my pencil and pad…

Mary Morrison lies next to her husband and their sons, James who died the day of his birth, and John aged 29. Mary's grave is a special one, for it is said to be the first. But was it?

Mary Morton, daughter of missionaries, married China's first Protestant missionary, Robert Morrison, in Macau in 1809. She died in childbirth in 1821. At the time of their first son's death, the Morrisons had buried him on the hillside outside the city walls, the Portuguese Roman Catholic cemetery not being available to Protestants. But now the Chinese would not allow Robert Morrison to open his son's grave to bury his wife. The Select Committee of the East India Company was prompted by the awfulness of the situation to bargain with the Portuguese authorities for a site for a Protestant cemetery.

The cemetery was created the other side of Casa Garden (or Casa da Horta) from the public gardens. The mystery is that Casa Garden (now the Camões Museum) was already rented by the Company and two Company graves existed in its grounds – an embryo cemetery.

James Moloney, a Company supercargo between 1807 and 1821, writes quite clearly in his unpublished memoir, at the India Office, London, of a day in January 1813 when another supercargo, Mr Roberts (not to be confused with Mr Robarts who died in 1825 and whose grave is in the cemetery), 'was buried in the beautiful garden of Casa Horta where he resided; the funeral service was performed by me – a tomb was placed on the grave.'

Moloney also knew of the second burial. He noted that Sir Theophilus Metcalfe, then acting President of the Company's Select Committee, had visited Bengal and married there the daughter of Sir Charles Russell. 'He brought her to Macao,' Moloney wrote, 'where she died and was buried in the same garden as Mr Roberts.' The Metcalfes, the records show, were married in 1804, and Sophia died in 1809.

There is no sign now of the Roberts and Metcalfe graves, though they still existed when the merchant Gideon Nye visited Macau, for he wrote of Casa Garden and the Grotto of Camões, 'where may still be found the tombstones of Mr Robartes [sic] and Lady Metcalf [sic]... as may also be found in the adjoining cemetery those of ... Revd

Dr Morrison'. Nye was more probably talking of the time when he was writing his book (a transcript of public talks he gave in the 1870s) than of the time about which he was writing (the 1830s).

It seems likely that before 1821 the Company broke the rules prohibiting Protestants from being buried within the city walls at least twice, but perhaps only when the dead had lived in the nearby house, Casa Garden. If it had applied to everyone associated with the Company, Mary Morrison would have qualified, her husband having been the Company's official translator since the time of their marriage.

I am haunted by the question, where is Sophia Metcalfe's grave? Others who died there have become part of history, because their graves exist, and with them the names and dates on the tombstones. They somehow come alive whenever they are visited.

Death seems to have come early on the China coast. Elizabeth Fearon's grave is next to that of 20-year-old Louisa, wife of Christopher Fearon's partner, James W.H. Ilberry. But there is barely a hint of the cause of death in either case. William Jardine wrote to James Matheson on 22 August 1837 describing how 'Mrs Ilberry has died, niece of Mrs Crockett, strong willed lady refused to be blistered or take doctors' prescriptions'. She left at least one child, a daughter born just over a year earlier.

On 31 March 1838, aged 44, Elizabeth Fearon died at Lintin, the island between Macau and Canton where the opium hulks were stationed; through them the opium was transferred from the clippers that brought it from India to the small fast boats which clandestinely disposed of it. The women of Macau used to go to Lintin for a break, and many wives of sea captains lived on board at anchor there for quite long periods. Away from her comfortable home, Elizabeth would have been more vulnerable. Her fifth child had been born the previous year.

Two of Mrs Crockett's children are buried in the cemetery close to her niece Louisa Ilberry, one aged 21 days in 1835, the other, a few months later, aged six years. So is her husband John, a sea captain, who died a few months before her niece, aged 51, leaving Mrs Crockett with five other children to look after.

Caroline Shillaber, who came to visit the young American Harriett Low and stayed to marry the English Dr Thomas Colledge, buried three of her children there – one aged 18 months in 1837; one aged 17 months in September 1838; the third aged eight months in December the same year. These little graves with their big headstones make a deep impression on the visitor. It is augmented by reading Harriett's account of their girlish days before Caroline's marriage.

When Mary Morrison died in 1821, the other women in the community rallied round. Mary had spent some time in Britain over the years since her marriage trying to regain her health. In 1819 she travelled out to Macau with Mrs Moloney. James Moloney had recently married Harriet Harding; a year earlier, Harriet's sister Catherine had married another Company supercargo, W.H.C. Plowden. The two

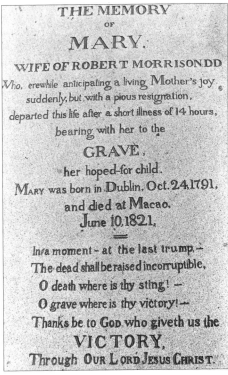

Mary Morrison's tombstone,
Old Protestant Cemetery, Macau

sisters and their husbands were to live together in Macau, making life very much easier and more pleasant for both of them. When Mary Morrison died, they offered to do what they could for her daughter Rebecca, as did Janet Livingstone, wife of the Company's surgeon whose six-month-old daughter, Charlotte, had been buried three years earlier – presumably on the hillside. Little Charlotte's grave, like other similar ones, was later moved within the cemetery.

The Moloneys left China later that year because of Harriet's ill health – James sacrificing his career, as he makes clear, for his wife. Catherine Plowden died in Macau, aged 35, in 1827. When W.H.C. Plowden was deposed as President of the Select Committee at the end of 1829, he was probably ready to go home. When he returned as President in 1830, he brought a new wife, the widow Annette Nixon. She went back to England six months later because of ill health.

And yet, one must not get Macau's mortality rate out of perspective. The enclave was hot and humid in the summer – much as Hong Kong and Macau are today; it was plagued by mosquitoes and cockroaches; and the narrow Chinese streets were filthy, as Lady Napier reported before the death of her husband (who lay buried beside Mary Morrison before his body was taken back to Scotland). But Catherine Plowden's sister, Harriet Moloney, died a year before her in England of typhus, as their father had died just before Harriet arrived home.

When Harriett Low eventually married, after her five-year sojourn on the China coast, and went with her American husband to live in England, she had eight children there, four of whom were dead before they were six years old. And, notwithstanding so many deaths of young women, perhaps worn out or weakened by childbearing, many who had lived for years in the East lived to a better than average old age. Harriett Low lived until she was 67; Emily Davis, wife of the Company man who became the second governor of Hong Kong, and mother of seven children, lived until she was 65; Julia Baynes, who had her sixth of seven children in a typhoon, lived to be 88; and Eliza Napier (eight children) died at 89!

Written 1989

CANTON, BEIJING AND SHANGHAI

CHAPTER 6

A DAY IN THE
RECONSTRUCTION OF
A LIFE
Whampoa, December 1993

Slithering up the muddy clay slope, I clutched at long grass stems and finally reached the top. There, the sunlight filtered into a bamboo grove, abandoned it seemed since time immemorial. Pushing aside fronds, we made for Alexander Everett's grave. The headstone was wedged upside-down in the ground. I had to cock my head to decipher that he was United States' Minister to China and had died in 1847.

Foreigners were buried on Dane's Island, Whampoa (Huangpu), from the early nineteenth century. The cemetery was vandalised during the Second Opium War (1857-1860), and again a century later during the Korean War. It was not until 1983 that the Canton (Guangzhou) authorities rediscovered it during a heritage survey. Only a visit from members of staff of the American Consulate in August this year had preceded ours.

But I had wanted to visit the cemetery ever since I read that Lydia Hale Devan had been buried there in 1846. Cemeteries are somehow not morbid to the historian; they reek not of putrefaction and grief, but of the essence of that long ago life that you are striving to reconstitute.

More than once on a visit to Canton I resolved to get to Whampoa and search for Lydia. But nothing came of it. There are no organised tourist trips down the river that I could discover, even if I could find Whampoa on a modern Canton map, no public transport, no description in a tourist guide.

Funny when you consider how once it was a port in its own right. There the foreign sailing ships, forbidden to go up the Pearl River as far as Canton, would tie up and unload their cargo. Round about, the First Opium War raged between 1839 and 1842. Charles Elliot passed in his cutter dozens of times, perhaps moored for a while, on business or to take a walk, so difficult anywhere else in the delta. And Clara, too, passed this way at least twice, to and from Canton in May 1841.

I know now, even if I had persisted in trying to find Lydia Hale Devan, a very minor character in my history of Western women, I would have been disappointed. It was only with the discovery of Alexander Everett's grave, and news filtering out about it on the grapevine, that the director of the Hong Kong Museum of History resolved, through contacts with Canton colleagues, to take a Royal Asiatic Society group there.

The bamboo-festooned cemetery has been well and truly vandalised, but I went looking for Lydia nevertheless. I think I found her tombstone. Just above that of Everett was a slab on its face. The name was buried in the ground but the obverse inscription reads, 'This monument is erected by her bereaved husband.'

I have a list here, from H.S. Smith's *Diary of Events ... on Shameen* (1938), of burials on Dane's Island. Eliza Jane Wilden, buried in 1850, is just before Everett on the list; after him comes Agnes Ball, infant daughter of Rev. J. Ball, 1850. Lydia's name is the one before Eliza Jane. Beside this unnamed tombstone in the cemetery is the anonymous one of a child. Just the three are fully visible.

Of Eliza Jane Wilden I know nothing, but of Lydia I know a little. She was one of the earliest women to spend time in Hong Kong. In November 1844 she had recently arrived and was staying with the missionaries Lewis and Henrietta Shuck. The latter, aged 27, was pregnant with her fifth child.

Henrietta described Lydia in a letter home as 'a sweet sister. We seem to be agreed on all points, and I pray and believe that we shall be assistants to each other. When I am laid by, which will be I expect in a few days, she will be able to aid me very much.' Sadly, Henrietta did not survive her confinement.

The following April, Lydia accompanied her missionary husband, Thomas, to Canton and there, hardly settled, she died. Henrietta Shuck, unusually for that time, was a missionary in her own right. So too was Lydia, I learn for the first time. The records describe her as 'the first Lady Missionary to the people of Canton'.

A fellow missionary, William Dean, describes how, 'Uniting high mental gifts and culture with the kind words and genteel bearing of a true Christian woman, [she] commanded respect and wielded an influence for good all around her.'

This little knowledge of her, squirrelled away for five years, has been fanned into new eagerness. That is why I hope the tombstone is hers, so that, when the Chinese authorities dig that heavy slab from the ground and restore it the right way up, Lydia Hale Devan, Baptist of New York, will, in a sense, live again.

Perhaps the whole cemetery will be revived, on that gentle hill, under that bamboo bower, but it will never again be like finding her, as I am sure I did, face down and forgotten.

<hr />

Later I discovered that in the same cemetery were buried William Couper and Ellen Couper. The entry on the 1938 list for the former suggests that he was 'cruelly dragged from the side of his wife and daughter by a crew of Mandarin Braves, and is supposed to have died in prison at Canton, year 1850.'

Of Ellen Couper the record says that she was the wife of 'the above WJ Couper'; she died aged 24 in 1858. Beware of records! Untangling these strands is some consolation for having missed the Couper Docks. These were on the list of visits we were to make in Whampoa and, knowing what I do about the Coupers, I was looking forward to the dry docks which John Couper, father and son, had constructed between 1851 and 1854.

There are conflicting stories about the Couper incident, but one thing appears incontrovertible: husband and wife lived on a chopboat – a sort of Chinese houseboat – moored off Whampoa, presumably close to the docks on Dane's Island. The story has it that at 5 pm on Saturday, 20 December 1856, a sampan came alongside the Coupers' chopboat with a letter for John Couper senior. Walking with his wife and daughter on the deck, he leaned down to take it and was pulled overboard, never to be seen again.

That he had a grave on Dane island comes as news to me; that he is supposed to have died in prison in Canton is fascinating and requires further investigation. But it cannot have been in 1850, since he was apparently still around until 1856.

In some versions of the story, particularly a caption against a picture of their chopboat, Mrs Couper was killed at the time her husband disappeared, felled on the deck of the chop. However, the impresario Albert Smith met her in September 1858 and his description not only contradicts the story of her murder in 1856, but also that she died in 1858 aged 24. For Smith writes of how he breakfasted on young Mr Couper's chop and how 'His mother and sister joined us. The old lady was very weary of China and longed to be home again.'

So, who was Ellen Couper aged 24 in 1858 when she died? Was she the daughter of Mr and Mrs John Couper senior? Perhaps she was the one on the deck with her parents when the fateful incident took place?

Now I turn to the St John's Cathedral birth, deaths and marriages records of early Hong Kong kept in the public record office. Two weddings took place on 25 November 1857, a year after John Couper's disappearance. One was of Jane Couper to John Gibson, the other of Williamina Cowper to Henry Castilla. John C. Cowper was one of the witnesses. (No confusion should be felt by the change of spelling: Couper and Cowper were interchangeable.)

Six months later, on 5 June 1858, John Cardno Cowper married Ellen Kitchen. It is obviously she who died on 18 October 1858, four months after her marriage. Why, I shall keep an eye and an ear open to find out.

So when the Chinese authorities have cleared up the cemetery on Dane's Island, I hope Ellen Kitchen Couper's tombstone will be among those found under the eroding soil and bamboo leaves of over a century. Perhaps it was the one of which only a corner was showing, and which I tried to scrape clean with a constantly snapping bamboo twig. At all events, there are worse places in which to lie.

But why didn't we see the Couper Docks? An oversight, it seems. As we went to step once more into the sampans, having moved from one part of the island to another, I asked, 'Are we going to see the Couper Docks now?'

'No,' answered our expert companion. 'There isn't time. They're somewhere else and we have to go for lunch.'

I saw later on the map that they were close to an earlier port of call. Now, as I went to step from the quay down to the sampan, I felt transported back to childhood, to that moment when you were told that you couldn't go to that party, couldn't have that toy. I felt thwarted in a way that I have rarely felt as an adult. I stepped across the dangerous gap and ropes unseeing and uncaring. My eyes vainly scoured the horizon for the Couper Docks.

This time I took no notice of the person who sat behind the motor of the sampan, expertly plying it through the Whampoa waters. Her ancestors, her grandmothers, had been doing it for generations around the waters of the Pearl River Delta. The artist George Chinnery had sketched and painted her innumerable times; every account of the area by soldier, sailor or merchant had mentioned her flashing eyes and merry laugh.

Mrs John Henry Gray, wife of the vicar of Christ's Church Shameen, the foreign enclave in Canton after the foreign factories were destroyed in 1857, spent 14 months in Canton between 1877 and 1878. She describes how, on a visit to Whampoa, the women skulled and rowed the boats dressed in tunics, wide short dark blue trousers, but no shoes or stockings. By then there were no large ships at Whampoa, and the docks had been sold to the Chinese.

Our boatwoman particularly caught my attention when we first set out on our journey for Dane's Island. She looked so absurdly right historically. She grew tired of me taking photographs, however, and rather sulky.

*Pearl River boatwoman and child,
Whampoa, 1993*

When we finally tied up, I turned back and saw her feeding her little son. She was laughing happily, and I took another photograph. It's much better than one of the Couper Docks!

Why had the timetable for that morning in Whampoa gone adrift? There was an unforeseen visit which, in itself, was pure compensation. Walking from the Parsee cemetery back to the shore, we came upon the Whampoa Military Academy. For a feminist pacifist, the attraction this complex of buildings provided may seem strange, but it had a direct connection with a book review I had just written, a piece of research I was about to carry out and a book I had planned.

Upstairs in the shell that remains of an administrative building is a small room off the main museum hall. Poking your nose curiously into someone's bedroom you see a simple iron double bed with snowy white sheet and pillowcases, and a pristine mosquito net caught back to reveal it. There is, too, an ordinary desk and chair and, above it, a portrait.

Standing, is Sun Yat-sen (Sun Zhongshan), father of the Chinese Revolution of 1911, and sitting beside him is his wife, Soong Ching Ling (Song Qingling). Born 100 years ago this year, she is the object of my interest and to come across her bedroom here was a real bonus.

Of course, nostalgia is open to manipulation and this is no exception. Soong Ching Ling slept here on perhaps one occasion for a night or two. What is more, the building was bombed and badly damaged by the Japanese before they took Canton in 1938. The air of seediness that pervades all these rooms hung with fading photographs is relatively modern, and even the bed is probably a replacement from government surplus stores. Even so, the effect of simplicity and asceticism is striking.

Sun Yat-sen set up the Academy in June 1924, with Soviet help, to train officers not just to command but to be imbued with revolutionary principle as well. Ironically, in view of what was to follow, its director was Chiang Kai-shek, not yet Soong Ching Ling's brother-in-law, nor even claiming to be Sun Yat-sen's political heir.

Ironically, too, Sun was not of a military bent. A photograph of the opening shows him in what is now called a Mao jacket, and Chiang in full and spanking military gear.

Soong Ching Ling, who had been Sun's wife since 1915, was constantly at his side and providing inspiration during what should have been the beginning of a successful period of his revolution. It was not only that she had a beautiful face, a graceful carriage and a pleasing disposition. Those attributes alone would probably have kept her at home in the traditional woman's role.

Somewhat younger than her husband, she inspired younger Chinese, particularly students; committed to the advancement of women, she provided an essential role model for her 'sisters'. Beyond her hard work at her husband's side and in his office, she had earned her spurs.

Two years before, Sun had been driven from his revolutionary base of Canton by a local warlord. Soong Ching Ling, pregnant at the time, urged her husband to flee without her. 'China can do without me,' she argued, 'but it can't do without you.' She followed him some hours later, under fire, and losing their child as she did so, in such a way that she could never again conceive.

It was on the warship that took the couple to safety in Hong Kong that Chiang Kai-shek forged the relationship with Sun Yat-sen which allowed his later rise to power.

Back in Canton in 1923, Soong Ching Ling went up in the small two-seater plane – reputedly the first built in China – that was the pride of Sun's exiguous airforce. The plane was thereafter called *Rosamunde* – Soong Ching Ling's Western name. Photographs of this event and many other similar acts of commitment and example line the walls.

That same month, Soong Ching Ling accompanied her husband in a gunboat to Humen, the Bocca Tigris fortifications at the mouth of the Pearl River which epitomise China's lack of success in the First

Soong Ching Ling at the time she married
Dr Sun Yat-sen, 1915

Opium War. Sun's mission there was to see to their strengthening for the future defence of China.

Close by, Commissioner Lin had ordered the foreign opium to be destroyed in June 1839. I had visited the place 150 years later, in 1989, and seen in my mind's eye Charlotte King. With her American husband Charles, the anti-opium trade activist, she was allowed to watch the sickly-sweet balls of opium being drenched and dissolved in wide troughs rather like a sewage disposal plant.

Now, as well as seeing Charlotte there, in her hooped skirt, an umbrella or sunshade protecting her against the summer heat and rain, I saw Soong Ching Ling in traditional white tunic and long black skirt.

They would probably have had much in common, both being women before their time. While Charlotte King had, in the 1830s, when it was forbidden by the Chinese, learned Cantonese and involved herself in the lives of Chinese women in Macau, Soong Ching Ling's English was fluent as a result of her North American education, and her understanding of Western culture was of use to her throughout her life and revolutionary activities.

At the end of 1924, Sun Yat-sen and Soong Ching Ling left Canton to travel round the coast and up towards Beijing. But, instead of success in the negotiations for national unity that were planned, Sun became ill, was diagnosed with cancer and was dead by March 1925.

It is these events, and that outcome to their marriage and, indeed, to the Revolution, which make the iron bed in that shabby building on Dane's Island so poignant.

CHAPTER 7

OF PALACES AND JADE
The Permanence of Things

Sometimes you don't choose whose life you are going to explore and write about; a character throws herself at you, and she may bring all sorts of excess baggage in her train. So it was with Madame Wellington Koo, a woman of some interest perhaps, but not necessarily one worthy of many hours of work.

'Are you free at 6 o'clock tomorrow?' Linda asked. She went on to invite me to a Christie's 'on view' at which the jade necklace of her grandfather's second wife, Madame Wellington Koo (Oei Hui-lan), would be displayed before auction.

Linda calls her the second wife and her own grandmother, daughter of T'ang Shaoyi, a minister under the 1911 Republic, the first. For purists, and those who have read Madame Koo's autobiography *No Feast Lasts For Ever* (1975), there was an earlier wife. 'Yes, but that was annulled,' Linda explains sternly. 'It doesn't count.'

Like many young Chinese men, V.K. Wellington Koo (Ku Wei-chun) had a wife chosen for him and went through with the marriage because that is what you did; in this case, there was also a debt of honour to be paid. According to Madame Koo, the marriage was ended by mutual consent of both families as soon as it was clear that it could not work. Koo then married Linda's grandmother, an educated woman more suitable for a high-flyer. These second marriages were a common phenomenon of the period.

I tend to get interested in the families of my Chinese women friends, especially if they are colourful, and Linda's certainly is. The necklace invitation was only the latest development in my interest. Wellington Koo, as well as being a distinguished diplomat (ambassador in Paris,

London and Washington), a member of the Chinese government before Liberation in 1949, and afterwards a Judge of the International Court of Justice, had another claim on my attention: Sun Yat-sen died in his Beijing palace in 1925.

It is known as Wellington Koo's palace, but Madame explains the real situation: 'The palace had been bought for me and Papa had paid for all the renovations, but it was registered in Wellington Koo's name. This arrangement was necessary in those days because if it had been in my name he as a Chinese man would have looked ridiculous.'

Madame Koo's father, Oei Tiong Ham, was very rich and he made sure that she had plenty of pin money. With it she bought fabulous jewellery. She describes in her book the irresistibly beautiful jade pepper carved for an emperor's homesick Persian concubine which she bought from the last emperor, Pu Yi, when he was broke, and later had made into a pendant by Cartier. Until I actually saw the necklace now for sale, I thought it was that pendant and revelled in knowing how Madame Koo had come to own it. But it patently was not the same piece. She does not mention the provenance of these 65 apple-green jade beads, but the catalogue suggests that the necklace was bought by her from Pu Yi's mother. Indeed, Linda's father has since confirmed that he was with his stepmother when she acquired it. Although she does not refer to it, there are photographs in the book that appear to show her wearing the single long strand twined in two.

We had a jolly time at the 'on view' because Christie's knew of Linda's association and were happy to take the necklace out of the glass case for her to try it on. While Linda was doing so, Baroness Dunn, Senior Executive Councillor and Chairperson of Christie's Swire Hong Kong, arrived and her eyes widened with delight and covetousness as it was transferred from Linda's neck to hers. Lydia Dunn proceeded to do her hostly duty wearing the slinky beads — and they did suit her!

Three days later, Linda and I met for the auction. Madame Wellington Koo's jade necklace was the *pièce de résistance*, lot number 1900, the last of many pieces of jade jewellery. It went for HK$6.3 million (£546,210). We don't know who sold it, but we found out later that the purchaser

*Madame Wellington Koo, wearing her jade necklace,
with Edda Ciano in Beijing, 1929*

was from Singapore. Not altogether surprisingly there was a family connection – not with Madame, who had two sons with Wellington Koo,
but with the branch of her predecessor, Linda's grandmother.

There was an irony in the event in the Hilton ballroom that evening
probably only apparent to Linda and me. Linda is not without her own
fame, or notoriety, depending on your point of view. She had the courage to sue an academic colleague for plagiarism – with all the unpleas-
antness over many years that it involved – and won at each stage of the
case's progress through the courts. Linda's costs in the High Court
alone were also HK$6 million or so; at the time of the auction she had
recovered none of it.

At the auction, I had followed the jade necklace to its next historical resting place. Now I wanted to visit the palace in Beijing where Madame Koo was living when she bought it, not so much to see where her hundreds of Pekinese dogs romped, as to see where Sun Yat-sen died. And there Soong Ching Ling, his wife of only ten years, had sat at his side easing his last days before taking up his revolutionary mantle which she was to wear with such distinction.

Madame Koo, who was interested in the supernatural and set store by dreams, adds her own drama to Sun Yat-sen's death. She tells of how, early in 1925, she had a 'horrible dream'. She saw 'a dead pig with goat's feet lying in Wellington Koo's reception room under his black carved table. Everything was so vivid I felt I could not bear the sight, and in my dream I fled to the courtyard of our palace. There I was met by a row of soldiers with drawn bayonets.'

Shortly after that dream, the Koos were banished from the palace when Feng Yu-hsiang, the warlord known as the Christian General, took Beijing. The army comandeered the Koo palace and there, on 12 March, Sun Yat-sen died in that same reception room.

So Madame Koo's palace saw the bifurcation of twentieth century Chinese history, a moment that left behind one of its 'ifs' — what if Sun Yat-sen, who brought about the fall of the Ch'ing dynasty, had not died then? Three centuries earlier, the woman for whom the palace had been built — Ch'en Yuanyuan, known as 'the Round Faced Beauty' — was the cause of the fall of the Ming dynasty.

Ch'en Yuanyuan was the 'favourite' concubine of General Wu San-kei (1612-1678). How they met seems somewhat distorted by the mists of time. One version talks of an affair she had with the 'celebrated literatus' Mao Hsiang in Soochow which ended in the spring of 1642. This version suggests that 'the girl was then carried off by a relative of the emperor to Beijing where she became the concubine of General Wu Sangui'. From this reference, one assumes that she was rather young, not yet a woman.

Another version suggests that Wu bought her, as he would have to if she were an indentured singing girl, for a 'fabulous sum' in Soochow. Yet another, that Wu met her in Beijing at a banquet at the house of a minister of state where she was employed as a maidservant. He fell immediately in love with her, as much for her voice as for her beauty.

What then happened in 1644 is also open to interpretation. Beijing and the Ming dynasty were under pressure from the rebel leader Li Tsucheng and from the Manchus. General Wu, ordered by the Ming emperor to come to the rescue of Beijing, hesitated. He then learned, however, that Li had not only taken his father hostage but also, more crucially, Ch'en Yuanyuan.

Wu set off to face Li but was driven into the arms of the Manchus. Changing sides in order to rescue his favourite, his forces and those of the Manchus defeated Li. Li, retreating, executed Wu's father and his family; Ch'en Yuanyuan, however was spared. The Manchus became the Ch'ing, the final, dynasty.

L.C. Arlington describes in *In Search of Old Peking* (1935) how a pile of rocks in the garden of General Wu's father is the only memorial to Ch'en Yuanyuan. He seems unaware that the Koo palace was built for her. So I resolved to visit both the pile of rocks and the palace in an effort to retrace her steps as well. On the same trip to Beijing, I wanted to visit Soong Ching Ling's last residence, to draw yet another strand into the story. Not only had Soong Ching Ling spent the worst hours of her life in the Koo palace nursing her dying husband, but her own last residence was part of the complex where Emperor Pu Yi was born.

There is another link as tenuous as Pu Yi, his birthplace and his jade necklace, and the palace where Sun Yat-sen died, between Madame Koo and Soong Ching Ling – two otherwise very different women. When France fell to Germany in 1940, Wellington Koo was China's ambassador there. Stored in the Paris embassy were crates of antiques that had been sent over from Hong Kong to be sold to raise money for the China Defence League. Soong Ching Ling founded and chaired the League following her flight to Hong Kong when the Japanese took Shanghai in 1937. It was Madame Koo who rescued these crates and sent them back to Hong Kong.

Soong Ching Ling's biographer, Israel (Eppy) Epstein, reminded me of this connection – which I had read about before I knew of Madame Koo's existence – when we met on the eve of my expedition to see the places involved in my concocted story. Soong Ching Ling had been most grateful and, as was her way, sent Madame Koo a graceful note of sincerest thanks.

Eppy was his usual fund of knowledge, and he and his wife, Huang Wanbi, did their best to find out where the pile of stones commemorating the Round Faced Beauty might be. Arlington gives the location as Shan Tzu Shih Erh Hutong (Rocky Mountain Lane), but that means nothing in real Chinese. He adds that this *hutong* (lane) is 'south of Tung Chih Men, under the city walls'. The city walls have gone and the second ring road runs where they stood. Derek and I agreed, therefore, that a stinking hot day in June, with neither of us speaking Chinese and with several other places to visit, was not the time to go scrabbling for a pile of stones which undoubtedly no longer exists. In the cool of the autumn, who knows …?

Visiting Soong Ching Ling's last home was as poignant an experience as I had expected. The large bedroom where she died is set up as a working room too, with a desk and all the lampshades slightly askew to provide better reading light. But in a way, it was the garden that I most wanted to see because of an anecdote which somehow, of all the brave and worthwhile things she did, seems to convey the essence of that very special woman.

Eppy tells the story of how, when she was old and infirm, before her death in 1981, her gardener would put out new potted plants to tempt her to exercise. 'Sometimes she would ask "Can I pick this flower?" and when he once answered, "Of course, they're all yours," she said, "But it's your labour."' So it was those flower pots that I wanted to find. And I did. Not only were there rows of bright red potted salvia near the front door, but under a bower of trees near a red-lacquer pavilion (the souvenir shop!) there was also a gardener with a cart on a bicycle filled with potted plants.

Eppy had added a charming tailpiece to the story of the plant pots. He reminded me that he wrote much of his biography in Soong Ching

Ling's house, conjuring up her ghost. What is more, even now, when one of his own plants sickens, he transfers it to her garden to be revived.

We took a taxi from Soong Ching Ling's. Linda Koo's husband had given me very precise details in Chinese characters of how to find the Koo palace. Linda had warned me not to be disappointed; it was no longer as it was in Madame's day. For one thing, there was a high-rise building abutting it. Linda had visited it in the early 1980s and taken photographs, mostly of the exterior. Using these, her father, adding his own childhood memories of the palace, had commissioned a painting in traditional style of the complex as it had been. He had presented it to Wellington Koo, who did not die until 1987 just before his 100th birthday, as a birthday present. A copy of this picture now hangs over Linda's desk and I had taken a photograph of it to help in my search.

Eppy had marked on the map where he thought the palace was, and that was lucky because the written address and directions did not suffice for the driver. But then no one we asked in Zhangzizhong Lu was too sure of its exact location either. They tried to be helpful though and sent us back and forth along the main road. Finally, near to despair, we stopped an older man in a straw hat who looked not only as if he could read but also as if he might know where Sun Yat-sen had died.

He turned out to be almost blind and rather deaf, but he spoke a little careful English, and he knew what we were talking about. He took us almost to the gate and left us. We were revived. But the caretaker would not let us in. We flashed the photograph of how it used to be to show our good faith; we flashed Eppy's card which he had given us to smooth our path at Soong Ching Ling's; we flashed smiles, and glances of anguish. Nothing worked. We could not get beyond the red-lacquer entrance, could not see more than the first courtyard.

It is always hard to admit defeat when you are straining at the historical leash; but sometimes you have to. We took photographs of the entrance and of a sign to show what authority or ministry was so private. Using those, we hope to make better arrangements for the future. And then we followed the surrounding grey stone wall along its full square, through *hutongs* empty save us and the past. They were as they had long been, and so were the magnificent trees uninhibited by the high walls. The ten acres of grounds now seem parcelled up, including a couple of small coal-driven factories, all equally inaccessible. Upon reflection, we should have talked our way into the clinic overlooking the complex; there might have been something interesting to see.

At one of the gates, we managed to peer over and saw two men playing chess in a brightly coloured pavilion. They sat there, we fantasised, just as Ch'en Yuanyuan had done 350 years before. Derek saw her painting her nails, I, writing poetry or painting. There is no evidence that she did either, but Tongpai, who had a longer relationship in Soochow with Mao Hsiang, and came from the same background – 'a rare beauty among singing girls' – practised calligraphy and painted and was represented in a 1988 exhibition of Chinese women artists.

Fifteen years or so after her beauty decided the fate of China, having accompanied General Wu to Yunnan which he governed, the Round Faced Beauty became a nun.

There is one other link between Ch'en Yuanyuan, Soong Ching Ling and Madame Wellington Koo: love, marriage and concubinage in traditional Chinese society. Margaret Wang, writing a story for the Chinese housewives to whom I teach English, explains how in China 'you were more likely to love your concubine than a wife who was often introduced to you only on your wedding day. You could choose your concubine but not, normally, your wife. You could come to respect and admire your wife, but love was thought to be an emotion that was unreliable and fickle and could not form the basis for sound relationships.' (See also Chapter 17, 'The New Concubines'.)

The Ming dynasty had fallen because of a general's love for his beautiful concubine. Sun Yat-sen 'amicably and legally' divorced his first wife, chosen for him when he was 17, to marry Soong Ching Ling, 27 years his junior. Great pressure was put on him to take her as his concubine, following tradition. But he demurred; he and Soong Ching Ling believed strongly in the equality of women and men. She then had to prove herself as a meet consort, as a fearless revolutionary, before she was accepted as his wife. There is plenty of evidence to suggest that theirs was a real love match.

As for Madame Wellington Koo, she seems to have fallen between tradition and modernity. In 1919, a year after Linda's grandmother died in the influenza epidemic that swept Europe and the United States where Wellington Koo was then posted, she was deemed an ideal replacement wife and mother to his two children. Wellington Koo, according to her, courted her somewhat frantically, almost as if it were a love match; but she married him because it was expected of her. She seemed surprised when, eventually, he found love elsewhere, calling her replacement a concubine, and refusing to acknowledge that she had been legally divorced.

Madame Koo's father had many concubines, and the author of *The Soong Dynasty* (1985), Sterling Seagrave, must have confused the father with the husband when he wrote that Wellington Koo was 'a diplomat trained at Colombia University, who nonetheless was celebrated for keeping twenty six concubines.' When informed by a family member of this apparently outrageous misrepresentation, the 98-year-old diplomat replied, 'Is that all?'

Koo's former wife, calling herself Madame Wellington Koo to the last, outlived him by five years. Legend has it that she was 12 years older than she admitted – his age, in fact. Most of her fabulous jewellery had been stolen when she was old and living in New York. But the jade necklace lives on.

Written June 1994.

BIBLIOGRAPHY

Arlington, L.C. and Lewisohn, William, *In Search of Old Peking* (Hong Kong, Oxford University Press, 1987; 1st published 1935).

Boorman, Howard L., *Biographical Dictionary of Republican China* (New York, Columbia University Press, 1970).

Bredon, Juliet, *Peking* (Hong Kong, Oxford University Press, 1982; 1st published 1919).

Epstein, Israel, *Pioneers in China's Modernization*, (Beijing, China Peace Publishing,1987).

Epstein, Israel, *Woman in World History: Soong Ching Ling (Mme Sun Yatsen)* (Beijing, New World Press, 1993).

Hummel, Arthur (ed.), *Eminent Chinese of the Ching Period 1644-1912* (Washington DC, US Government Print Office, 1944).

Koo, Madame Wellington (with Isabella Taves), *No Feast Lasts For Ever* (New York, Quadrangle, 1975).

O'Neill, Hugh B., *Companion to Chinese History* (New York, Facts on File Publications, 1987).

Seagrave, Sterling, *The Soong Dynasty* (New York, Harper Row, 1985).

Weidner, Marsha et al., *Views From the Jade Terrace: Chinese Women Artists 1300-1900* (Indianapolis, Indianapolis Museum of Art, 1988).

CHAPTER 8

THE SEVENTH
GENTLEMAN
Shi Liang

'The Communist Portia' is how Shi Liang has been described.[1] The cliché attempts to denigrate the politics and sex of China's Minister for Justice between 1949 and 1959, but at least it does get her gender right. Describing her earlier activities, the labels are more ambiguous.

Shi Liang, hitherto only one of the shorter footnotes in Chinese revolutionary history, is known for two contributions. She was appointed Minister for Justice after Liberation although she was not a Communist. More intriguingly, in November 1936, she was one of 'the Seven Gentlemen' arrested in Shanghai on the orders of Chiang Kai-shek.

That the detained leaders of the National Salvation Association were called the Seven Gentlemen was not to denigrate Shi Liang's sex, nor to dismiss it. The phrase had strong Confucian resonances and was used to honour her and her fellows.[2] Following Liberation, the Seven Gentlemen became known as the Seven Patriots[3] – perhaps precisely to dispel those same overtones. The symbolism and importance of names make it, therefore, all the more ironic that Shi Liang should, in some quarters, be embalmed for ever as a 'gentleman'.

One reference book refers to her consistently as 'he';[4] and James Bertram, whose personal accounts of that period are much relied on by historians, writes of the National Salvation leaders as 'eminent professional men and scholars of some distinction.'[5]

But Shi Liang was very much a woman. In the traditional sense, she was described by the French Prime Minister Edgar Faure, following his 1955 visit to China, as 'very beautiful and very chic'.[6] More usefully, she was an obvious role model for the emancipation of Chinese women – unremarked so far as I can determine – from the 1930s until at least 1959. She deserves to be more than a historical footnote or a gentleman. What is more, her life, and the causes in which she was involved, throw some light on today's issues, particularly the dialogue between the West and China over human rights, and the effects of galloping economic modernisation, including foreign investment, in China. Shanghai of the 1930s becomes a backdrop to the horrific and avoidable factory fatalities of the 1990s (see also Chapter 2).

Although the date of Shi Liang's birth is in dispute, 1900 is the most likely.[7] In addition, details about her life in various reference books – in Chinese and English – are so at odds that the only reliable source is her own short account, 'The Road I Travelled', published in English as both a magazine article and a chapter in a book about revolutionary heroines. Other sources are, therefore, used to supplement and extend Shi Liang's version. The inclusion of the lives and writing of some of her progressive contemporaries provides a wider context for the momentous events in which Shi Liang played so important a part.

EARLY REBELLIONS AND THE MAY 4 MOVEMENT

Shi Liang came from a Mandarin, or scholarly, background on both sides. But, for reasons she does not explain, her father refused to sit for the exams, reducing his eight offspring to a life of deprivation as he tried to care for them on a teacher's salary in Changchou (Changzhou)[8], Kiangsu (Jiangsu) Province. Three of his daughters died from malnutrition and lack of means to seek medical treatment.

There was some attempt to rectify this when Shi Liang was seven; her mother wanted to betroth her into a rich family named Liu. 'Child-brides' were a common institution in feudal China, but Shi Liang refused to comply. This was to be the first of many rebellions and presaged, too, a 'modern' attitude towards marriage. In spite of rarely having enough to eat, Shi Liang was well educated at home, her father introducing her to the Chinese classics, stories of Chinese heroes and principles of patriotism and integrity.

The education of girls in schools had only recently begun, following the reforms of 1900. At 14, Shi Liang was enrolled in a primary school at nearby Wusih (Wuxi). One source suggests that she was a year younger than that and that there her rebellion entered the public domain. She is said to have led a 'student movement' which got rid of a teacher who had neither learning nor skill.[9]

In 1918 or 1919, Shi Liang entered the local teacher training school, or Women's Normal College.[10] The same Chinese source that details many rebellious exploits describes how she led a students' strike and protest. They drove away the school's president, surrounded the county magistrate and created a disturbance at the county government.[11]

Again, Shi Liang does not mention this event. She does mention 'student activities' following the May 4 Incident of 1919; but she says little more than that she was 'drawn in' and 'became engrossed in current books and magazines and dreamed of a just society where people could live secure'.[12]

Under the Treaty of Versailles, the Chinese province of Shantung (Shandong), formerly in Germany's sphere of influence, was given by the negotiating powers to Japan; this high-handedness sparked the incident which grew into a movement. Descriptions of Shi Liang's anti-Japanese activities at this time are, therefore, probably true. She is said to have been associate head of the Student's Association in Wujin County which led a local boycott of Japanese goods. She is also said to have taken a pair of socks made in Japan from a girl student and thrown them into the fire.[13]

SHI LIANG'S CONTEMPORARIES

May 4, 1919 was a monumental moment for all China; the movement which grew out of a student demonstration began to erode the constraints of both patriarchal Confucianism and foreign domination. Women, particularly, began to find a voice; and schoolgirls were almost as much involved as the students who led the way for the whole country.

The writer Hsieh Ping-ying (Xie Bing-ying), born in 1903 or 1906 (sources vary), describes her own involvement at a school in Changsha Province run by Norwegian missionaries. The girls were not allowed to join the students' demonstration, but of that time Hsieh writes:

> While we heard the drums and bugles, and the shouting of the slogan 'Down with Imperialism' from outside, we also wanted to do something on the same lines. We wrote our slogans on pieces of paper torn from our exercise books and pasted them on chop sticks. We organised a parade going from the playground to the upstairs floors, and then from there to the ground again. While we were parading we, like the students in the streets, were equally excited and full of enthusiasm. We shouted loudly, 'Down with Imperialism!' 'We want Freedom of Speech!' 'We want to join the Students Union!' 'We must wipe away our National Shame!'[14]

Young factory girl with bound feet, 1936

Teng Ying-chao (Deng Yingzhao), with whom Shi Liang was later to work, was born in 1903 and was a student at the First Girls Normal School in Tientsin (Tianjin) in 1919. She was involved in activities regarded as subversive by the government. In an interview with Dymphna Cusack in the 1950s, she described how 'Patriotism was already a green shoot in my heart, so I set aside my books temporarily and came out of my class-room to organize girl-students and housewives of Tientsin into a patriotic society.'[15]

Students from her school and Nankai University also established the Awakening Society (*Chueh-wu she*), the tenets of which included humanitarianism, socialism, anarchism and the belief that social progress should draw upon the self-awakening of the individual.[16] Teng Ying-chao gives an example of the student demonstrations that were taking place:

> We decided to hold a big demonstration on 10th October, anniversary of the Revolution of 1911. We girls prepared banners and banner-holders of bamboo. We didn't know at the time that they would also serve for self-defence. The meeting was surrounded by soldiers who threatened us with bayonets, then the police rushed out and we used the bamboo poles to knock off their caps.[17]

They were rescued by male students from Nankai, among whom was Chou En-lai (Zhou Enlai), later Teng Ying-chao's husband.

As a result of the May 4 Movement, temporary Girls' Patriotic Associations sprang up, though they existed only in 'small, scattered groups' until the May 30 Movement of 1925. Feminist Women's Rights Associations, which talked of suffrage and equality, were formed in Beijing, Tientsin, Shanghai, Canton, 'and a few modern cities'.[18]

LAW STUDIES AND MAY 30 MOVEMENT

By 1923, aged 23, Shi Liang had moved to Shanghai to study law at the Shanghai College of Political Science and Law. That she managed to read law, and later practised both informally and formally, is a story in itself. Alison Conner, in her paper 'Early Lawyers: The Shanghai Bar' (1991), makes it clear that she was something of a phenomenon, equalled only by her contemporary Tcheng Soumay (Zheng Yuxiu) who described her legal (and illegal) adventures in *My Revolutionary Years* (1943). Unfortunately, if the two met, neither mentions it.

The 1912 Regulations limited the status of lawyer, and thus the practice of law, to *male* citizens. Conner describes how, in the early 1920s, the Shanghai Women's Rights Movement announced that a 'law school for girls' had been established. But the courses were 'designed to prepare women for the duties of citizenship', rather than to practise law.[19] Tcheng Soumay studied law in France; Shi Liang explains how she managed to enroll in Shanghai: she was sponsored by Su Chien (Xu Qian), a notable jurist.[20] How she knew him is, however, unclear. The enactment of the 1927 Regulations, the year of Shi Liang's graduation, did not specify gender, allowing both women to practise.

Shi Liang's success in graduating suggests the political atmosphere of the times, for she was hardly a model student in the traditional sense. In May 1925, Shanghai police under British officers shot dead 13 Chinese demonstrators. Shi Liang describes how, in the 'mammoth' student-worker demonstration that followed the incident, 'We marched shoulder to shoulder, shouting the slogan: "Down with the imperialists, down with the traitors." I was arrested along with a few others, but was released the next day.'[21]

The revolutionary incidents which then proliferated became known as the May 30 Movement. At Shi Liang's college, the students' council set up the journal *Avenge* of which she was made editor-in-chief. It had considerable influence on Shanghai students more generally.

THE EVENTS OF 1926-1927

Upon graduation, in 1927, Shi Liang says that she began working 'in a training centre for political personnel run by the KMT [Kuomintang]'.[22] However, she does not say where. It is interesting to note how the changing political situation of this time is reflected in the differing and sometimes partisan accounts of Shi Liang's activities. One Chinese source states that she became 'an instructor, a member of the Nanking political work staff'. It goes on to suggest that,

> on the charge of being suspected as a Communist Party member, she was arrested and put in prison. Being rescued from prison, she avoided the fate of death. Later she was appointed to work as a law clerk in the secular local court of Jiangsu province. But because of the fact that she was once jailed, her job as a law clerk was terminated.[23]

Another Chinese source says that she was arrested for 'contradicting her superior'.[24] Of two English-language reference works, one states:

> Clerk Nanjing Special Criminal Court; instructor for women students in the training class established by Kiangsu government to train administrative heads of districts; mem. Standing Cme, Kiangsu; failed to pass physical examination selection of Kiangsu magistrate (a communist publication claimed that this was a case of discrimination but several other sources claimed she was suffering from venereal disease).[25]

The other suggests for this period that Shi Liang

> joined the KMT and during the Northern Expedition of 1926-27 she headed the Personnel Training Section under the Revolutionary Army's General Political Department. She held several minor posts with the KMT in the late twenties in Kiangsu ...[26]

To try and reconcile accounts of Shi Liang's activities following her graduation, it is as well to look chronologically at China's political history of the period, and the part that women played in it.

The Northern Expedition was a march north from Canton in 1926-1927 by forces under Chiang Kai-shek in a bid to crush the recalcitrant warlords, unite China and form a stable government. To do so, it was designed to involve, for perhaps the first time, the people of China — peasants, workers and women. One of the platforms of the KMT, which was then still under the influence of the revolutionary ideals of the recently deceased Sun Yat-sen, was the emancipation of women. The Communist Party, which was still in alliance with the KMT, specifically called on women, as an oppressed group, to support its goals.

Women were involved in the Northern Expedition at many levels. Their part in its military wing is poignantly evoked by Hsieh Ping-ying in *Autobiography of a Chinese Girl* (1943). She maintained:

> All girl students who wanted to join the Army had as their motive, in nine cases out of ten, to get away from their families, by whom they were suppressed. They all wanted to find their own way out. But the moment they put on their uniform and shouldered their guns, their ideas became less selfish.[27]

And, of life in the field, she wrote:

> Our hair had been cut very short, especially Shu Yun's who had shaved her head making it look very much like a bald pate, and because of that, no matter what masterly disguise she assumed, one could tell at a glance that she was a woman soldier and had carried a rifle. Then, too, we were all sun-tanned and our skins were very dark, and because we had been handling rifles for such a long period, our hands gave us away immediately.[28]

Shi Liang seems to have been involved in the more civilian side of the Northern Expedition, an aspect captured by Anna Louise Strong in her 1928 article, 'Some Hankow Memories: Of a Women's Union that Busied Itself with Slave Girls, Bobbed Hair and Divorce'. In it, she describes a 1927 visit to the Wuchang Women's Union and to the attached 'political school established by Mme Sun Yat-sen [Soong Ching Ling] for the training of woman propagandists'.[29]

She talked to 'many young women who had done active fighting for women's rights in the rural districts of central China'.[30] They were, in fact, taught at the school how to spread the word about women's rights. What these activists had to contend with, as a reaction to their work, is told through the stories of Miss Ma and Miss Lang who had escaped from the scene of military reaction in northern Hupeh (Hubei). They had been jeered at and jostled by the soldiers; one of them had been forced to parade the streets between mobs that shouted at the sight of her bobbed hair.[31]

Meanwhile, the events that form the background to Shi Liang's imprisonment of the period were building to a climax. As a result of the Northern Expedition, the National Government had been inaugurated at Wuhan (incorporating the cities of Hankow [Hankou], Wuchang and Hanyang) on 1 January 1927, but with tensions between the various factions. On 12 April, in preparation for Chiang Kai-shek and his wing of the KMT entering Shanghai, they turned on their erstwhile allies and sought to eliminate anyone there accused of being a Communist. Following this *coup d'état*, Chiang set up his (anti-Communist) government in Nanking. A period of violence and uncertainty began and in July a purge of Communists in Wuhan followed.

Women soldiers such as Hsieh Ping-ying felt their sudden and unexpected demobilisation as a result of these events thus:

> This great, majestic women's army was now demobilised, but the spirit of the movement would live for ever. In 1927 the seeds of revolution had already been sown all over China. In every city and in every village I believed that in future the flowers of the revolution would spring up, and final victory would certainly be ours![32]

She was somewhat sheltered, in spite of having to return home. Women such as Teng Ying-chao,[33] who had joined the Communist Youth

League in 1924, and the Party in 1925, and had been vice-chair of the Women's Department in Wuhan, went underground. But her evasion in Canton involved her in great personal tragedy. 'Our home was searched and sealed,' she explained to Dymphna Cusack. 'I had just given birth to my first baby after a difficult labour. It died and I had hardly time to drag my weakened body out of bed and flee.'[34]

The Women's Department, chaired by Ho Hsiang-ning (He Xiangning), widow of Sun Yat-sen's close colleague assassinated two years earlier,[35] was destroyed. Many girls and women working in it were imprisoned, tortured and executed. Then nearly 50 and a veteran of the movement, Ho resigned her posts in the KMT, never to trust its leaders again, and moved to her ancestral home in Hong Kong.[36] Some women were killed simply for having their hair bobbed in the revolutionary style first favoured by Ho Hsiang-ning.

In her own account, Shi Liang discusses Chiang Kai-shek's burgeoning influence on the KMT at that period, and the reactionary path down which the party proceeded; she continues:

> Deeply angered by their actions, I voiced my protest against their surrender to the foreign powers while butchering the people. I was not affiliated to any political organization at that time, but when I was taken to prison with a few Communists, some of whom were badly tortured and others shot after three or four days' imprisonment, I felt proud to be among those brave and dedicated men and women. ... Before long, the then Minister of Education Cai Yuanpei [Ts'ai Yuanpei] who knew me personally, went bail for me. I was released after two months' imprisonment.[37]

As for Shi Liang's alleged venereal disease, that sounds like the sort of misinformation put about to ruin the name of a radical woman. She and her kind were, after all, fighting against institutionalised attitudes that for centuries had subjected women to footbinding, concubinage, female infanticide and the cult of chastity.[38]

CIVIL RIGHTS LAWYER

By 1931, there is general agreement that Shi Liang was practising law in Shanghai, and Conner notes that in that year she joined the Shanghai Bar Association.[39] Without naming the date, Shi Liang talks of starting her 16-year career which she 'loved from the first day'.[40] Her main concerns in the Tong Kang law firm were marriage and political cases and she was one of a very small number of women lawyers.

She set up practice at a crucial time for the city and the country's civil and political development. On 18 September 1931, Japan invaded Manchuria (the Mukden Incident), and the course of events was set in motion that was to lead to the arrest in Shanghai of the Seven Gentlemen in November 1936, the Sian (Xi'an) Incident of December and the Marco Polo Incident of 7 July 1937 that started the Sino-Japanese war in earnest.

Following the crackdown on Communists in 1927, the political situation had become polarised, with continuing repression from Chiang Kai-shek's government against radicals, particularly those advocating resistance against Japan, as well as Communists. Nanking's thugs, known as Blue Shirts, led what was known as the White Terror. At the centre of the radical movement, and increasingly active in attempts to protect civil liberties, was Sun Yat-sen's widow (and by then Chiang Kai-shek's sister-in-law), Soong Ching Ling.

In 1932, she was instrumental in setting up a formal structure for the protection and defence of political prisoners throughout the country – the China League for the Protection of Civil Rights. In March 1933, their first case was that of Liao Cheng-chih (Liao Zhengzhi), son of Soong's close friend Ho Hsiang-ning. As a result of the League's intervention, Liao was released into the hands of his mother who was herself one of its activists.[41]

The tasks of the League, enumerated by Soong Ching Ling, were to:

I. Fight for the liberation of political prisoners in China and against the current system of imprisonment, torture and executions. [It] concerns itself first of all with the masses of unknown and nameless prisoners.

2. Give counsel and legal assistance to political prisoners, and arouse public opinion by investigation of prison conditions and the publication of the facts.

3. Assist the struggle for ... rights of organization, free speech, press and assembly.[42]

It was now, if not before, that Shi Liang was drawn into this milieu. She was commissioned on behalf of Deng Zhongxia, one of China's longest-established and ablest Communist labour leaders, after Soong Ching Ling's rescue efforts had failed. He had been arrested by Shanghai's French Concession police, and Shi Liang argued in the French court that he be freed. But Chiang Kai-shek insisted that he be handed over to the government in Nanking and the French complied; he was shot in 1933, aged 39.[43] Shi Liang says that she did not know at the time who her client was. She was still in bed one morning when a messenger brought a letter asking for help from someone called Shi Yi.[44] But, as a result of Deng Zhongxia's treatment at the hands of the KMT, 'I began to see that the law was never a binding force for them, but merely an ornament, a sham.'[45]

The Civil Rights League was more successful in saving the life of the woman writer, Communist and feminist, Ting Ling (Ding Ling), whose lover had been executed the previous year. By calling international attention to her kidnapping in May 1933, the League undoubtedly prevented her murder, though she was apparently subjected to 'the kerosene and feces' torture.[46] She was to resurface in 1936 in Yan'an (Yenan).

The work of protecting victims of the White Terror was itself dangerous, and Shi Liang showed considerable courage in being involved. Agnes Smedley, one of only two Western members of the League, wrote about one of its efforts: 'Of the two lawyers who volunteered their services, one dropped out when he received a warning following the first hearing, the other fled when the Blue Shirts threatened to destroy his business and kill him.'[47] The League paid for its efforts when its secretary was shot down in the street in 1933; it was forced to disband.

NATIONAL SALVATION ASSOCIATION

Also involved in the League's work were at least two others of the future Seven Gentlemen, and it is clear that, in the years between the end of its formal activities and the formation of the National Salvation Association, Shi Liang continued her work as a lawyer among similarly radical activists. The journalist Tsou T'ao-fen (Zou Taofen), perhaps the best known of the Seven Gentlemen, consistently focused attention on the Japan issue through magazines that were closed down by the government and restarted under other names. And Soong Ching Ling and Ho Hsiang-ning were among those supporting the call in August 1935 by the Communist Party, then nearing the end of its Long March, for a United Front against Japan. In spite of this continuing trend, the anti-Japanese student demonstration in Peking on 9 December 1935 marked the symbolic beginning of a new phase – the end of China's non-resistance.

Before demonstrating, the students sent a message to Soong Ching Ling asking her advice. 'Show your mettle and swing into action', was her reply.[48] During the demonstration, gendarmes flourishing tommy guns 'pushed into the throng and indiscriminately clubbed boys and girls alike', wrote the observer Edgar Snow.[49] Tsou's magazine of the time picked up on the demonstration, and the publicity ensured that knowledge of the incident spread. As a result, throughout December 1935 and January 1936, national salvation groups were set up. The English-language and uncensored news bulletin of the Society of the Friends of China reported that streams of students set off throughout North China to hold meetings and conferences and to present modern national revolutionary plays in villages and towns. At the same time, study groups were set up in educational institutions.[50]

On 12 December, intellectuals, including those who were to become the Seven Gentlemen, organised the Shanghai Cultural Circles' National Salvation Association. On 21 December, several hundred women, including Shi Liang and Ho Hsiang-ning, organised the Shanghai Women's National Salvation Association, with Shi Liang in the chair. The women marched to demand that civil war be replaced by united resistance against Japan, proclaiming 'women can save themselves only through participating in national resistance'.[51]

This was not the first time that the women of Shanghai had marched against Japanese aggression. Shi Liang recalls how on 8 March 1931, the International Working Women's Day following the Mukden Incident, women 'from all walks of life gathered for a celebratory meeting'. Their slogan was, 'Free our people first, or there can be no real emancipation for women'.[52] The KMT moved in to scotch this demonstration which, as Shi Liang says, was supported by the Communist Party. As the women marched from the hall, they were rounded up by gendarmes armed with clubs and truncheons and many were injured.

In the days that followed in December 1935, the National Salvation Association formed branches for professionals, students, workers and housewives. It published journals and established links with other organisations such as the YWCA (Young Women's Christian Association) which were later to prove invaluable.

Then, on 28 January 1936, several thousand people at a rally celebrated the formation of the All-Shanghai National Salvation League. This was followed, on 31 May, by the formation of the All-China League of National Salvation Associations. Shi Liang was elected to its executive committee, as was Soong Ching Ling who also became its national symbol. It called on all parties and factions to stop civil war activities, release political prisoners, and send representatives to a conference which would discuss the best means to fight the enemy and establish a democratic authority.[53]

The Women's National Salvation Association was not simply a group of women calling for resistance against Japan. It soon became a national women's movement whose concerns grew in all directions and it continued its work through the war years. Israel Epstein, a journalist in China at the time, describes some of its influence in *The People's War*:

The women are learning to read and write. They give plays and entertainments. And they have begun to vote and take part in the administration of their villages, these former creatures without rights. In the district of Tanghsien, twenty women have been elected to be heads of villages. In Fuping district, there are more than ten who hold this office. To their new tasks, the emancipated women bring an impressive conscientiousness and seriousness. They walk miles through snow rather than miss a meeting to which they are delegated. For the first time in centuries, the women of North-east Shansi can hold up their heads. Equal citizens, they are marching in step with the men out of feudalism and oppression. They have their rights now and they acknowledge their responsibilities, which they bear proudly and with honour.[54]

Between 1927 and 1937, 26 women's organisations, described by Bobby Siu in *Women of China: Origins of Repression*, were set up to carry out a variety of tasks connected with the growing crisis.[55]

In Shanghai in 1936, the immediate task was actively to unite China against the Japanese threat, contrary to the designs of the Nanking government. The national salvation movement was so widespread that only the Kuomintang and the Communist Party were larger and more influential. It was said to have 'no membership books, no formal or systematic organisation. ... The movement spread like wildfire.'[56]

In July 1936, four leaders of the National Salvation Association published a platform for the movement: 'A Number of Essential Conditions and Minimum Demands for a United Resistance to Invasion.' The writers demanded that Chiang Kai-shek 'halt the war against the Communists, drop threats against the Southwest, and restore freedom of speech to Chinese to proclaim resistance'.[57] Chiang remained unmoved, but the document's wide circulation aroused considerable national interest. On 10 August, Mao Tse-tung (Mao Zedong) announced the Communist Party's support for the proposal, a move which further encouraged the Nanking government to label the united front movement Communist.

At about this time the story goes that Ho Hsiang-ning went to the Executive *Yuan* in Nanking to demand an interview with Chiang Kai-shek. Although attempts were made to thwart her intention, she persisted and was eventually shown into his presence. There she harangued him on his policy to 'conclude the civil war before fighting the external enemy'. Finding him unmoved, Madame Ho reached into her basket and, taking out a woman's *cheongsam* (dress), held it out to him. 'Put this on!' she ordered coldly and walked out.[58]

That summer, as Japanese aggression increased so did the momentum of the Salvationist cause. Shi Liang describes a 'giant' demonstration on 18 September, the fifth anniversary of the Mukden Incident:

> When we reached the Small Eastern Gate, groups of KMT gendarmes suddenly stormed us, yelling and beating us up. I quickly stepped into a rickshaw standing in the street and shouted at the top of my voice: 'Chinese shouldn't fight Chinese' and 'Let's fight the aggressors together'. The gendarmes moved towards us. They viciously struck at the head of a young woman nearby and she began to bleed profusely. I too was badly injured and was spitting blood. I learned later that my lung had been hurt. A group of workers came up in time to rescue me. They linked arms to shield me from the attack, and later escorted me to the French concession. I owed them my life.[59]

She adds an interesting tailpiece to her story when she writes of her time as Minister for Justice:

> Twenty years later, long after China was liberated, I happened to meet an old worker at an out-patient clinic one day. 'Comrade Shi Liang,' he said much to my astonishment. 'Do you remember that demonstration in Shanghai? Well, I

was one of those workers who got you out of the way.' Waving away my expressions of thanks, he said simply, 'There was nothing else we could have done — as Chinese we share a common cause.'

On 19 October, Lu Hsun (Lu Xun), the most loved and radical of Chinese writers, died and his funeral was turned into a public protest against the Japanese by the National Salvation Association, in which he had been a tireless worker. Soong Ching Ling, Shi Liang and other leaders were in the forefront of the 10,000-strong procession.

WOMEN FACTORY WORKERS *(See photograph on p. 95)*

The end of October saw the beginning of the Japanese invasion from Manchuria of Suiyuan in Mongolia, heightening tension between China and Japan. Then, on 8 November, strikes began in Shanghai's Japanese-owned textile mills. At the time, wages and working conditions were the stated cause, but by 20 November, the nature of the strikes had changed: now over 20,000 workers were involved, and the strikes had begun to spread to other cities. What is more, they had become overtly anti-Japanese.

From the point of view of women's history, the preponderance of women (over 70 per cent)[60] in the Shanghai textile mills is as crucial as their involvement in the strikes themselves — for those women were to become highly politicised and to have their endurance and courage finely honed.

Shi Liang became involved because the strikers turned to the National Salvation Association for financial assistance and moral support. Progressive people in Shanghai, including Western supporters, started to raise funds. Ruth Weiss, a young Austrian who had arrived in Shanghai in 1933 and had been taken up and radicalised by Agnes Smedley, describes how 'some of us were approached not only to give our contributions but possibly to get some from our acquaintances'.[61] Ruth also remembers Shi Liang speaking at demonstrations organised by the National Salvation League to garner further support.

The plight of women in the Japanese-owned Shanghai textile mills was one waiting to find a revolution. Anna Louise Strong, reporting from China a few months later, writes first in *China Fights for Freedom* of the situation in 1926-1927. Then, the trade unions were strong and the highest wages known were US$10-15 monthly. Once the Japanese started taking over factories, wages in general dropped in the industry because of their uncontrolled wage cutting. By the time war broke out in 1937, the women were only getting US$3-6 monthly and were without trade union protection.[62] (See also Chapter 2.)

Even before the intervention of the National Salvation Association, the women workers were not totally without support. Ruth Weiss, who was part of a study group of which a YWCA secretary, Cora Deng, was also a member, writes, 'Since the YWCA had classes for the women workers … teaching them reading and writing, helping them in every way possible, when the oppression increased with the growing encroachment of Japan, naturally the YWCA was trying to support the strikers in every way, money included.'[63] It was Cora Deng who, as a member of the Industrial Section of the YWCA, organised the night schools.[64]

Anna Louise Strong, meeting 'graduates' of these classes at the beginning of the war, reported how they told her that,

> the freeing of workers and of women must be worked out in connection with the freeing of the Chinese people as a whole. Workers and women suffer the most from Japanese oppression. The Japanese mills are the worst; they often made us work sixteen to eighteen hours, and until noon on Sunday without extra pay. Now the Japanese have destroyed all our homes and factories. So the working women are strongest to help the army. We go in the very front lines.[65]

Emily Honig suggests in *Sisters and Strangers: Women in the Shanghai Cotton Mills 1919-1949* (1986) that, although the teachers at the YWCA schools did not actively instigate strikes, they played an important role once strikes developed.[66] It was not only moral or financial support that were important; the classes also acted as a grapevine, and thus as a catalyst. One striker, Koo Lian-ying (Gu Lianying), explained how this happened during a strike that started at the Japanese-owned Tong Xing Mill:

> At our school there were some women who had worked at Tong Xing, so they told us about their strike. We all went to have a look, and we went to where workers lived, to try to persuade them not to go to work. All of us from the school went together, in the evening when we had free time.
>
> The Japanese finally conceded, and raised their wages. When we saw that they got five fen ... raise, we all said 'We have to think of a way to demand this too.' We at Yong An ended up striking as well.[67]

Honig reports how the emergence of the National Salvation Association prompted the YWCA to include patriotism, nationalism and anti-imperialism in its classes. People who knew the conditions in the occupied northeast of the country were invited to describe Japanese aggression to women workers at night school. And then, when there were anti-Japanese demonstrations, workers and teachers attended them together.[68]

Soong Ching Ling, for ever with her finger on the pulse, wrote of the women strikers:

> Their courage was even greater than that of the students because they faced not only violence but immediate starvation. These miserably underpaid factory girls — with patched clothing and wisps of cotton in their hair, working 16 to 18 hours a day from early childhood, many of them already coughing from the tubercular seeds of death in their chests, will always remain heroic figures in the annals of our awakening.[69]

THE ARREST OF THE SEVEN GENTLEMEN

Pressed by the Japanese, the Nanking government now used Salvation-ist support for the anti-Japanese strikes as an excuse to act. During the night of 22 November, they arrested seven leaders of the National Sal-vation Association, the Seven Gentlemen – leaving out only Soong Ching Ling and 97-year-old Ma Hsian-po (Ma Xianbo).

These arrests, the repercussions of which were so great at the time, but which have since become subsumed under the more dramatic and devastating impact of War and Liberation, are now usually described only in passing. For the human drama, particularly as it affected Shi Liang, Ruth Weiss's firsthand account in her autobiography (not yet published) is invaluable:

> I got wind of this through the weirdest means – a phone call at 4 am in French. The caller was Shi Liang's boyfriend [later her husband] Lu Chao-hua with whom I could con-verse under normal circumstances in French. But at 4am my French is not even so fluent as in plain daytime. So it took quite a while to realize that it was Mr Lu calling and then to get at the reason for his frantic appeal. He wanted to know if my boss, Li Shi Zheng, the Chinese version of Santa Claus, was in town so as to bail Shi Liang out – she had been arrested!
>
> This piece of news was foremost in my mind till day-break. If Shi Liang was arrested who was not such a wild and woolly radical, weren't there others involved, too? As soon as I could, I went to the *Voice of China* and there the Graniches [the editors] confirmed my suspicions, yes, there were six others taken in at the same time.[70]

As for Shi Liang herself, she remembers that late in the night of 22 November she 'had been wakened by a noise, only to find myself arrested without a reason'.[71] The arrests were carried out with the co-operation of the International Settlement and French Concession police, without warrants and without specific charges.

Although several Salvationist journals were closed at the same time, the effect of the arrests was electric. Soong Ching Ling, whom the Japanese had reported as also detained, proclaimed to reporters:

> There are still 475 million Chinese people whose patriotic wrath and righteous indignation cannot be suppressed! Let the Japanese militarists beware! They may cause the arrest of seven leaders, but they must still reckon with the Chinese people.[72]

The Seven Gentlemen were charged by the Bureau of Public Safety of the Chinese City Government with 'communistic behaviour' and 'suspicion of instigating the strike in the Japanese cotton mills.'[73] However, the case was adjourned on 28 November because of unsatisfactory evidence and the seven leaders were released on personal bonds signed by their defence lawyers. Six of them were rearrested 24 hours later charged with 'committing acts with intent to injure the Chinese Republic'.[74] Shi Liang evaded the net and became a wanted woman with 50,000 yuan on her head; she saw posters advertising the prize money.[75] She spent her period of freedom winding up 'organisational work' in the National Salvation Association.

On 2 December, 27,000 textile workers in Tsingtao (Qingdao) struck, closing all six Japanese mills in the city and proving the counter-productive nature of the arrest of the Seven Gentlemen.

Soong Ching Ling had immediately made her home (at 29 Rue Molière in Shanghai) the headquarters for the defence of the Seven and a post box for the threatened Salvationist movement. Through regular advertisements headed 'HELP CHINA!', she invited funds and messages to be sent to her personally.[76] To remove them from the hotbed of Shanghai, on 4 December six of the Seven were taken to Soochow (Suzhou) prison.

On 6 December came the dramatic kidnapping of Chiang Kai-shek in Sian, where he had gone to step up his campaign against the

Communists. Afterwards, his supporters always denied that his release had anything to do with undertakings he gave concerning the Seven Gentlemen. Mao Tse-tung agreed in a statement he put out on 28 December that Chiang did not sign a specific agreement; nevertheless, he tacitly agreed to a six-point programme, one of which was to release the patriotic leaders.[77] And, while there were many reasons for the military leaders responsible to have arrested Chiang, certainly they were converts to the Salvationist cause.[78] Although the Seven Gentlemen were eventually tried, from the time of the Sian incident China presented a united front against Japan.

On 30 December, Shi Liang gave herself up to the court in Soochow. In her version she travelled in disguise; in another she was dressed in the height of fashion and likely to attract the maximum attention.[79] She asked that she be imprisoned with the other 'Six Gentlemen' for 'being guilty of loving the nation'.[80] She writes of how,

> I was thrown into a cell with more than 60 other women. The next seven months in prison was one of the busiest periods of my life. I got to know every one of the inmates and the ins and outs of their case histories. In many ways I became their lawyer, helping each of them to study her own case and suggesting ways to present it in court. I also taught some women to read and write. Most of them had been driven to committing crimes after an unsuccesful marriage. Their tragic experiences exposed for me the seamy side of the old society.[81]

Another account adds a gloss to her story:

> Shi Liang felt a bit awkward facing these strange 'partners'. She learnt that by custom the older inmates bullied newcomers, so she wondered if they would attack her and how she could defend herself. She did not know how to greet them and asked, 'How are you, Sisters?', realising as she did

so how inappropriate it was.

Before she could change the wording, one woman answered, 'How well could we be in prison?'

Shi Liang reddened to her neck and did not know what to reply. Someone else asked, 'Are you a lawyer?' Shi Liang nodded.

A young woman of about twenty years old added, 'Do lawyers go to court?' Once the topic changed to her own profession, Shi Liang became lively and talkative again, forgetting that she was in prison. She told them that the duty of lawyers was to help wronged and oppressed people and that if any of them were wronged she could help them. 'That is my job,' Shi Liang said.

'Good.' One woman came up and caught Shi Liang's arm. 'Let's go. I want to tell you something. They say that I murdered my husband. But I was wronged.'[82]

The indictment of the Seven in Soochow in April, and the trial which followed, starting in June, were something of an anti-climax. But they gave students the chance to demonstrate and the press to stir up public opinion. In the hearing on 11 June, the judge asked Shi Liang, 'You have been advocating uniting various parties, isn't that the slogan of the Communist Party?'

Shi Liang replied, 'What the National Salvation Association wants is that all parties form an alliance to fight againt the Japanese. We don't mind if it's the Kuomintang or the Communist Party. It is an alliance without regard to party, class or sex. What matters is whether or not one fights against the Japanese. Fighting against the Japanese to save the country is called for by the public all over China. It is not a slogan we learned from the Communist Party.'[83]

On 5 July, Soong Ching Ling and others travelled to Soochow prison and demanded to be arrested and tried too, since their beliefs were the same as those of the Seven Gentlemen. Not surprisingly, in view of Soong Ching Ling's mystical immunity, the authorities failed to oblige, but the 'Go to Prison to Save the Nation' movement was still a publicity coup. The Seven were released on bail when the Sino-Japanese war erupted later that month.

How much the Seven Gentlemen had suffered in prison is a question raised by Ruth Weiss's contention that 'the head of the Soochow jail was a personal acquaintance of some of the arrested [which] guaranteed them not too bad treatment'. Her account of Shi Liang at a rally on 4 August to welcome the Seven Gentlemen home gives an even more vivid picture:

> Shi Liang was the only one I knew relatively well. As usual,
> she was bubbling over with excitement. Thus I learned that
> she was incarcerated in Suzhou jail with prostitutes and
> other victims of social oppression and that they all cried
> like everything when she left them – obviously, it must have

The Seven Gentlemen on their release from prison,
1937

been a great help to have a woman lawyer, and a progressive one at that, at their elbow. In those days, there were no defence lawyers for the peccadillos of the common people.[84]

The Seven came out to a country at war and issued their individual manifestos. Shi Liang's, reported in *The Voice of China*, proclaimed, under the heading 'This is the War for Life or Death':

The aggressors, having disturbed the peace of the world, and the League of Nations standing impotent before the aggressor, we can but use our own strength to resist. This is the war for life or death, destruction or existence of our nation; a war between the oppressed and imperialism. This kind of war will inevitably be a protracted one. We have to concentrate all our forces, mobilize all the masses of our country to build an iron-strong fort and a steel strong front, so that with a dare-to-die determination and guided by the world forces for peace and righteousness, we can firmly cope with our enemy. As long as the enemy does not forsake its aggressive atrocities we shall not stop our war. We must seek righteousness through sacrifice, and win real peace and existence through struggle.[85]

AFTERMATH

Shi Liang moved to Chungking (Chongqing) for the war, together with the government, foreign diplomats, the military and journalists, and anyone else who could get there or who had business there, including some leaders of the Communist Party. She headed a liaison committee of the Women's Advisory Committee under the New Life Movement in which Mme Chiang Kai-shek (Soong Mei-ling) was a leader. She was also associated with Soong Ching Ling in work for women. Anna Wang, the German wife of the Communist leader Wang Ping-nan (Wang Bingnan), tells two stories of Shi Liang in Chungking which add humour and non-conformity in her personal life to the picture of a serious dissident. Wang writes of the woman whom she, and many others, called 'Older Sister':

> The energetic, clever woman was particularly noticeable because she did not give one the feeling of being Americanized like so many modern Chinese women. She was an example of Chinese women's emancipation and was said to be one of the best lawyers in Chungking.
>
> Through this eminence, she had earned the esteem of Mme Chiang Kai-shek in whose women's committee she took part for a while, although she was also a member of the National Salvation Association. That Shi Liang had a sense of humour was shown one day when Mme Chiang told her that some people might not like her 'marriage-like relationship' with a young lawyer. At that time in China there was no registry where you could legally register a marriage. Moreover modern Chinese accept co-habitation as a marriage but usually the plighting of the troth is made known by a feast.
>
> 'All right,' said Shi Liang. 'For the sake of the United Front I will play bride.' The marriage celebration became one of the funniest gatherings in Chungking's war years. Shi Liang, married for years, even if not according to Mme Chiang's understanding, played an old-fashioned bride, while her guests, politically and socially as progressive and lacking in prejudice as she and her husband, but with the innate thespian talent of the Chinese, made the feast a comedy to bowl you over.[86]

When a few months later, Shi Liang's mother died, there was, astonishingly to Anna Wang, a huge funeral ceremony held according to Buddhist ritual. With, as she put it, 'Western directness', Anna Wang asked her, 'How can you square this with your principles that you don't belong to any religious group? You are openly against the old customs, and yet you call in priests and behave like any other conservative Chinese woman.'

'My mother was a conservative,' explained Shi Liang. 'A Buddhist funeral is the most expensive and, out of respect for her, I have chosen that. The promise of such a funeral was her last joy.'[87]

Towards the end of the war, Shi Liang was among the organisers of the radical China Women's Association which, at Liberation, was to be placed under the All-China Federation of Democratic Women. It was in this task that she worked with Teng Ying-chao. In 1944, she was among those who formed the China Democratic League (CDL), what was to become the main non-Communist political party following Liberation.[88] In 1946, she returned to practise in Shanghai, remaining there after the CDL was outlawed by the KMT in the autumn of 1947. (She was to become vice-chair of the CDL in 1953.)

In April 1949, Teng Ying-chao's husband, Chou En-lai, and Mao Tse-tung sent a telegram to Soong Ching Ling at the Rue Molière in Shanghai urging her to come to Beijing to give them support. That and other telegrams and letters were ignored. But when Teng Ying-chao herself came, Soong Ching Ling responded. She left for the north, taking with her 'non-Communist women of standing and influence such as Shi Liang'.[89] Shi Liang was appointed Minister for Justice under the new government set up that year.

One of the first pieces of legislation to be promulgated, only nine months after Liberation, was the 1950 Marriage Law. The drafting process had begun before Liberation was completed, views being solicited from all over China, within the rapidly expanding liberated areas.[90] Shi Liang was involved at that time in the formulation of the law; later she was responsible for its implementation, both as Minister and vice-chair of a special committee.[91] She commented on it thus:

> Women need special support if they are to attain real equality. After land reform, women who had been victims of unreasonable marriage arrangements in the past, now have land

in their own right. Their economic status has been raised and they are no longer subject to their husband's economic bondage.[92]

Using that quotation, and in response, Ruth Weiss writes, 'how much suffering and oppression is hidden behind these sober words! China's women had indeed much cause to rejoice.'

There was more to the Marriage Law than mere rhetoric, or even legislation. On 23 October, Chou En-lai dispatched a team of investigators led by Shi Liang to observe its implementation. They not only visited places at all four points of the compass, but they also organised a network of teams at the lowest provincial level. In small gatherings throughout the country, women were urged to discuss the past and look to the future. Many meetings were held at which judicial officers offered explanations and judgements on model divorce cases.[93]

Writing later of that time, Shi Liang noted that, 'When I was appointed Minister of Justice and witnessed the exhilarating scenes of women cheering the first Marriage Law in 1953, I could still see in my mind's eye the lingering shadows of Mrs Zhen [imprisoned for murder] and my other fellow inmates [in Soochow].'[94] Her own experience of nearly being a child-bride is only mentioned by implication.

Shi Liang's career over the 30 years that followed progressed conventionally enough for her time and place, as a senior member of the National People's Congress, for her province, and of the Democratic Women's Federation. She maintained close ties with old friends and associates, as evidenced by two enchanting photographs of her with Soong Ching Ling and Ho Hsiang-ning, one in 1951 (see page 122), the other in 1961.

By 1951, Soong Ching Ling was one of three non-Communist vice-chairs of the government; she died in 1981, named on her deathbed honorary chair of the People's Republic, and given membership of the Party. In August 1960, Ho Hsiang-ning, back in China since 1949, was elected, at the age of 80, to chair the central committee of the KMT Revolutionary Committee (another of the non-Communist

Soong Ching Ling (centre), Shi Liang (left) and Ho Hsiang-ning (seated), 1951

democratic parties), and she was honorary chair of the China Women's Federation. She wore her hair bobbed till the end, dying in 1972.

Shi Liang did not join the Communist Party and apparently survived the Cultural Revolution without coming under attack. She was probably one of those protected, as Soong Ching Ling was, by Chou En-lai.[95] In her older age, she lived in a 'hospital' and continued to attend meetings from there. One obituary notes:

> At the Fifth Session of the China Democratic League, when Shi Liang appeared in her wheelchair on the platform, all those in the meeting hall stood up to show their respect. Despite her ill health, Shi Liang finished her inaugural address without a rest.[96]

She died, still in harness in 1985, probably as old as the century.

A reference book published in Taipei (Taibei) depicts Shi Liang as a vain person having a strong desire for personal fame and gain and 'ganging up' with the Chinese Communist Party long before 1949.[97] The use of that term is ironic, or intentional, for an unsubstantiated anecdote, told me by a Chinese legal scholar, makes a tenuous connection between Shi Liang and Chiang Ching (Jiang Qing), leader of the Gang of Four. When Mao Tse-tung's widow was put on trial in 1980, the judge said that she could have any lawyer she liked. She replied that there had not been a decent lawyer since Shi Liang, a story that certainly ties in with at least one account of the trial.[98]

But, of those dramatic times in 1936, and appropriately to sum up the woman, Ruth Weiss writes:

> She was an intrepid person, even political cases did not scare
> her. … She was one of those democratic personages who
> are such an endearing feature of China, like the other six
> gentlemen, who had no fear to speak out although they had
> no armed forces to back them up.

CONCLUSION

Alison Conner mentioned Shi Liang's name to me some years ago when she was starting her work on Shanghai's legal community and I was concentrating on Western women in Hong Kong. I remember being surprised that there was a Chinese woman lawyer in Shanghai in the 1930s; there was not one in Hong Kong until well after World War II. I put the name away in a drawer, knowing that one day Shi Liang would surface in my work.

Last autumn, I reviewed Israel Epstein's biography of Soong Ching Ling, and read the manuscript of Ruth Weiss's autobiography. Shi Liang featured in both. My interest was roused, but still the vital spark was missing – I was concentrating on Western women in revolutionary China.

In November 1993, I attended a human rights seminar at the Chinese University of Hong Kong. There, a most beguiling scholar from the Mainland asked Western human rights scholars and activists to be patient with China on the issue. Human rights, in the sense of civil and political rather than social and economic rights, were a new concept in

China, he explained. I wanted then to mention Soong Ching Ling and the China League for the Protection of Civil Rights, but I could not remember the details well enough for such a scholarly forum. Afterwards, I went back to the material to refresh my mind, and there was Shi Liang. Her time had come for me.

John Fairbank, the doyen of Western historians on China, was there in the 1930s and peripherally involved with the League through Agnes Smedley and Helen and Edgar Snow. On reflection in his autobiography, he is impatient with some of its attempts to highlight the conditions of political prisoners then, and to call for reform. He writes:

> How do you define and assert civil rights among cart pullers on the street and sick soldiers in barracks? The China League was a pressure group on behalf of political prisoners, who would be primarily of the student class or intelligentsia. The implicit claim was that these vestiges of the old scholar ruling class should be treated better than criminals, coolies, and soldiers. Sound enough in traditional terms.[99]

His argument is similar to the one often used by China's representatives today when countering 'Western' criticisms.

One has to sympathise with the mindset that sees the vastness of China, the extent of its social and economic problems and its history before Liberation. And yet, the foregoing chapter shows what civil rights are really about, and that those who fought for those rights in China in the 1930s, including Communists, were equally concerned with social and economic rights and political and civil ones. The two campaigns are not mutually exclusive but compatible, even essential to one another.

While I was collecting material on Shi Liang, there was yet another fire in a foreign-owned factory in China. On 13 December 1993, 61 sleeping workers were killed in the Taiwan-funded Gaofu Textile Company in Foochow (Fuzhou). Nearly all the victims were women. The *Legal Daily* reported that the company's general manager did at least 'acknowledge responsibility for having the dormitory and warehouse so close together, despite official warnings from fire safety officials earlier in the year'.[100]

In November, the barbaric behaviour of managements in foreign-owned factories in China had been more sharply etched when 84 workers, again mostly women, were killed in the Hong Kong-owned Zhili toy factory located in the Shenzhen special economic zone. A survivor reported, 'Everybody was crowding on to the second floor when we realised the gates were locked.' She jumped from the second floor window 'after rescuers prised open security bars'. More than 50 bodies were found 'piled on the staircase and behind one of the two locked downstairs gates'. A Chinese government official said, 'We have warned the factory several times to take action to improve their fire prevention safety standards.'[101]

A resident of the area explained that 'the factory always locked the gates in order to prevent the workers escaping'. In a recent fire in a Hong-kong owned factory in Thailand it was so that the workers could not steal the tawdry goods they were making. Recently, I have been reliably informed, a Hong Kong industrialist said that, if the women workers from the countryside were not locked in at night, they would work as prostitutes.[102] If there is any truth in that suggestion, it may also be a comment on pay and conditions.

And if there is any truth, it should be put against the story of Zhang Feng, a woman worker at a Japanese electronics factory in Hainan Province. There she found pay and conditions reasonable. Then she found her duties 'extended to helping win over clients by using her feminine charms'.[103]

Following the several fires, details of pay and conditions have emerged that seem hardly better than those in the Japanese-owned factories in China in the 1930s. Guangdong Province, adjoining Hong Kong, has 3,000 toy manufacturers, most of them with Hong Kong owners.[104] There, labour is cheap; life, apparently, is cheap too.[105]

Following the Zhili fire, survivors were 'held prisoner to stifle bad publicity'.[106] Given that reaction by the authorities, and the incident that sparked it, one has to ask, can economic progress be secured at the expense of civil rights? From the protection of civil rights to the recognition of human rights, and their protection, is not even a step. The campaign for civil rights and against the abuses of foreign factory owners in the 1930s also shows that the examples and lessons of history cannot be disregarded.

In bringing these threads together, I am convinced that recreating history does not have to be a static craft – the recording of what happened, or even its objective analysis. It is more interesting and useful if it shows the past as part of the present, of an organic continuum and challenge. History also shows you where your real roots are.

Written July 1994.

NOTES

1. Carsun Chang, *The Third Force in China* (1952), p. 80.
2. Parks M. Coble, *Facing Japan* (1991), p. 339.
3. Soong Ching Ling Foundation, *The Great Life of Soong Ching Ling* (1987), p. 51. 'The Six Gentlemen' were martyred for protesting against official misconduct during the Ming dynasty.
4. Max Perleberg, *Who's Who in Modern China* (1954), p. 187.
5. James Bertram, *Crisis in China* (1937), p. 19.
6. Edgar Faure, *The Serpent and the Tortoise* (1958), p. 8. The Indian diplomat K.M. Panikkar wrote in *In Two Chinas* (1955), p. 86, that 'though a radical in her politics and a member of the government, she does not evidently follow the directive about lipstick and makeup. Whenever I have had the pleasure of seeing her, she was dressed with great care and taste.'
7. The following dates are given by the following sources: 1900: Wolfgang Bartke, *Who's Who in the People's Republic of China* (1981), p. 320; 1900: Xu Youchun, *Who's Who in the Period of the Republic of China* (1991), p. 8; 1907: Donald Klein, *Biographical Dictionary of Chinese Communism* (1971), p. 764; 1908: *Who's Who in the Chinese Communist Party* (1967), p. 81; 1908: Union Research Institute, *Who's Who in Communist China* (1970), p. 569. Shi Liang herself does not give a date, but does confirm dates of landmarks in her life.
8. Shi Liang, 'The Road I Travelled' (1981), p. 18.
9. Shan Yuyue, 'Shi Liang Gave Herself up to the Court' (1987), p. 85. All translations from the Chinese for this chapter have been done by my dear friend Zhao Yuhong.
10. Shan Yuyue, 'Shi Liang Gave Herself up to the Court', p. 85.
11. Shan Yuyue, 'Shi Liang Gave Herself up to the Court', p. 85.
12. Shi Liang, 'The Road I Travelled', p. 18.
13. Shan Yuyue, 'Shi Liang Gave Herself up to the Court', p. 85.
14. Hsieh Ping-ying, *Autobiography of a Chinese Girl* (1986), pp. 67-68.
15. Dymphna Cusack, *Chinese Women Speak* (1985), p. 185.
16. Howard L. Boorman, *Biographical Dictionary of Republican China* (1967), p. 264.
17. Cusack, *Chinese Women Speak*, p. 186.
18. Helen Foster Snow, *My China Years* (1984), p. 19
19. Alison Conner, 'China's Early Lawyers', p. 8.
20. Shi Liang, 'The Road I Travelled', p. 18.
21. Shi Liang, 'The Road I Travelled', p. 18.
22. Shi Liang, 'The Road I Travelled', p. 18.
23. Xu, *Who's Who in the Period of the Republic of China*, p. 159.
24. Shan Yuyue, 'Shi Liang Gave Herself up to the Court', p. 85.
25. Union Research Institute, *Who's Who in Communist China*, p. 569.
26. Klein, *Biographical Dictionary of Chinese Communism*, p. 764.
27. Hsieh, *Autobiography of a Chinese Girl*, p. 93. Hsieh also published her *War Diary* in 1928. New *War Diaries* are available in English in *Girl Rebel: The Autobiography of Hsieh ping-ying*.
28. Hsieh, *Autobiography of a Chinese Girl*, p. 93.
29. Anna Louise Strong, 'Some Hankow Memories' (1928), p. 794.
30. Strong, 'Some Hankow Memories', p. 797.

31. Strong, 'Some Hankow Memories', p. 797.

32. Hsieh, *Autobiography of a Chinese Girl*, p. 135.

33. For the uninitiated reader it may have made recognition easier to call Teng Ying-chao, Mme Chou En-lai; however, it is essential to realise that women such as Teng Ying-chao, Ho Hsiang-ning and Soong Ching Ling were revolutionary figures in their own right and used their own names.

34. Cusack, *Chinese Women Speak*, p. 188.

35. Her husband was Liao Chung-kai (Liao Zhongkai); her son, also a well-known revolutionary, Liao Cheng-chih; and her daughter, Cynthia Liao (Liao Meng-hsing), later secretary to Soong Ching Ling.

36. She spent her early years in the British Colony where her family was in the tea business – Boorman, p. 67.

37. Shi Liang, 'The Road I Travelled', p. 18.

38. Accusations of immorality were not confined to women involved in politics, and suffering for it; Yang Chien, the secretary of the League for Civil Rights assassinated in 1933, is just one example of its use as black propaganda against men – John Fairbank, *Chinabound* (1982), p. 77.

39. Conner, 'China's Early Lawyers', p. 10.

40. Shi Liang, 'The Road I Travelled', p. 18.

41. Israel Epstein, *Woman in World History* (1993), pp. 277-278.

42. Epstein, *Woman in World History*, pp. 279-280

43. Epstein, *Woman in World History*, p. 282.

44. Shi Liang, 'The Road I Travelled', p. 18.

45. Shi Liang, 'The Road I Travelled', p. 18.

46. John Fairbank, *Chinabound* (1982), p. 75.

47. Agnes Smedley, *China Correspondent* (1970), p. 84.

48. Epstein, *Woman in World History*, p. 307.

49. Edgar Snow, *Journey to the Beginning* (1960), p. 144.

50. Ruth Weiss, unpublished manuscript. See note 61.

51. Epstein, *Woman in World History*, p. 382.

52. Shi Liang, 'The Road I Travelled', p. 19.

53. Epstein, *Woman in World History*, p. 308.

54. I. Epstein, *The People's War* (1939), pp. 249-250.

55. Bobby Siu, *Women of China* (1982), p. 134.

56. Coble, *Facing Japan*, p. 296.

57. Coble, *Facing Japan*, p. 336.

58. Percy Chen, *China Called Me* (1979), p. 288.

59. Shi Liang, 'The Road I Travelled', pp. 19-20.

60. Ono Kazuko, *Chinese Women in a Century of Revolution* (1989), p. 113

61. Ruth Weiss, unpublished manuscript (work in progress in English and German). All quotations from Ruth Weiss come from the same source. I would like to thank her most warmly for her generosity in allowing me to use this material before she has published it herself.

62. Anna Louise Strong, *China Fights for Freedom* (1939), p. 73.

63. Ruth Weiss, unpublished manuscript.

64. Rewi Alley, *At 90* (1986), pp. 276-277.

65. Strong, *China Fights for Freedom*, p. 172.

66. Emily Honig, *Sisters and Strangers*, p. 223.

67. Honig, *Sisters and Strangers*, pp. 222-223.

68. Honig, *Sisters and Strangers*, p. 223.

69. Epstein, *Woman in World History*, p. 382.

70. Ruth Weiss, unpublished manuscript. The other six were: Li Gongpu, Wang Zaoshi, Shen Junru, Zou Taofen, Zhang Naiqui and Sha Qianli.

71. Shi Liang, 'The Road I Travelled', p. 20.

72. Epstein, *Woman in World History*, p. 315; Coble, *Facing Japan*, p. 339.

73. Ruth Weiss, unpublished manuscript.

74. Ruth Weiss, unpublished manuscript.

75. Shi Liang, 'The Road I Travelled', p. 20.

76. Epstein, *Woman in World History*, p. 315.

77. Edgar Snow, *Red Star Over China* (1972), p. 433; Snow, *Journey to the Beginning*, p. 186.

78. Snow, *Red Star Over China*, p. 427; Coble, *Facing Japan*, pp. 340-341. The leaders were Zhang Yue-ling and Yang Hu-cheng.

79. Shan Yuyue, 'Shi Liang Gave Herself up to the Court', p. 83; Shi Liang, 'The Road I Travelled', p. 20.

80. Hu Yuzhi, 'Mourning the Last of the "Seven Gentlemen"', (1985), p. 5.

81. Shi Liang, 'The Road I Travelled,' p. 20.

82. Shan Yuyue, 'Shi Liang Gave Herself up to the Court', p. 86.

83. Hu Yuzhi, 'Mourning the Last of the "Seven Gentlemen"', p. 5.

84. Ruth Weiss, unpublished manuscript.

85. *Voice of China*, 15 August 1937, p. 12.

86. Anna Wang, *Ich Kampfte fur Mao* (1964), p. 371; found and translated for me by Ruth Weiss. Shi Liang's husband, a Shanghai lawyer, had several names: Lu Chao-hua, Lu Diandong, Andre Loh. They were apparently separated by 1949 and, by 1956, she had remarried.

87. Wang, *Ich Kampfte fur Mao*, p. 371.

88. Another member of the League was Chou Chingwen (Zhou Jingwen); see the chapters on Xiao Hong. As a member of the League, Shi Liang was subject to harassment in Chungking.

89. Han Suyin, *Eldest Son* (1994), p. 207.

90. Cusack, *Chinese Women Speak*, p. 200.

91. Klein, *Biographical Dictionary of Chinese Communism*, p. 765.

92. Ruth Weiss, unpublished manuscript. The Marriage Law abolished the traditional, feudal Chinese marriage system. For example, it legalised freedom of choice, monogamy, and equal rights for women and men; it prohibited bigamy, concubinage and child brides (Kazuko *Chinese Women in a Century of Revolution*, pp. 176-186).

93. Kasuko, *Chinese Women in a Century of Revolution*, p. 182.

94. Shi Liang, 'The Road I Travelled,' p. 20.

95. Epstein, *Woman in World History*, p. 550.

96. Xi Zhongxun, 'Deep Mourning Over a Close Friend of the Chinese Communist Party,' (1985), p. 4.

97. *Who's Who in the Communist Party*, pp. 81-82.

98. Ross Terrill, *Madame Mao* (1992), p. 378.

99. Fairbank, *Chinabound*, p. 71.

100. *South China Morning Post*, 9 January 1994.

101. *Sunday Morning Post*, 21 November 1994.

102. Reported by Professor Derek Roebuck, Faculty of Law, City University of Hong Kong.

103. *South China Morning Post*, 21 January 1994.

104. *South China Morning Post*, 20 November 1993.

105. Japanese factory owners moved into China early in the century because a 1916 law in Japan protected women from night work (Kazuko, p. 113). Comparatively higher wages for factory workers in Hong Kong, and less stringent protection in China have had the same effect.

106. *South China Morning Post*, 22 November 1992.

107. This chapter does not set out to be a comprehensive account of Shi Liang's life. Apart from her work on the implementation of the 1950 Marriage Law as Minister for Justice, and a brief sketch of 1937-1985, it concentrates on her role as the Seventh Gentleman. What it does hope to do is to support further work on her life.

BIBLIOGRAPHY

Alley, Rewi, *At 90: Memoirs of My China Years* (Beijing, New World Press, 1986).

Bartke, Wolfgang, *Who's Who in the People's Republic of China*, pp. 320-321 (Armonk NY, M.E. Sharpe, 1981).

Bertram, James, *Crisis in China: The Story of the Sian Mutiny* (London, Macmillan, 1937).

Boorman, Howard L., *Biographical Dictionary of Republican China* (New York, Colombia University Press, 1967).

Chang, Carsun, *The Third Force in China* (New York, Bookman Association, 1952).

Chen, Joseph T., *The May 4th Movement in Shanghai: The Making of a Social Movement in Modern China* (Leiden, E.J. Brill, 1971).

Chen, Percy, *China Called Me: My Life Inside the Chinese Revolution* (Boston, Little Brown, 1979).

Coble, Parks M., *Facing Japan: Chinese Politics & Japanese Imperialism, 1931-1937* (Harvard, Council on East Asian Studies, 1991).

Conner, Alison, 'China's Early Lawyers: The Shanghai Bar' (paper prepared for 12th IAHA Conference, Hong Kong, 1991).

Cusack, Dymphna, *Chinese Women Speak* (London, Century Hutchison, 1985; 1st published 1958).

Epstein, I., *The People's War* (London, Victor Gollancz, 1939).

Epstein, Israel, *Woman in World History: The Life and Times of Soong Ching Ling (Mme Sun Yatsen)* (Beijing, New World Press, 1993).

Fairbank, John, *Chinabound: A Fifty-Year Memoir* (New York, Harper & Row, 1982).

Faure, Edgar, *The Serpent and the Tortoise* (New York, Macmillan, 1958).

Han Suyin, *Eldest Son: Zhou Enlai and the Making of Modern China 1896-1976* (London, Pimlico, 1994).

Honig, Emily, *Sisters and Strangers: Women in the Shanghai Cotton Mills 1919-1949* (Stanford, Stanford University Press, 1986).

Hsieh Ping-ying, *Autobiography of a Chinese Girl* (London, Pandora, 1986; 1st published 1943).

Hsieh Ping-ying, *Girl Rebel: The Autobiography of Hsieh Ping-ying* (New York, Da Capo Press, 1975).

Hu Yuzhi and Shen Zijiu, 'Mourning the Last of the "Seven Gentlemen" – Shi Liang' (Daonian "Qi Jun Zi" de Zuihou yige – Shi Liang Tong Zhi", in *People's Daily*, 13 October 1985).

Israel, John and Klein, Donald W., *Rebels and Bureaucrats: China's December 9ers* (Berkeley, University of California Press, 1976).

Kasuko, Ono, *Chinese Women in a Century of Revolution, 1850-1950* (Stanford, Stanford University Press, 1989; 1st published 1978).

Klein, Donald and Clark, Anne, *Biographical Dictionary of Chinese Communism*, pp. 764-766 (Cambridge, Mass., Harvard University Press, 1971).

Mackinnon, Janice R. and Mackinnon, Stephen R., *Agnes Smedley: The Life and Times of an American Radical* (London, Virago, 1988).

North China Herald

Panikkar, K.M., *In Two Chinas: Memoirs of a Diplomat* (London, George Allen & Unwin, 1955).

Perleberg, Max, *Who's Who in Modern China* (Hong Kong, Ye Olde Printerie, 1954).

Shan Yuyue, 'Shi Liang Gave Herself up to the Court', in *The Seven Gentlemen*, vol. 10, 1987, pp. 83-89.

Shi Liang, 'The Road I Travelled', in *Women of China*, part 8, pp. 18-20 (Beijing, 1981).

Shi Liang, 'The Road I Travelled', in *When They Were Young* (Beijing, New World Press, 1981).

Shieh, Joseph, *Dans Le Jardin Des Aventuriers* (Paris, Seuil, 1995).

Siu, Bobby, *Women of China: Imperialism and Women's Resistance, 1900-1949* (London, Zed Press, 1982).

Smedley, Agnes, *China Correspondent* (London, Pandora, 1970; 1st published 1943 as *Battle Hymn of China*).

Snow, Edgar, *Red Star Over China* (London, Penguin, 1972; 1st published 1937).

Snow, Edgar, *Journey to the Beginning* (London, Victor Gollancz, 1960).

Snow, Edgar, *Red China Today: The Other Side of the River* (London, Penguin, 1970).

Snow, Helen Foster, *Women in Modern China* (The Hague, Mouton, 1967).

Snow, Helen Foster, *My China Years* (London, Harrap, 1984).

Soong Ching Ling Foundation, *The Great Life of Soong Ching Ling* (Beijing, 1987).

South China Morning Post.

Strong, Anna Louise, 'Some Hankow Memories: Of a Women's Union that Busied Itself with Slave Girls, Bobbed Hair and Divorce', in *Asia*, 1928, pp. 794-833.

Strong, Anna Louise, *China Fights for Freedom* (London, Lindsay Drummond, 1939).

Sunday Morning Post.

Tcheng Soumay, *My Revolutionary Years* (New York, Charles Scribner, 1943).

Terrill, Ross, *Madame Mao: The White-Boned Demon* (New York, Simon & Schuster, 1992).

Union Research Institute, *Who's Who in Communist China*, pp. 569-570 (Hong Kong, 1970).

Van Slyke, Lyman P., *Enemies and Friends: The United Front in Chinese Communist History* (Stanford, Stanford University Press, 1967).

Voice of China.

Wang, Anna, *Ich Kampfte fur Mao* (Hamburg, Christian Wegner, 1964).

Wang Ying, *The Child Bride* (Beijing, Foreign Language Press, 1989).

Weiss, Ruth, *Lu Xun: A Writer for All Times* (Beijing, New World Press, 1985).

Weiss, Ruth, *Autobiography* (ms in preparation).

Who's Who in the Chinese Communist Party (Zhongqong Renming Lu) (Taipei, International Relations Research Institute of the Republic of China, 1967).

Xi Zhongxun, 'Deep Mourning Over a Close Friend of the Chinese Communist Party – Shi Liang' (Chentong Daonian Zhongguo Gongchandang de Qinmi Zhanyou – Shi Liang Tongzhi) in *People's Daily*, 16 September 1985.

Xu Youchun, *Who's Who in the Period of the Republic of China* (Shijiazhuang, Hebei People's Press, 1991).

CHAPTER 9

REMEMBERING A DAUGHTER OF SHANGHAI
Agnes Smedley's Centenary

Scratched on a desk in a well-known Beijing university is the name 'Smedley'. Perhaps it was a crib for an exam; more likely, a lecture that included the exploits of the American activist and writer Agnes Smedley had struck a chord with a Chinese student.

For it was in China that Smedley lived her best years and about it that she produced her best non-fiction writing. It was because of her and her fellow Americans, Anna Louise Strong and Edgar Snow, that the Chinese revolutionary activities of the 1920s and 1930s became known, admired and supported in the outside world.

As a result, the ashes of the two women are buried in Babaoshan, the Cemetery for Revolutionaries in Beijing; the visitor comes across Snow's tomb by the willow-fringed lake in the grounds of Peking University.

They are known in China as 'the Three SSS' and there is a society to honour them, now called the China Friendship Study Society. It was under the auspices of the local branch that the centenary of Agnes Smedley's birth has just been celebrated (December 1992) in Shanghai where she lived when she arrived in China in 1928 as a journalist.

From Beijing and further afield came people who had known Smedley before her death in Oxford in 1950, and those who now devote their scholarship to her life and work.

First she was remembered in papers given at a symposium. Ruth Weiss, 84 years old the following day, proved the importance of her

Agnes Smedley in Kuomintang uniform,
1937-1940

own presence, and that of her contemporaries, with her opening comment, 'There are very few people left who knew Agnes Smedley face to face.' And she described her first view of Smedley in a way that surviving snapshots cannot convey because they lack subjectivity: 'A tall woman wearing a broad-brimmed hat pulled down over her face; she was not beautiful but impressive.'

Weiss knew Smedley in Shanghai from the end of 1934 and was soon roped into her political activities. Holding up an ageing copy of 'Economic Conditions in China', she told how 'Agnes gave me the job of sending out a big drawerful of these pamphlets to various people in Shanghai.' And she remembered how, when the Beijing student movement of early 1936 caught on in Shanghai a week later, 'everyone whom Agnes knew got involved in gathering news' which was then 'gathered and sent out by Agnes to progressive circles'.

Israel Epstein, an expert on Soong Ching Ling (Mme Sun Yat-sen) with whom Smedley worked against the Japanese incursion, knew her in Tianjin in 1935-1936, in Wuhan in 1938 and after the war in the United States. Following Ruth Weiss, he developed the physical impression of Smedley on a different level when he suggested that 'Agnes, becoming a historic figure, is sometimes presented in reportage as tall and physically strong – a sort of superhuman type in every respect. In fact, while her courage and spirit were unquenchable, and she worked hard and incessantly, she was weak physically and often ill.'

In the hotel lobby before the symposium, the writer Ayako Ishigaki, with her long sable coat and impeccable coiffure, was supported on both sides as she walked; she gave the impression of pampered ill health. On the platform, she raised her arms above her head like a prize-fighter, then handed her speech to a male companion to read. In it she apologised to the audience: at 89, she did not feel up to delivering it herself.

Ayako Ishigaki had settled in the United States in the 1920s and met Smedley at Yaddo, the retreat for creative artists near New York, during the war. She and her husband, the painter Eitaro Ishigaki, were part of a small group of anti-militarist Japanese exiles trusted by the government. It was all the more courageous, therefore, that they should have remained loyal to Smedley when, in 1949, she was accused of being a Communist spy.

Against Smedley's advice, Ayako saw her off at the docks when she left the United States for the last time. Smedley was remembered then as a haggard, exhausted figure wearing an empty smile as she said good-bye. The Ishigakis were later deported.

Then there was the Chinese composer Meng Bo who had first come across Smedley in Jiangxi dancing and singing Russian folk tunes. They exchanged songs and 'I was very touched that some of those pieces (of mine) were found in her things and are now kept in a museum in Beijing'.

He remembered of her, 'She wasn't like a foreigner, but a Chinese. … She was so kind to me, so easy to make friends with.' Her vocal rendition for him of Beethoven's Ninth Symphony had inspired him in his life's work. She relaxed hard, but she also worked hard, 16 hours a

'Smedley' scratched on a desk, Beijing, 1992

day, he said, and she was always asking questions about conditions in Shanghai, which she was missing.

There were papers, too, specifically about her work – fundraising, publicity and nursing – with the Eighth Route Army; her translations of Lu Xun's writing; and her encouragement of younger, less-established Chinese writers, including the woman novelist Xiao Hong who died in Hong Kong a few months after Smedley had left there for home and safety and a few weeks after the Japanese invasion of the colony.

Retiring to Hong Kong in 1940 primarily for health reasons, Smedley was looked after by friends such as Hilda Selwyn-Clarke whom she had met through their mutual support of the Chinese war effort.

In spite of restrictions by the British authorities because of her long-standing support of Indian nationalism, and with the research help of Hilda Selwyn-Clarke, Smedley produced a damning critique of Hong

Kong's social conditions signed 'American Observer' and published in the *South China Morning Post*.

The one area that did not seem adequately covered in the symposium was Smedley's concern for ordinary Chinese women: her attempts to start a birth control clinic for them in Shanghai; her writing about the difficulties of their traditional life; and her keen consciousness-raising among them.

There was an opportunity to remedy that omission the next afternoon when 200 schoolchildren – half of them girls – were introduced to the life of Agnes Smedley. She had been in the vanguard of those campaigning to give women in China a chance; in celebration of her birth 100 years ago, they owed it to her, now, to take hold of that chance.

The climax of the two-day celebrations was the unveiling of a plaque in her honour on the building where she had lived. The inscription was in both Chinese and English. In her life, too, East and West had been united, for Smedley was an internationalist, as well as a supporter of Chinese wartime patriotism.

It was a cold winter's day, but the elderly who remembered her, and the young who had cause to be grateful to her, were undeterred.

Smedley herself was deterred by little in life – from her childhood of poverty in the United States which inspired the novel *Daughter of Earth*, to her death on her way back to China to celebrate a liberation that she had not only recorded but in which she had also played a warmly-acknowledged part (see also Chapter 21). They call her there 'Daughter of Shanghai'.

Published in *Window*, Hong Kong, 5 February 1993.

THE SILK ROAD

CHAPTER 10

SPIRIT OF PLACE
Chinibagh, Kashgar,
1898-1992

The sky was star-spangled black velvet and vaulted. We lay half sprawled on the flat wooden cart, clutching at the sides to stop ourselves slipping into the path of donkeys coming behind. Our own donkey, bells tinkling, clipped along at a fine pace, encouraged by the whip of the driver who sat to one side of its haunches.

I was approaching the gates of what had been the British Consulate in Kashgar on the old Silk Road. It was an important moment; for many years I had hoped to follow in the footsteps of Catherine Macartney, the first British woman to live there, in 1898.

After her had come Ella Sykes, whose brother had taken over as Consul General while the Macartneys were on leave in 1915, and Diana Shipton who had gone there with her husband in 1946. Then there were the intrepid travellers who had arrived there after crossing the deserts of Chinese Turkestan on foot and horseback – Eleanor Lattimore and Ella Maillart (see Chapter 11).

But that first night in Kashgar, although we disembarked at the gates of the old consulate, we did not go in. Instead we were headed just down the road, to The Bistro, to drink coffee and Turfan port and eat chocolate cake. The Western eating place was something of a novelty in Kashgar in 1992, and something of a necessity for less hardy travellers.

We were staying at the Seman Hotel, what had once been the Russian Consulate, the only other diplomatic compound in that isolated centre of the 'Great Game' where British India, Russia and China met. The food at the Seman was so unappealing that we had left before

The front door of the British Consulate-General, Kashgar

attempting to eat it. And, while we had dined reasonably at a trellised café just inside the gates of the hotel, we needed a nightcap to enable us to face unlovely sheets on our hotel bed.

Finally, though, I did go through the gates. I wrote to my mother about that moment for which I had long waited:

> Lunch was to be the highlight of my trip because it was to be held at a hotel which used to be the British Consulate, still called what it was then, Chinibagh. Unfortunately, it was not quite as it was.
>
> Firstly, as you go in, there's this big modern block which I ignored; then, leading round to the back, are some of the

nastiest lavatories I've ever had to cope with. Wincing out of
them you reach the remains of the old Residence. It is now
a hostel for Pakistani long distance lorry drivers. Many were
stranded because the pass over the Karakorams had been
closed for some reason or other, whether an early snow fall
or something more political was unclear. The Afghan who
later talked to Derek comes to catch hawks to sell to rich
Saudi Arabians, and also wanted to exult over any passing
Englishman for being inferior to Pakistanis at cricket.

When you've passed those dormitories, trying not to
look in because it's rude, but looking in like mad nevertheless because you have travelled thousands of miles to see
that house, you come to a room used as a hotel dining room.
And there we had a meal which was not the worst we had on
the trip but all the dishes were served with such dirty accou-
trements, and all the food somehow tasted dirty.

I climbed around outside as much as I could to try and
get an impression of what Chinibagh must have been like,
and the surrounding countryside, but the imagination was
in over-drive because it's now in such a sorry state. Not surprisingly, the view has quite disappeared, and nothing is left
of the beautiful garden that Catherine Macartney created,
nor of the English atmosphere that used to welcome travellers and make them go into ecstasies in print.

But then, why should anyone perpetuate in that or the
Russian Consulate what used to be? Though they would if
they realised how financially rewarding it would be. Can you
imagine an English country house hotel in the middle of
the desert? But it's too late now.

I did not try to discuss with the waitresses at Chinibagh how it
used to be, but there was one question with which I persevered. Where
was the Mazzar of Bibi Anna? Ella Sykes wrote how the grave of this
female saint was situated on a bluff opposite the consulate. She

described it as a mud tomb on which a white flag fluttered, and surrounded by a mud wall.

She explained how, there, 'widows and divorced women who desired remarriage and girls anxious for a husband were wont to resort; putting their hands into holes built in the tomb, they would implore the holy woman to aid them.' (p. 92)

Ella had been unable to find any further information about Bibi Khanum; I was unable to find out anything at all about the tomb – no one had heard of it; it has obviously become a victim of 80 or so years of Kashgar's urban development.

Ella Sykes had given me another lead: she mentions silver buttons bordering embroidered caps. After lunch at Chinibagh, therefore, while the rest of the party were taken to the mosque, Derek and I peeled off to Gold and Silversmiths' Road beside it to look for silver buttons.

Up and down the road we traipsed, past scribes writing letters for clients, pavement barbers, a woman selling piles of unleavened bread, tailors and seamstresses also open to public gaze, and dozens of little stalls, carpeted cubby holes, full of craftspeople, mostly in gold – rather crude but clever and intriguing to watch – and new or ageing knick-knacks, with just a few silver buttons. Eventually, what with bargaining and matching, I found eight or so at a reasonable – though not a knock-down – price. Who once wore those buttons? Now one adorns my black and silver evening jacket.

Back at the Seman Hotel on our last evening, after a day trip to Yarkand and into the Taklamakan desert, I became anxious about failing to find the ghosts of the Russian women who had lived there a hundred years earlier, and the British women who visited them.

The hotel is a conglomerate of ugly modern blocks on one side of the old consulate courtyard. Another side is the entrance and our trellised, life-saving café; on the third side are old Russian, ochre-painted buildings that are now offices, staff quarters and the souvenir shop – all rather ghostless. The fourth side is the hotel's avoidable restaurant, in front of which the drains were all being dug up so that you could get no feeling of what the courtyard had been like.

As it grew dark over dinner at the café, I got into conversation with a member of our group whose grandmother had spent time in Kashgar in the 1930s. She told me that she had found some more of the Russian Consulate by climbing over the dug-up drains and going round the back. She took me there and, though it was too dark for the photographs I took to be any use at all, I did have a rewarding journey backwards in time and felt that I had assuaged something of my disappointment at how the past had been replaced by sleazy present. There was a portico, and a columned verandah leading on to a wild garden where roses still bloomed and a huge hundred-year-old oak still flourished. That was a really good moment.

I know nothing yet about the Russian women, except the very little that the British women have told me. Of 1898, Catherine Macartney wrote:

> Then I must call at the Russian Consulate on Mme Kolokoloff, the wife of the Secretary of the Consulate. Mons. Petrovsky had not his wife with him. There were two other Russian ladies, wives of the Cossack and Customs Officers, but as they spoke only Russian I could not get on very well with them, and the visits we paid each other were rather painful ordeals. Mme Kolokoloff spoke French, and so I set to at once to improve my French and we got on splendidly with her and her three children. (p. 48)

Ella Sykes, 17 years later, was a little more forthcoming in her descriptions, but even she had her problems:

> Nice and friendly as the Russians all were, my brother and I led lives of such a different kind that we could not well coalesce. If we dined with them we could never leave before midnight, and they themselves said that they liked to stay on till five o'clock in the morning, the domestics serving up a supper, or rather an early breakfast, from the remnants of

the dinner, and possibly they would stroll out to see the sun rise before they repaired to their homes. Owing to their love of late hours they did not rise till mid-day, and as they could not enjoy the cool of the mornings as we did, they need to 'take the air' by moonlight. (p. 49)

I could not blame the Russians for wanting to be out in the moon-light in that garden, no matter how faded the remains I saw in the gathering dusk.

By 1946, Russia had long been the Soviet Union, but some things about Russian hospitality had little changed, as Diana Shipton noted:

Our efforts to leave were vigorously resisted. This was not polite protesting, a matter of form, but aggressive refusal. Every hour we would make another attempt to leave until by 2 or even 3 am we would abandon politeness and go. I never understood the meaning behind this half-humorous, half-angry fight to keep us until the early hours. It was ob-vious that everyone had exhausted their powers of conversa-tion. Interpreters were drooping, many guests were frankly asleep but still our host whipped on the flagging spirit of the party. (p. 102)

Certainly, in 1992, we could not wait to get away from what had been the Russian Consulate.

———•◦•———

I've been rather unkind about Kashgar, particularly about the Chinibagh and Seman hotels. But I had so longed to go there and, although I knew I should be disappointed, I had not quite prepared myself for the depths of my disillusion. Partly the problem was how we arrived in Kashgar, compared with how my women did before Libera-tion in 1949.

We had stayed in a surprisingly civilised hotel in Urumchi, the capital of the Uygur Autonomous Republic (Singkiang or Xinjiang) – a hotel to which we were to repair from both our forays, west to Kashgar, and east to Turfan, as if to an oasis. As I wrote, 'Just the joy of a shower and washing one's hair and soft crisp clean sheets on a king sized bed and a clean floor, and BBC World Service television!' My women had travelled for weeks overland, two through pre-Revolutionary Russia, one over the Karakoram Pass from what was India in the days before the Highway, and two from the east, through the deserts of China. For them, Kashgar and Chinibagh were the oasis. That was so even for Catherine Macartney who created Chinibagh as it was to become known.

'Spirit of place' becomes crucial in the re-creation of the lives of the past, and that spirit is made up of a myriad refractions. The travel writer sees and experiences a place through her own experience and personality, and yet, as the following accounts of my women show, the place also seems to have its own intrinsic reality. What processes create the spirit? – that is the question.

The non-Russian Western women who arrived in Kashgar and then at Chinibagh had an experience that was so uncannily similar that it must illustrate something about the place itself. I hobbled along behind and could barely catch at a wisp as I wrote of that first moment:

> It was really quite extraordinary to come in to land and see the desert come to a halt and the oasis take over at a quite specific point, and in a straight line. I do love that contrast of what Gertrude Bell called the Desert and the Sown, the dry sand and the wet green of lush vegetation. And then a particular feature of Kashgar, from the records of my travellers as they arrive, is the poplar avenues. Can you imagine what that gentle silver rustle of the leaves and the tinkle of the irrigation channels beneath must have meant to them after a gruelling desert crossing? The quite extraordinary thing was that we were driving along those same avenues *to the same place*; well, not to the British Consulate, but to the Russian, which is even more exotic.

I am conscious that, in concentrating only on the route to the British Consulate and the place itself, I am omitting the whole of the Kashgar experienced by the indigenous people (and even the Han Chinese!) and those people seen through the experience of my women travellers; that would take at least a book – the book which took me to Kashgar in the first place. But Chinibagh was a phenomenon that deserves a page or two of its own.

Catherine Macartney arrived in Kashgar as a new bride, give or take a wedding journey through Southern Russia. She was 21 and had never been out of England before. Her husband, George, born of a Chinese mother and a Scottish father, was Britain's first Consul General there when he arrived in 1890. He had set up a bachelor establishment rather different from the gracious family home that was to greet later travellers. Catherine wrote of her arrival in 1898:

> When at last we arrived at Chini Bagh (Chinese Garden), my new home, we found decorations up, the courtyard carpeted with bright rugs, and hung round with beautiful Benares brocade, to welcome us. A number of Hindus, dressed in spotless white, were drawn up as a guard of honour in two lines, and as we walked between them they bowed and salaamed, calling us 'Ma Bap', which means Father and Mother. I was very puzzled by their offering me rupees in the palm of their hands, and started to make a collection, when I saw my husband frowning at me and signalling to me that I was only to touch the money and pass on. Afterwards he explained that they were honouring me by paying me tribute and were not offering me tips!
>
> It was a very kind welcome, but I did wish I had been able to tidy myself up first. I was conscious all the time of looking like a dust heap, and could feel my hair walking down my back. Knowing that one is thoroughly untidy and dirty does not make one feel at all dignified.
>
> In the drawing-room Mrs Hogberg [wife of a Swedish

missionary] was waiting for us with a very hearty welcome, and a real English tea prepared. And so we had reached home after six weeks' journey from London. (pp. 30-31)

For 31-year-old Ella Sykes and her younger diplomat brother Percy, the journey had been a little shorter:

On 10 April, the thirty-sixth day after leaving England, we rode across the stony plain towards a long green line on the horizon that indicated the goal of our journey ...

Some miles out of the city a fine saddle-horse and a rickety hooded victoria met us. My brother mounted the one and I got into the other, to be jolted over stones and in clouds of dust towards Kashgar. As we entered the Oasis with its avenues of willow, poplar and mulberry that surrounded the town for miles, Sir George Macartney and his children appeared to welcome us, and we also had a greeting from the Indians, when we entered a garden and sat down at a table on which a lavish meal had been spread.

We halted farther on to exchange greetings with the Swedish missionaries, then drove in the red dust to where the Russian Consul-General and his staff hospitably entertained us, and afterwards to the Chinese reception, where more tea had to be sipped. This was the last stopping-place, and it was a joy that I heard the children who shared my carriage say, as we skirted the castellated city wall, that we were at last nearing the British Consulate.

We drove into a large garden planted with trees, where Lady Macartney came down the steps of a big, pleasing house, and giving us the kindest of greetings, led us into the dining-room. Here it was so delightful to be once more in an English atmosphere and to talk to a countrywoman that I could not resist partaking of afternoon tea, though it was the fourth time since we had entered the Kashgar Oasis. (pp. 37-38)

The American Eleanor Lattimore had lived a lifetime of adventure in the months since she left Bijing in 1927. She had caught up with her new husband in Urumchi, and I later tried to find a flavour of the backstreets of the old town where, against all odds, they ran into each other's arms. Of their arrival in Kashgar, she wrote:

> After fifteen breathless sticky vagabond days of desert we have reached an oasis of civilization, of all Central Asia the most civilized, the British Consulate General in Kashgar. For the first time in our travels we arrived ahead of schedule, not because we travelled fast but because we were misinformed as to the length of the journey and our host and hostess are still in the hills. They will be back in a few days, however, and they left cordial word for us to make ourselves

Eleanor Holgate Lattimore, 1927

at home in their guest house. We are loving the contrast of its comfort with our recent vagabondage – hot baths, clean sheets, dainty food, nice dishes, white-robed servants, a library of books, shady terraces and an enchanting garden riotous with fruit and flowers. (p. 239)

Eleanor then backtracks to bring the reader up to that point and concludes the chapter:

New escorts joined us at the Chinese city and we rode in cavalcade along the shady avenue which leads through irrigated fields and villages from the Chinese to the Turki city. We rode through the city gate and wound through streets still sleeping, all the way across the picturesque old town and out a far gate and past some Russian buildings and up to a gate adorned with lion and unicorn. Inside we found warm welcome from the Chinese and Indian secretaries of the consulate, the guest house ready for us, stacks of mail and a good English breakfast. (p. 255)

Later she observes, 'My one regret now is that Owen isn't an Englishman so that he might one day aspire to be consul in Kashgar.' (p. 259)

And Ella Maillart, the Swiss traveller arriving with Peter Fleming in 1935, wrote:

A rare feeling of joy possessed me. It has always seemed natural to me to be wherever I happen to find myself, but I knew that though we had often speculated as to what it would feel like to arrive at Kashgar, at Peking it had seemed crazy even to think of such a thing as possible. ...

There was going to be a perfect welcome in a friendly house, a long month's holiday to be spent in the Himalayas – and no worries just yet. Incapable of expressing the joy that rose within me in any other fashion, I broke into the uncontrolled laughter of a high-spirited girl, and gave Peter a few digs in the ribs with my elbow.

Below the massive walls of the Old Town where there were little kitchen gardens, a handsome cavalier in raw tussore clothes and a topee was coming forward to meet us. He introduced himself and bade us welcome. His name was Arthur Barlow and he was the Vice-Consul. We followed him to a gateway crowned with the coat of arms that has *Dieu et mon droit* inscribed on it. We were at the British Consulate General. Himalayan mountaineers of the Hunza Company stood on guard beside the laurels. I noticed that they had ibex-heads on ornaments in their white caps.

The garden was a riot of flowers. Young ducks waddled about on the English lawn. And then, the house! It was a long house with a verandah, a cool hall, and well-polished furniture; armchairs covered with chintz, books and newspapers everywhere. ... There was a youngish man, the English doctor at the Consulate, and a slight old lady who seemed to emerge out of a lace collar. 'May I introduce ... Miss Engwell of the Swedish Mission.' And last of all, there was a table piled high with sandwiches and hot scones swimming in melting butter. ...

Behold me, obliged to try and keep my cup of tea straight on a slippery saucer, and saying with my very best 'fashionable society' smile: 'Two lumps, please ... Yes, thanks, we had an excellent journey.' (pp. 249-251)

Diana Shipton arrived in Kashgar in 1946 with her husband, the mountaineer Eric Shipton, who had been Consul General there between 1940 and 1942, and was now to take up his post again. Her journey over the Karakorams and across the border into China on horseback was little different from that of her predecessors, and her reaction to the end of the journey was similar:

At about 9 o'clock that night the massive walls of Kashgar loomed up out of the dark. The city gates were opened for us and we drove in. The little oil lamps of the bazaar twinkled all round us. It seemed unbelievable that we had arrived. To be entering the ancient town which had been our goal for so long, felt like a dream. It was nearly three months, to the day, since we had sailed from Southampton. (p. 39)

In her next chapter, Diana writes:

In 1946 air travel to Kashgar was still restricted to the use of a few Chinese officials. From whichever direction the ordinary traveller approached it, the journey was rough and the comforts few. Arriving at the British Consulate the sudden transition from the harsh desert to a well-appointed English home, seemed, literally fantastic – as if by a turn of some magic ring, the whole place would disappear. This sounds over-lyrical, and by some Western standards the house left plenty to be desired. But for me the first impression of luxury and comfort, after the hard journey, was never quite dulled. The present house was finished in 1913, and whatever its faults in design (for instance many of the rooms were dark and sunless, two guest-rooms were at the end of a rough, stone corridor, beyond the kitchen regions), it was a solid, well-built house, very superior to the modest, native-style mud house which Lady Macartney describes as her first home in Kashgar. Such things as glass in the windows, which I took for granted, were a luxury to her; her furniture was mostly home-made and comical. I walked in to a completely furnished, ready-made home. It was strange to think of the many ideas and tastes which had built up this whole. Now I was free to add my own individual touch. (pp. 40-41)

Diana left Kashgar two years later, when the consulate was closed following India's independence. I met her nearly 40 years later to talk about her Kashgar days and how her view of them differed from that of her former husband. Six years after that, a couple of weeks before I left for Chinese Turkestan, I dropped her a note letting her know that I was going. But I had not really left her time to reply and I did not think she would want to; what could she tell me to look out for? When we met again a year or so after my visit, we barely discussed it. She already knew from others how her Kashgar and her Chinibagh had changed, and she did not want to relive the hurt. (Diana Shipton Drummond died while this book was being published. I miss her.)

I had to go to Kashgar, and I thoroughly enjoyed the Sunday Market which all visitors now go for, but Chinibagh and its environs live more vividly in my mind through the accounts of my predecessors than they do in my memory.

How then does one define 'spirit of place'? To describe a place as 'steeped in history' is not only a cliché, it is also misleading. 'Spirit of place' comes not from a place being dunked in history for a while to stew; it comes instead from the people who have been steeped in that place over time, as if they were peppercorns or lemon rind. Their aura, or essence, pervades it then, and now. That may be obvious in a place like the Forbidden City in Beijing, where every marble alleyway reeks of what has happened there over centuries. In Chinibagh today, 'spirit of place' may have to be absorbed through the mind's eye – something in addition to imagination – of the beholder. Training the muscles of the mind's eye is one of the pleasurable exercises of the historian. The test will come when finally I start to write at greater length about Western women in Kashgar.

BIBLIOGRAPHY

Bell, Gertrude, *The Desert and the Sown* (London, Virago, 1985; lst published 1907).

Lattimore, Eleanor Holgate, *Turkistan Reunion* (London, Hurst & Blackett, 1934.

Macartney, Lady, *An English Lady in Chinese Turkestan* (Hong Kong, Oxford University Press, 1985; lst published 1931).

Maillart, Ella, *Forbidden Journey: From Peking to Kashmir* (London, Heinemann, 1937).

Shipton, Diana, *The Antique Land* (London, Hodder & Stoughton, 1950).

Sykes, Ella, *Through Deserts & Oases of Central Asia* (London, Macmillan, 1920).

CHAPTER II

DIFFERENT WAVELENGTHS
Ella Maillart and
Peter Fleming, 1935

Ella Maillart and Peter Fleming only came together – against the better judgement of both lone travellers – because their proposed journey across China was to be so fraught with obstacles. They needed to pool resources and, having bumped into each other on assignment in Manchuria, they admired each other's talents sufficiently to risk a joint venture. Maillart held the trump card of having found a Russian couple (the Smigunovs) who knew an obscure way through and, desperate to return to their home in the Tsaidam on the southern rim of Chinese Turkestan, were prepared to act as guides. Maillart sets the scene of her co-operation with Fleming:

> Hearing me speak of the Tsaidam and the Smigunovs, he had said coldly: 'As a matter of fact I'm going back to Europe by that route. You can come with me if you like …'
>
> 'I beg your pardon,' I had answered. 'It's my route and it's I who'll take you, if I can think of some way in which you might be useful to me.' (*Forbidden Journey*, p. 18)

While the last chapter, 'Spirit of Place', suggests a close relationship between the published accounts of women travellers in the same place over time, this one contrasts the accounts of a woman and a man travelling together at the same time. On their return home, Ella Maillart wrote *Forbidden Journey*, and Peter Fleming, *News from Tartary*.

When she set out with Peter Fleming from Beijing in 1935, Ella

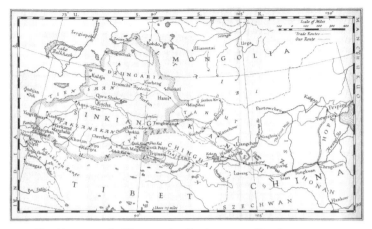

*Maillart and Fleming's Beijing to Kashgar route
from* News From Tartary, *1936*

Maillart had already established three reputations: as an Olympic yachts-woman (1924); as a world-class skier for Switzerland (1931-1934); and as a traveller, with her book *Turkestan Solo* (1934), the account of a hazardous and determined journey she made alone in Soviet Central Asia in 1932.

Maillart – called 'Kini' in Fleming's book – is different from most women travelling with a male companion: she was not married to Fleming, nor was she related to him in any other way. So, we have a strong, independent professional woman of 31 joining forces as an equal with a 27-year-old man already admired for his *Brazilian Adventure* (1933) and *One's Company* (1934) (describing a search for Communist rebels in Southern China). His *Times* obituary (1971) remarks that, 'as a stylist he was in the top flight; as a traveller he was *sui generis*, for his journeys and his manner of recounting them belonged to a school of his own devising.'

Eight years after Eleanor and Owen Lattimore had made the rela-tively easy journey from Beijing to India across Chinese Turkestan de-scribed in complementary books and glimpsed in the previous chapter, the political situation there had radically changed. This meant that, first, the two reporters, Maillart for a French newspaper, Fleming for the

London *Times*, felt they should bring back an account to the outside world of what was going on and, second, they would be unable to obtain permission to do the journey at all. Thus they came to do it covertly, a fact which gives a distinct edge to both accounts.

And yet, a woman such as Maillart could write a few months later when, because of an enforced delay, Fleming had gone off hunting:

> Ever since we had reached the flat solitude of the Tsaidam [the] mountains [to the south] had been beckoning to me, but there was no persuading Peter to sacrifice a week to go exploring, and I had given up the hope of getting to know them. Now, with my rucksack on my back I could spend three days in going, at any rate, some little distance up the valley. It was a way of becoming my own master again, of ceasing to be a mere fragment of a caravan. Of course Peter was chivalrous and pretended that I was very useful, but he could not realize how much I longed to shake off the inertia that had taken hold of me since I began travelling with him. I no longer took the lead, no longer shouldered any responsibility. I was one of a group, and my capacity for decision was blunted.
>
> But it was no use, Peter returned from his hunting, happy at having had a good day while I minded the house ... Peter said he wanted to get on. (p. 122)

How had that happened? The paradoxical key seems to be in their relationship. A paradox because they did not have one in the way that most other travelling couples did: they had no legal or formal emotional tie, nor did they have a romantic one. They were comrades in arms. Their relationship was, therefore, in theory, unimportant to their journey. And yet it is crucial. Maillart half realised that in one or two of her asides, but she is ultimately left baffled and frustrated.

The following passages from Maillart are essential to an understanding of their journey and of Fleming's ability to travel as he wanted to, rather than as she wanted:

Every night Peter would repeat his refrain: 'Sixty *lis* nearer to London.' He did it to annoy me, and I would tell him to shut up, for I wanted to forget that we had, inevitably, to return home. I even lost the desire to return home. I should have liked the journey to continue for the rest of my life. There was nothing to attract me back to the west. I knew I should feel isolated amongst my contemporaries, for their ways had ceased to be my ways. In London I had thought that Peter was in revolt against town life. Now I saw him impatient to get back to it and I wondered whether he had only been indulging in a well-bred affectation. Yet how was I to know whether he was being sincere now or merely para-doxical, or trying to mystify me? Only his own compatri-ots, I thought, would be able to resolve these riddles. What is certain, however, is that Peter seemed to be less afraid of finishing up in the depths of an Urumchi prison than of getting home too late to shoot grouse in Scotland. We were about to cross one of the most magnificent hunting grounds in the world. Yet the fact that Tibetan yaks and wild asses, ibexes and markhors of the Hindu Kush were within range would not change his mood. A surprising companion! Or was it only that he wanted to accomplish the unique exploit of shooting, in the same year, 'tur' in the Caucasus, duck in Shanghai, antelopes in the Koko Nor and deer in Scotland? (p. 89)

On 15 August 1935, Maillart writes:

We had been six months travelling that day and we opened a bottle of brandy to celebrate the occasion. Peter, a dilet-tante, like all good Etonians, remarked that it was the first time in his life he had stuck to anything for more than six months. (p. 270)

Maillart was right about his dilettantism – Fleming will confirm that in a passage praising Maillart; what was perhaps not so obvious was that it was both true and untrue. He was a professional dilettante. His kind of Englishman had been trained – firmly but unobtrusively – for generations to be both a dilettante, and to lead, to rule and to win. Percy Sykes, educated at Rugby, was in a similar tradition; but Fleming, as an Old Etonian, was expected to and would expect himself to perfect the art.

Maillart notices little signals:

> I listened to Peter, noting that an unwritten law has decreed that it shall be considered a sign of good breeding for an Old Etonian never to speak of 'Eton' unnecessarily but always of 'School,' without saying what school. (p. 165)

Percy Sykes, who worked for the British government in Iran before he relieved George Macartney as Consul General in Kashgar, had a nose for understanding local custom and manipulating it to his own advantage when he persuaded a Persian administrator that his reputation in Europe for hospitality would suffer unless he allowed Sykes to have his own way. There are numerous examples of Fleming doing the same. The behaviour of these two men confirms Paul Fussell's description in *Abroad: British Literary Travelling Between the Wars* (1980) of a certain mode of British male travelling as 'a powerful strain of lawless eccentricity and flagrant individuality' and a 'commendable distrust of authority'.

Fleming's biographer – Duff Hart-Davis – also Fleming's godson and son of his close friend Rupert Hart-Davis, understands those matters; he writes, introducing an illustrative text:

> By that stage of the journey Peter had developed to a high degree the art of manipulating 'face' and using its subtle but very real pressures to secure food, animals, free passage, or whatever the expedition needed at the moment. As they entered Khotan, for instance, they needed fodder for the

animals. The mayor was out and 'the shrewd old-fashioned Chinese in charge of his yamen was very properly alienated by my vagabond appearance – dirty shorts and Red Indian face and knees and arms. But I took his rebuffs cooley and, after referring to my friendship with several men of consequence in Khotan, I not too ostentatiously wrote down his name and rank; then I made as if to leave him, my demeanour expressing well-bred regret at such churlish treatment of a foreign traveller. This mild and oblique intimidation shook his nerve, and before long we got the fodder.' (Duff Hart-Davis, *Peter Fleming*, p. 180; Peter Fleming, *News From Tartary*, p. 294)

Maillart is conscious of Fleming's background; it would be difficult not to notice it superficially for, as she writes, 'Peter warned me that his affected manner and languid Oxford accent had driven his last travelling companion nearly crazy.' (p. 9) She makes frequent references, too, to the 'Old Etonian', one of them following an incident similar to that noted by Hart-Davis. Fleming sets the scene:

Towards dusk we came to Chira, a fairly considerable bazaar. I dragged myself along, too hot and tired to care that I was losing face by travelling on foot. Just outside the bazaar there was a parade-ground, equipped ... with a hundred-foot-high wooden tower. ... From the summit of this tower an officer with a megaphone was drilling two or three hundred cavalry. ...

When I moved on along the edge of the parade-ground I was spotted from on high. There were shouts from the tower which I knew were meant for me, but I ignored them and it was not until two panting orderlies were on my heels that I turned and registered polite surprise. They led me back. ... when we reached the foot of the tower the officer shouted (but not to me) an order; and a man who looked like a sergeant left the ranks and addressed me in Russian. I judged it prudent to conceal my knowledge of this language and said facetiously to the bystanders 'What kind of aboriginal speech is this?' The feeble sally got a laugh, and in China once you have got a laugh the battle is half over.

The officer on the tower asked me, in loud and peremptory Chinese, if I was a Russian. Mimicking as best I could his over-bearing tones, I replied that I was an Englishman. Had I a passport? Yes, of course; 'passport have not, this remote place what manner arrive' (The audience was with me, now). The officer said he wanted to examine the passport. I replied that when I had reached my inn, and washed, and drunk tea, I would be glad to show my passport to anyone; at present I was hot and tired and dirty and in no mood for affairs of this kind. In the end, after further exchanges on these lines, I was allowed to go. I felt –

The professional: Ella Maillart, traveller and reporter en route across China

though one can never be sure – that I had not lost face. ...
(pp. 291-292)

Maillart, who had arrived earlier in the town, was only told about this charade when she joined her. Giving only spare details of it, she sums up:

> The situation might easily have taken a nasty turn, but the old Etonian succeeded in extricating himself with flying colours. He got the laughs on his side by addressing the officer on his high perch, not inappropriately, as '*Do Ta jen*' ('very great man'). (p. 203)

Maillart may well not have realised then the full significance – how Fleming, from his background, manipulated her too; a manipulation which he describes bare-facedly and self-deprecatingly, as only his kind could:

The amateur: Peter Fleming at camp during his journey with Maillart

Perhaps one of the main reasons for our getting on so well was that Kini always had a certain friendly contempt for me and I always had a sneaking respect for her; both sentiments arose from the fact that she was a professional and I was eternally the amateur. The contrast showed all the time. Kini believed that the best way to get a thing done was to do it yourself; I believed that the best way to get a thing done was to induce somebody else to do it. It was I who shot the hares; but it was Kini who, noticing that if Li or a Mongol skinned them the liver and kidneys were always thrown away, taught herself to do the job. If anything wanted mending or making fast, if a box needed repacking, if one of the saddles was coming to bits, it was always I who said, 'Oh, that'll be all right', always Kini who expertly ensured that it would be. On my side it was partly laziness and partly incompetence; on Kini's it was the knowledge, acquired from experience, of how important the little things can be. In so far as you can audit a division of labour, ours would have worked out something like this:

I did: all the shooting; most of the heavy manual labour; all the negotiating; all the unnecessary acceleration of progress; all the talking in Chinese and (later) Turki.

Kini did: all the cooking; all the laundering; all the medical and veterinary work; most of the fraternizing; most of the talking in Russian.

I suppose I was the leader, because I made decisions more quickly, guessed more quickly, knew more quickly what I wanted than Kini did. But she did all the work that required skill or application, and almost all the work that was distasteful or annoying rather than merely arduous, the work that gets left undone if there are only second-rate people to do it; we both knew that she was, so to speak, the better man, and this knowledge evened things out between us, robbed my automatically dominating position of its power to strain our relations. We had complete confidence in each other. (pp. 167-169)

All that flattery was real, and yet it was not real. A little later he says that he could not talk fluently, except nonsense, but he prided himself on his writing, on telling a good story, and that was a very good, very English, very male, very Old Etonian good story. While on the journey he was turning over in his mind what he would write about Maillart in his book, he also knew what he had written home to his friend Hart-Davis about Maillart and his fiancée, the actress Celia Johnson (whom he calls 'Crackwit'):

The fourth member is a dashing Swiss girl, who (this is important) may take some explaining to the Crackwit if she hears about her. Her name is Maillart. ... I met her in London in the summer, said 'see you in China,' and forgot about her. But at the time I ragged the Crackwit about her, pretending to have been greatly struck, and that is why I have said nothing to her (the Crackwit) about this woman. ...

We remain on speaking terms without difficulty, but as far as the Affections go she will never mean more to me than a yak. All the same I feel guilty towards the Crackwit and worry a lot about not having told her about the Other Woman, though I'm sure it was better not to. So if, Peking being what it is, the news comes through and the Crackwit asks with a forced laugh 'What about Peter's Swiss?', will you explain? It's a silly situation and would never have arisen if I hadn't cracked jokes about the girl last summer.

On re-reading this, I seem to have been unduly deroga-tory about the Swiss. She is very enterprising and what you might call a good trouper. It's just that she isn't my cup of tea. (p. 158) (Duff Hart-Davis, *Peter Fleming*)

And in a later letter to Hart-Davis (the biographer does not give dates for these letters, and Fleming may well have chosen to write differently later):

> The Swiss is bearing up well, and we remain on speaking though not always in my case on listening terms; she is an honest soul and quite useful. I do hope Celia is all right.
> (p. 164)

Perhaps Fleming thought that Celia might read that letter or surely he would not have been so patronising; it certainly puts a damper on his published panegyrics.

It is obvious that Fleming admired Maillart – he could not fail to; but he would make no concessions to her way of travelling. She could dominate on some matters, such as health; when she persuaded him in Beijing to be inoculated against typhus she writes:

> Peter maintained that no louse would dare attack his 'iron' skin, and I had great difficulty persuading him to go. But I pointed out that if he were taken ill it was on me it would fall to nurse him and that he must therefore obey orders.
> (p. 12)

But on the central issue she had no effective weapon. She realised that she had made a mistake – even though, when she made the decision to travel with him, there seemed little choice. She wrote early on in her account, even before they had left 'civilisation':

> Though I liked the companionship and it had considerably ameliorated the anxiety of our wait at Lanchow, it nevertheless deprived me of the greatest thrill the sense of discovering had given me on previous journeys. I had lost the intense joy, the intoxication, of blazing my own trail and the proud sense of being able to get through alone, to which I

had become accustomed. Above all, a piece of Europe inevitably accompanied us through the mere fact of our association. That isolated us. I was no longer thousands of miles from my own world. I was not submerged by, or integrated into, Asia. Travelling in company, one does not learn the language so quickly. The natives do not make their own of you. You penetrate less deeply into the life about you. (p. 46)

Fifteen years later she wrote those insights into her 'philosophy of travel' when she contributed a chapter with that title to *Traveller's Quest*, edited by M.A. Michael, and she elaborated further, still drawing on that Chinese Turkestan experience:

Detachment was slowly becoming part of me. It was normal to belong nowhere, or everywhere; to feel one is an eternal traveller. ... I discovered I was richly contented, away from my people and my friends – without a roof, without a wood fire, without bread even. In winter at twelve thousand feet of altitude with two cups of barley flour a day; at ease in a reality which was a void. (pp. 121-122)

That word 'reality' is essential to an understanding of Maillart's travel. Her friends realised that when, to honour her on her 80th birthday, they compiled a book and called it *Voyage Vers le Réel* (Voyage towards Reality) (1983).

'Was I typical of our age when I wanted to learn how to grasp reality?' Maillart had written, and continued:

What goes under the name of spiritual problems of the modern man became a fact for me when I saw that having had all I wanted, I was nevertheless miserable. Material security, welfare, humaneness – they were not sufficient ideals to me. Now at least I know with absolute certainty that we travel to find ourselves. By placing ourselves in all possible

circumstances which like projectors, will illumine our
different facets, we come to grasp all of a sudden, which one
of our facets is fully, uniquely, ourselves. Through it, go beyond it, having then exhausted our particularism. (p. 124)

So in the end it did not matter so much that she travelled with
Fleming and that he wanted to travel differently and get different things
out of the journey; for she discovered her own truth through her own
perceptions:

When I crossed Asia with my friend Peter Fleming, we spoke
with no one but each other during many months, and we
covered exactly the same ground. Nevertheless my journey
differed completely from his. One's mind colours the journey as if one wore individually tinted spectacles. It is our
mind we project outside and ultimately decipher when we
think we meet the 'objective' world. (p. 118)

And what was Fleming thinking; what did he get out of it? He
explained:

Of certain stages of a journey in Brazil I once wrote, 'con-
tinuous hunger is in many ways a very satisfactory basis for
existence'; and in Tartary it proved its worth again.

But there were days, or parts of days, when no such
material stimulus to thought and conversation, no such
gross foundation for peace of mind, were needed: days when
we rode or walked for hours, singly or together, filled with
contentment at our lot. The sun shone, the mountains were
alluring on our left, and we remembered the virtues of
desolation and felt keenly the compensations of a
nomad's life. Each march, each camp, differed very slightly
from the one before; but they did differ, and we appreciated
the slight but ever present freshness of our experience as

much as we appreciated the tiny changes in the flavour of our food.

We took besides, a certain pride in the very slowness and the primitive manner of our progress. We were travelling Asia at Asia's pace. In Macaulay's *History of England* ... he speaks with smug Victorian condescension of 'the extreme difficulty which our ancestors found in passing from place to place'; and there was a certain fascination in rediscovering a layer of experience whose very existence the contemporary world has forgotten. We had left the twentieth century behind with the lorries at Lanchow, and now we were up against the immemorial obstacles, the things which had bothered Alexander and worried the men who rode with Chinghis Khan – lack of beasts, lack of water, lack of grazing. We were doing the same stages every day that Marco Polo would have done if he had branched south from the Silk Road into the mountains. (pp. 166-167)

The 'slowness' described in Fleming's narrative does not tally with the journey as it really was, at least as it appeared to Maillart, bridling against his constant urging onwards!

As for the 'objective' world which Maillart mentions, for all their differences, they had one thing in common, as Fleming explains:

... that was our attitude to our profession (or vocation, or whatever you like to call it). We were united by an abhorrence of the false values placed – whether by its exponents or by the world at large – on what can most conveniently be referred to by its trade-name of Adventure. From an aesthetic rather than from an ethical point of view, we were repelled by the modern tendency to exaggerate, romanticize, and at last cheapen out of recognition the ends of the earth and the deeds done in their vicinity. It was about the only thing we ever agreed about. (p. 27)

Maillart confirmed:

> I appreciated Peter's brilliant intelligence, his faculty of being able to eat anything and sleep anywhere, and also his sure grasp of the kernel of any situation, of the essential point in any argument. I appreciated still more his horror of any distortion of facts and the native objectivity with which he recounted them. (p. 9)

In spite of their shared passion for the truth, Maillart and Fleming did see things differently, even objectively; he writes of a meeting with a provincial governor:

> General Shao, an elderly but vivacious little man with stubbly grey hair and beautiful manners, welcomed us in the innermost of many courtyards with cakes and fruit and tea. With him was his young and attractive wife, formerly a Moscow-trained Communist, whom marriage (it is said) saved at the eleventh hour from execution. (p. 48)

And Maillart writes:

> Shao Li-tze proved to be an affable little man, dressed in Chinese clothes. He had made a stay of several days in Paris in 1916 and could recall a few French words. We were received in a room furnished with Spartan simplicity. Shao Li-tze's wife was young and lively. Having made a prolonged stay in Moscow, she spoke excellent Russian and it was in that language we exchanged the usual polite greetings. ...
>
> As the governor talked, I was studying his young wife. With her slim fingers she was peeling pears for us. I wondered whether she had not come back from Russia holding Communist beliefs and whether she did not secretly wish to see Shensi in the hands of the Reds. (pp. 24-25)

168

For Fleming, Mme Shao Li-tze was a 'Moscow-trained Communist'; for Maillart she had been in Russia and it was interesting to speculate about whether or not she held Communist beliefs and sympathies. So much for objectivity!

Other differences in their accounts are more obviously subjective. Fleming did not travel fast and furiously without effort; he suffered, and sometimes Maillart won, even if it was by default. Fleming writes of their first and last bus ride, which was much delayed, 'Occasionally one of the other passengers reappeared, announced that we were starting at once, and disappeared. I began to get angry.' (p. 50) She responds:

> Peter was furious. I was enchanted. The delay gave us an opportunity of lunching at the Chinese inn where the Smigs [Smigunovs] had stayed, and making the acquaintance of our friend Norin's old cook who had arrived from the north with Bokkenkamp, the ethnographer. (p. 28)

Very soon Fleming had earned the name of 'galloper'.

And yet, there was a different, controlled, side to the galloper; the one that could outwardly show British sang-froid, if he chose:

> Peter suffered more than I from our compulsory inaction. … He could, however, remain outwardly impassive and smiling. That was our greatest asset in dealing with the inn-keeper, with the inquisitive police, with the scratchers at our paper windows. Never did a gesture of Peter's betray the hastiness that often characterizes Occidentals. (p. 56)

Fleming was as able to manipulate himself as he was others to achieve an objective. But behind the scenes the reality was very different, as he writes of the same occasion:

So for a time I played endless games of patience on the k'ang while Kini read or sewed or wrote up her diary. But gradually, as the glow of breakfast faded in our bellies, we became restless.

'Let's go up to Lu's.'

'Wait till I've finished this chapter.'

'How much more have you got?'

'Ten pages.'

'Hell, that's too much. Come on. I'm going now.'

'Oh, all right …'

So off we went, giving our by now celebrated performance of caged tigers down the long main street. (p. 78)

Once again, it seems they are doing what Fleming wants but it would be a mistake to think that they had no fun together. Far from it. They laughed a lot and had the sort of joking relationship which in traditional societies may exist between, for example, a mother-in-law and son-in-law — those who have a relationship which requires them to be friendly, even though there are, by the nature of things, opportunities for tension. There are many incidents that illustrate their 'joking relationship'.

At Tangar they stayed with a missionary couple called Urech; he was Swiss, she was Scots. Maillart writes:

Visitors were so rare at Tangar that young Malcolm, aged three, had never seen any. He called us 'the Mongols,' the term being synonymous with 'foreigners'. He also had a great success when he called Peter 'the *old* Maillart.' Only Peter was not flattered. Mrs Urech was quite proud when she found that Fleming, the brilliant author by whom she had just read an article in *The Reader's Digest*, and the young man whose coming she had been warned of, turned out to be one and the same person.

'Malcolm!' she said. 'Take a good look at the famous

man we have the honour to entertain in our house.'

'Then he isn't a Mongol?' asked the puzzled little boy.

'No,' I said. 'He is what is called in Europe a "special correspondent." He writes in the newspapers about what he has seen. Only he has a curious way of doing things. For instance, he says my linen takes up too much room, though actually it consists of three sweaters and three pairs of woollen pants. And all the time it is he who has my cases bursting with his enormous boxes of tobacco …'

Then Peter: 'If you don't stop grouching I'll write to *La Vie Parisienne* to recall you!'

And I: 'Mrs Urech, I've told him a hundred times that *Le Petit Parisien* and *La Vie Parisienne* are two entirely different periodicals. And, just imagine, *he* thinks I ought to be satisfied with a camel crossing Asia! Of course that won't stop me from having a horse. I don't see why he should be the only one to play the lord.'

'Well,' he protested, 'you'd be a lot better off on a camel, since you are accustomed to it from your other journeys.'

'No,' Mrs Urech intervened, 'she ought to be able to get on ahead and prepare supper for the lord.'

'I know,' I said, 'I am to be cook to my interpreter … Peter, I've been given dried apricots, onions …'

'"Been given!" You've been robbing Mrs Urech, that's what you've been doing. I know the old sea-dog, Mrs Urech. Give her back those apricots, you! We don't want them.'

'Listen to him, Mrs Urech! He who wants to cross Tibet and doesn't even know what scurvy is …'

Just then I noticed something the Chinese servant had brought in and involuntarily I cried: 'Oh, two kinds of jam to-day.'

Peter was scandalized.

'Really, Maillart,' he protested. 'You are a disgrace to the expedition.' (pp. 70-71)

One of Fleming's accounts of their 'joking relationship' reads:

> Occasionally we discussed without relish the books we should one day have to write about this journey. The prospect of sitting down and committing our memories to paper was welcome to neither of us; but at least I knew that I could get the horrid job done quickly, whereas Kini was sure that she could not. Travel books in French (at least the ones that I have read) are commonly more vivid and exclamatory than travel books in English; and I used to tease Kini by concocting apocryphal quotations from her forthcoming work: '*Great scott!' s'écria Pierre, dont le sangfroid d'ancien élève d'Eton ne se froissait guère que quand ses projets sportifs s'écroulaient, 'Voila mon vinchester qui ne marche plus!*' (p. 170)

And it would be a mistake to think that Maillart came away from their journey resentful or regretful. It is this author who has teased out the moments of frustration and, in conjunction with Fleming's background, made out a case. Maillart experienced times of great pleasure with Fleming and she understood the differences in their temperament well enough for them not to be a constant bone of contention. The following passage, which fits chronologically into her account in much the same place as his long analysis of their relationship fits into his (pp. 167-170), shows, nevertheless, that Maillart's greatest moments of joy tend to occur when she is taking an initiative.

> ... a tent-pole had been lost *en route*. There was no timber in the region, so it could not be replaced, and I went off to look for it. Walking along at an even pace I felt in great form, filled with such joy as I used to experience setting out on my skis on very dry winter mornings. There on the high table-lands of Asia I was singing, *I'm sitting on top of the world.*
> I even laughed at the wide heavens. It was an odd situation Peter and I were in together at the centre of the

continent. Indeed, it was like a situation in a novel, and if I were writing a best seller, it should be that very day or never that the hero and heroine fell into each other's arms in mutual love and gratitude. ... Well, novel-readers would have to go without. Peter was the best of comrades and I had found that I could be absolutely frank with him. It is true that our enterprise bound us to each other to such a degree that, living as we did, like two castaways on a desert island, our conversation at supper, evening after evening, revealed the fact that the same thoughts had struck us simultaneously in the course of the day. But it was only our egotisms that worked together, each helping the other. I could see clearly where we parted company. We both liked to spend our leisure in the open air, he shooting, I ski-ing ... But then? Peter thought me too serious and I did not understand British humour (as serious in the eyes of an Englishman as it is for a Chinaman to 'lose face'.) I had the bad taste to lay down the law about the art of living. Peter was bored by my craving to understand the thousands of diverse lives that make up humanity and bored, too, by my need to relate my own life to life in general. How could anybody be so crazy as to want to find out whether men's efforts brought about an improvement in human nature? Peter was troubled by none of these things. In his imperturbable wisdom he looked on human beings as characters in a comedy. As for his deeper self, his timidity usually made him hide it beneath a facetious dignity. Except at rare intervals, he seemed persuaded that his concerns were of no interest to anybody. ...

I found the tent pole. That was what mattered then. And success made me sing as I returned to Peter, who stood waiting for me to appear in the plain he dominated. (p. 148)

Maillart and Fleming discuss their relationship in some detail in their books – partly, perhaps, to tantalise a prurient 1930s readership.

From the similarities in some of the passages, it is fair to assume that they also discussed it together. Fleming, for example, in the long passage about her superior qualities already quoted from makes a remark that has distinct echoes of that quoted from Maillart:

> By all the conventions of desert island fiction we should have fallen madly in love with each other; by all the laws of human nature we should have driven each other crazy with irritation. As it was, we missed these almost equally embarrassing alternatives by a wide margin. (pp. 167-169)

It is reasonable to suggest that, in the 24 hours previous to the tent pole incident, Maillart had broached her general unhappiness and that they had attempted to thrash it out. The passage of frustration at the beginning of this chapter is only 20-odd pages earlier. They came to some sort of accommodation. One of the problems was that Eton, for all it had prepared Fleming to sail through life – bravely and with style, it must be said – had not prepared him for Maillart. He might be comfortable enough with a respectable English wife of his own kind, and, perhaps, with a 'travelling wife', in the Chinese sense, but no matter how hard he tries to show otherwise – and he writes as a well-travelled, intelligent, sophisticated man – he found it difficult to think of women as equals or to come to terms with women who were. In yet another endeavour to give Maillart her due, he wrote:

> I had no previous experience of a woman traveller, but Kini was the antithesis of the popular conception of that alarming species. She had, it is true, and in a marked degree, the qualities which distinguish these creatures in the books they write about themselves. She had courage and enterprise and resource; in endurance she excelled most men. (p. 26)

What Fleming means by these remarks concerning other travelling women is not clear; the very ambiguity underlines his attitude. Then we see him distorting his account of a particularly difficult day. It had started with Maillart's horse, Cynara, evading capture for some hours; Fleming writes:

> Every man, provided that he does not raise blisters or other impediments on his feet, can walk in a day at least half as far again as he imagines. The muscles responsible for placing the left foot in front of the right foot, and the right foot in front of the left foot, do not tire quickly; it is the feet that count. My own feet are almost as little sensitive as hooves, and as the hours of march dragged into their early 'teens I had nothing to complain of save tedium, anxiety, and the staleness of sustained exertion. But water would have been welcome – doubly so when a keen north wind bore down our line of march, sweeping the valley with a chilly enfilade. When night fell we were past talking, past hoping, past thinking. We moved numbly, each bounded in a nutshell of discontent.
>
> At half-past seven we gave it up and halted, pitching the tent on a slope of stony desert. We had been marching, at a good pace for camels, for fourteen hours without food and with only two or three halts, none longer than five minutes; Kini had done the first seven hours – the most strenuous, because of catching Cynara – on foot. (p. 218)

She writes:

> At six o'clock we were still on the march. Lashed by an icy wind, I held on to the slight shelter provided by the camel's load. … we were going along a water course, but a dried-up water-course. … Peter had just torn the entire sole off one of his shoes and come up in great distress. What was the good of wearing out man and beast by marching vainly for fourteen hours on end? I put my foot down, and insisted that, water or no water, we pitch the tent before nightfall. (pp. 168-169)

Fleming ends his account with another tribute to his companion:

> I got, during our seven months together, so used to regard-
> ing Kini as an equal in most things and a superior in some
> that perhaps I have paid over-few tributes to her powers of
> endurance. ... I should like to place it on record that, at the
> end of fourteen hours' march in the middle of a hard jour-
> ney (rising almost always before dawn, eating almost always
> a little less than enough), Kini went supperless to bed with-
> out, even by implication, turning a hair. The best that I can
> do in the way of an eulogy is to say that I thought nothing
> of it at the time. (p. 218)

Fleming meant it as the highest praise; he would not know what you
were talking about if you pointed out that Maillart did not feel the
need to say the same sort of thing about him, particularly since her
account suggests that his endurance, on that occasion, was slightly less
than hers, contradicting his account in a kindly but convincing way.
And it was a tribute indeed, for in addition to his opinion of women
travellers in particular, an occasion described first by Maillart is his
more usual opinion of women in general:

> A decided-looking and heavily-laden young mother joined
> our caravan a little way out from Bash Malghun. Her baby
> was given to crying at night and to vomiting; in short, 'did
> all that the dear little things do.' Thus the somewhat peeved
> Peter. He went so far as to predict all sorts of difficulties.
> He did not like women. 'You have to be always helping them,'
> he said. 'The moment they appear, complications begin.' And
> he was afraid that this one might turn the men against us.
> However, as he looked at the child, tied on the donkey and
> getting shaken, Peter finished by observing: 'Poor little chap!
> He hasn't much of a life.' My compassion, on the other hand,
> went out rather to the mother. (p. 173)

Fleming's version:

> Shortly before noon we were joined by a lady with two don-
> keys, on one of which she rode; the other carried a light
> load of household goods, on top of which was more than
> firmly lashed a yearling child. This infant relished very little
> the delights of travel and lodged almost continuous pro-
> tests; but its mother — a domineering person with a harsh,
> masculine voice — abused the donkey so roundly that most
> of her offspring's cries were drowned.

For all that Maillart travelled as Fleming wanted, rather than as she
preferred, and that she did the washing, sewing and cooking, she was
not steered towards women and womanly affairs in the way that women
travelling under similar circumstances usually were. This was a disad-
vantage, at least for those hoping to use her account for the re-creation
of women's lives, for it meant few opportunities for gleaning women's
lore. Nor, anyway, could she speak the language of the Chinese or Turki
women. When she could communicate, as with Mrs Urech, there were
sisterly relations.

 Often Maillart's accounts of women are visual ones and usually it is
of the beauty of those she is observing. There was one glaring exception, and she could not avoid noticing it wherever she went and being
horrified anew each time. She writes of footbinding on more than one
occasion; of Tungkuan she wrote:

> The women had beautiful, regular faces, and round their
> heads, like a narrow turban, wore a black veil. They were
> all going in the same direction and I followed them. Their
> mutilated feet, looking like pointed stumps and hitting
> the ground with a dull clatter, made my heart sick. When
> they walk their knees seem to be devoid of flexibility.
> The effect was of a caricature of a ballerina dancing on
> her toes. (p. 21)

In Chingchow she noted in the main street that 'the ground was so slippery that the women, because of their stunted feet, had to carry long sticks to support themselves.' (p. 32) That evening, Maillart and Fleming spent the night with a missionary and his wife; the latter confessed to Maillart that because of lack of security in the area 'in four years she had never rested properly at night. But amongst the compensations for all the uneasiness there was one that I found touching. She had helped to abolish the torturing of the women's feet out of shape.' (p. 32) And again:

> Life in Kansu is really wretched. Squatting in front of their mud hovels the women were stitching at thick cloth slippers for their husbands. With vacant faces and dressed in dusty jackets and trousers, they seemed to have no sense of feminine coquetry except in the matter of their stunted feet. These they shod with embroidered materials attached to little curved wooden heels. Many times I saw mothers on the side of the road tying up the feet of tiny girls – poor resigned things! – with dirty bandages. (p. 44)

And what did Fleming make of bound feet? 'The streets of Lanchow are romantic. The women hobble round the puddles on bound feet, their sleek heads shining like the shards of beetles. ...' (p. 63)

As for their own appearance, there is a charming vignette which epitomises their relationship and their journey. Of their arrival in Kashgar towards the end of their journey, Fleming, until then all burnt knees, wrote:

> I opened my suitcase. Alas for foresight! A plague on vanity! The suitcase was full of water.
>
> And not water only. Thus diluted, the fine dust of the desert, which habitually found its way through the chinks of all our luggage, had become a thin but ubiquitous paste of mud. One by one I lifted out the soggy garments ... the suit, the precious suit, came last of all. Wet it was bound to

be, and soiled with mud; what I had not bargained for was that it should turn out to be bright green in colour. The dye from a sash bought in Khotan had run. ...

... I had now to decide whether to enter Kashgar disguised as a lettuce, or looking like something that had escaped from Devil's Island. It seemed to me that, if there is one thing worse than wearing bright green clothes, it is wearing bright green clothes which are also soaking wet; I therefore sadly resumed the shorts and shirt of every day and prepared to let down the British Raj. (p. 318)

Don't say he had his tongue in his cheek; he carried that suit all the way from Beijing for that moment. Maillart writes:

Every time he opened the case during these past months I had noticed the beautiful material and the impeccable crease of the trousers. I foresaw that in my pleated skirt (rolled up in a bundle ever since our departure) I could hardly expect to be taken for much more than Peter's cook when the time came for him, in his elegance, to take me out in Kashgar high society. Of course it was vexatious that his suit should have been ruined ... But I wonder whether I felt as sorry as I ought to have done. (pp. 248-249)

Following her experience with Fleming, not surprisingly, in spite of their comradeship and achievement, Maillart either travelled alone or with other women. In 1939, she went through Persia and Afghanistan with someone she calls only Christina (Annemarie Schwarzenbach), and in 1945 she took a short walk in Southern Tibet with a woman she calls B (Beryl Smeeton). In her introduction to Smeeton's 1961 autobiography, Maillart wrote a few simple but telling lines:

Once more I am convinced that it is really people who matter most. A landscape or an idea may be of great importance, but in the end it all depends on who sees the Yangtze River, for instance, or who talks about freedom.

POSTSCRIPT

When I sent this chapter to Ella Maillart, she was not concerned about any analysis of her relationship with Fleming. She wrote back, 'Here I am without *Forbidden Journey* ... but try to find the page on the way to the Pamir, I climb alone a steep mountain, try to see Mustagh Ata ... when descending ... am *very* afraid to slip ... & I say something *impor-tant*: that I cannot die before I have found why we live ... or the purpose of living ... I think you might use it.' (2 December 1987)

On the page of her book she was directing me to she wrote:

> ... what mattered was myself, I, who was living at the centre of the world – that 'I' who did not want to disappear without accomplishing something worthwhile. Something that would carry me on, that would save me from nothingness, and satisfy – however humbly – the craving that existed in me. (pp. 268-269)

Ella Maillart, 1982

The physical travelling – let alone the travelling companion – was, therefore, unimportant. It was the spiritual travel, or quest, that mattered. And so, for the subject, as opposed to the observer, the past and any attempt to rake over it, is irrelevant because the quest is still not ended.

Their relationship, and the contrast between Fleming's account and her own, may have been unimportant to Maillart at 84, but for the biographer to be able to stand Maillart against the other half of a double mirror, is to produce reflections that may be illuminating.

Following our correspondence, I had the chance to meet Ella Maillart. For her, a private woman, and one who had that day fallen and grazed her face, the meeting in London was probably only an irritation. For me, despite the passage of time, despite her air of distraction, she was the physical manifestation of the Maillart of her books.

And yet, in my writing, I have drawn out a dimension of her that she does not recognise. I was conscious from the start of avoiding a spiritual side of Ella, brought out more in some of her other books, that was essential to her. She recognised it clearly for she wrote to me after our meeting, 'Congratulations for the thoroughness you put in the way you work. Am glad we met: we "function" on different wavelengths.' I thank her for the colon which suggests that she is glad we met because we are different, not that she is simply identifying a gap between us.

Of course, we see ourselves differently from how others see us but, in the end, I may have been as far distant from Ella as was Peter Fleming, from whom I tried to protect her. The question then must be, how much validity is there to my view of her? That is the dichotomy of biography. Without corresponding with and meeting Ella Maillart, I might not have had to acknowledge it to myself so clearly.

Written 1987. Quotations come from *Forbidden Journey* and *News from Tartary*, unless specified.

BIBLIOGRAPHY

Fleming, Peter, *Brazilian Adventure* (London, Jonathan Cape, 1933).

Fleming, Peter, *News From Tartary* (London, Jonathan Cape, 1936).

Fussell, P., *Abroad* (Oxford, Oxford University Press, 1980).

Hart-Davis, Duff, *Peter Fleming* (London, Jonathan Cape, 1974).

Lattimore, Eleanor Holgate, *Turkistan Reunion* (London, Hurst & Blackett, 1934).

Lattimore, Owen, *The Desert Road to Turkestan* (London, Methuan, 1928).

Lattimore, O., *High Tartary* (Boston, Little Brown, 1930).

Maillart, Ella K., *Turkestan Solo* (New York, G.P. Putnam, 1934).

Maillart, E.K., *Forbidden Journey* (London, William Heinemann, 1937).

Maillart, E.K., *The Cruel Way* (London, William Heinemann, 1947).

Maillart, E.K., 'My Philosophy of Travel', in M.A. Michael (ed.), *Traveller's Quest* (London, William Hodge, 1950).

Maillart E.K., 'Tibetan Jaunt', in O. Tchernine (ed.), *Explorers' and Travellers' Tales* (London, Jarrolds, 1958).

Maillart, E.K. (*melanges dediés a*) *Voyage Vers Le Réel* (Geneva, Editions Olizane, Collection Artou, 1983).

Smeeton, Beryl, *Winter Shoes in Springtime* (London, Rupert Hart-Davis, 1961).

Sykes, Percy Molesworth, *Ten Thousand Miles in Persia* (London, John Murray, 1902).

HONG KONG

CHAPTER 12

IT MADE THEIR BLOOD BOIL

The British Feminist Campaign against Licensed Prostitution in Hong Kong, 1931

INTRODUCTION

'The things we heard made our blood boil,' wrote Stella Benson in December 1930.[1] She had been invited to sit on a local League of Nations subcommittee to prepare evidence on Hong Kong for a visit by the Travelling Commission Enquiring into International Traffic in Women. The subcommittee was chaired by Gladys Forster and these two British women were, as a result of what they began to learn about trafficking, to form an unshakeable alliance against government regulation of prostitution.

Benson and Forster's work between February 1931, when the formal subcommittee had ostensibly completed its task and been disbanded, and December that year when the Governor announced the phased abolition of state-regulated prostitution, provides a self-contained case study that is interesting from more than one historiographical angle. This chapter, therefore, will look at the research material based on interviews with Chinese women – many of them underage girls – caught up in the 'entertainment business' in Hong Kong, and Benson and Forster's campaign to stop what they saw as exploitation, from the point of view of feminist, social and colonial history.

Both British women considered themselves feminists, though their attitude towards prostitution differed. At a time when prostitution is again under scrutiny not only by feminists, but also by prostitutes themselves, as well as those concerned with the exploitation of Third World women, the work, attitudes and research of Benson and Forster have something to offer. Their background, motivation and relationship with each other, relevant to a feminist interpretation, will also be explored.

   Their insistence on social reform – change in the law to end exploitation – will be contrasted with the work of missionary women in Hong Kong who sought to provide relief and salvation to 'fallen women'. These differing approaches will be set in their British context, and reformers and relief workers will be seen as heirs to a tradition of concern among Western women at the condition of Chinese women under patriarchal custom. When campaigning and lobbying for social reform in our own time is so much a part of Western political culture, the Hong Kong campaigns offer an opportunity to note earlier progress of now familiar methods.

Stella Benson, c1931

In developing the colonial context, the views of Western women towards the Chinese and their relationship with the women they sought to help will be explored, as will the relations between the social reformers and those with whom they worked – Chinese Christian women – and those whom they opposed – the colonial authorities for whom maintaining stability and prosperity and protecting British forces from venereal disease were prime considerations.

But Benson and Forster and others involved in community work among Chinese women have been criticised as members of a privileged colonialist class who were incapable of true sisterhood because of 'the fundamental inequalities of colonial rule'.[2] It will be argued in reply that these activists must be judged in their own context – in their own time and circumstances; but the question must be asked, did colonial women have the 'right' to intervene in the affairs of women with their own long-established and distinctive culture? Or did they, indeed, have a duty? And, what were the results of their actions? Finally, where do Western women stand today?

WESTERN WOMEN AND THE CONDITION OF CHINESE WOMEN

From the beginning, indeed in Macau before Hong Kong existed as a colony, missionary women were concerned about customs which they saw as detrimental to Chinese women. Henrietta Hall Shuck, a missionary who arrived from America with her husband in 1836 had, within six months, adopted a *mui tsai* – a girl who had been sold by her mother to a buyer who kept her only a few months and sold her again to a couple 'who used her cruelly.'[3] Very soon, Mrs Shuck opened a school in which she would have preferred to teach only girls and was forging relations in nearby villages with those whom she described as the 'neglected and degraded women of China.'[4]

Mary Gutzlaff, an English missionary teacher married to the Pomeranian Charles Gutzlaff, started a school for blind girls at the same time. One of her first pupils was 'taken out of the hands of an inhuman person pretending to be her father, but who had evidently kidnapped her and was exposing her in the public streets to excite compassion by the display of sores purposely left open.'[5]

From 1842, in Hong Kong, Chinese women's education became the prime concern for missionary wives and, after 1860, also for single missionary women. But there are references to the iniquities of footbinding and the *mui tsai* system — known also as domestic slavery — in their writing.[6]

Until the turn of the century, footbinding and the *mui tsai* system were to be the focus of criticism by women and attempts to provide spiritual relief and refuge; but there was no attempt to seek abolition of either custom except expressed as hope or prayer. Even the missionary Miss Ada Pitts, who spoke out in public against child labour in 1918 from the breadth of her 17 years' experience in the colony, only implicitly attacked the *mui tsai* system of domestic servitude of girls.[7] She proposed remedies and instigated an inquiry which reached fruition in the *Child Labour Ordinance* enacted in 1922. But it placed restraints mainly on poor families who depended on the work of their children; that was less controversial than suggesting the abolition of the *mui tsai* system, which would have had more effect on the influential rich.

FROM RELIEF TO REFORM

With the arrival of Alicia Little, a merchant's wife, in China in 1887, campaigning for reform became more likely, for she was neither a missionary nor a doctor who might have treated the physical effects of footbinding, and she had experience of campaigning for women and children's rights in England.

By 1896 she had formed an anti-footbinding committee in Shanghai which became the Natural Foot Society and worked for the abolition of the practice throughout China. In 1900 a branch was set up in Hong Kong with the Governor's daughter, Olive Blake, as secretary. Indeed, a meeting organised by Lady Blake and addressed by Alicia Little was held at Government House, the first time Chinese women had been invited there; and they attended in large numbers.[8]

In spite of the involvement of the Blakes, the activities of reformers were to be anti-establishment, though this was not from choice. It was made quite clear to Alicia Little by the Europeans she questioned in advance that there were no bound feet in Hong Kong – a claim which she easily disproved. The same sort of attitudes were to dog her reforming successors. Even today, the reaction of the Western male historian towards that involvement of Western women in the traditional Chinese custom of footbinding is negative.[9]

Another feature of these campaigns was the gradual breaking down of barriers between Western and Chinese women and, indeed, the emergence of Chinese women into public life. In 1908, the Natural Foot Society in Shanghai was taken over by Chinese women – three years before the Revolution which would upset many aspects of the old society, including the position of women. While the atmosphere in the refuges for rescued prostitutes run by missionary women in the twentieth century reinforces the impression of unequal relations between Western and Chinese, righteous and sinning, the educational establishments that they set up in Hong Kong allowed Chinese women to develop their potential.

A third feature was to be a strong element of research. Throughout the campaign to abolish footbinding, Alicia Little knew what she was talking about because she was in touch with Chinese women and men whom she had prompted not only to think about the issue but also to write and act. Her reforming successors in Hong Kong were to follow a similar path.

That the *mui tsai* system was eventually abolished – legally and in practice – in Hong Kong is largely due to the campaign, orchestrated over many years, by Clara Haslewood and her husband. She was not the first woman to try and do something about it – Ada Pitts had spoken out only a year earlier; but the urgency of the Haslewood campaign, the methods they employed and the reaction to it in official circles in Britain and Hong Kong were without parallel.

The campaign started in Hong Kong where Clara Haslewood, newly arrived, heard of *mui tsai* for the first time and began her own research. As a result of a letter she wrote, published in four local papers on the same day in November 1919, her husband, superintendent of the Naval Chart Depot, was advised by the naval authorities, prompted by the Governor, Sir Reginald Stubbs, to restrain his wife or resign. He resigned and the couple transferred their campaign to Britain and waged it through Parliament, women's groups, the Anti-Slavery Society and the Church.

Later, when Haslewood took up the case of his forced resignation, Stubbs talked of the annoyance that Clara's letters had caused to the local Chinese community, and the assumption, because of her husband's position, that her attacks were supported by the government. In fact, many Chinese, even at that early stage, approved of her stand, and told her so. Stubbs suggested too that her evidence was fallacious and that she was 'well-known to be a person of unbalanced mind'.[10] So effective were his attempts to undermine her reputation in official circles that ten years later, when the matter was resurrected, a former governor's wife wrote to a former governor, 'I seem to remember that Mrs Haslewood was rather hysterical over it all.'[11]

The attempt to cast the Haslewoods in opposition to the Chinese community as a whole was a strong feature of colonial reaction. Very early on, Clara Haslewood had been warned, 'Oh but you see the whole question of the *mui tsai* system is based on an old Chinese custom with which it would not be wise to interfere.'[12] She learned, however, that it had been forbidden in China by law since the Revolution of 1911, even if this had not been successfully enforced – an invincible argument in the years ahead.[13]

The British-based campaign was also much assisted by a steady flow of research material from Hong Kong. Indeed, not only was Miss Pitts able to help, but also added weight was given in the summer of 1921 by the formation there of the Anti-*Mui Tsai* Society. One of the aims of the Chinese group was to counterbalance the effects on the Hong Kong government of the Chinese Society for the Protection of *Mui Tsai*, which did not want abolition since many of its members had several *mui tsai* and concubines (often former *mui tsai*). By 1922 the Anti-*Mui Tsai* Society had nearly 1,000 members. One of its committee members was Mrs

Ma Ying-piu who explained at a meeting that women too were responsible for the existence of a custom which exploited the vulnerability of young girls.[14] Her involvement, in terms of the emergence of Chinese women into public life, was a landmark. (See the chapter 'Mrs Ma: A Footnote' which follows.) The same can be said of the working together on social reform of Europeans and Chinese on an equal footing.

In the exploration of the campaign against state regulation of prostitution that is to follow, the different approach between those providing relief and salvation and those calling for the abolition of a social evil will again become clear. Nevertheless, it is worth noting that the *mui tsai* and prostitution campaigns provide evidence for the importance of a broad base in campaign work – the effectiveness of activity coming from several directions and of different kinds.

If the implication in this chapter is that abolitionists were more effective than those providing palliatives through a Christian mission, it should be said that Mrs Ma was a Christian, the daughter of the missionary-educated Reverend Fok Ching-shang; and Ruby Mow Fung, who was, with her 'School for Prostitutes', to be such a pillar of strength and information to Stella Benson (non-Christian and anti-missionary)

Ruby Mow Fung (centre, front) and her school for prostitutes, with Gladys Forster, 1931-1932

and Gladys Forster, was also closely involved with the Anglican Church. While it was Ada Pitts, of the Church Missionary Society, who started the serious process of education about the *mui tsai* system, who provided invaluable research to the campaign for abolition, and who is to feature in the exploration of the work on behalf of prostitutes and against venereal disease.

BACKGROUND TO PROSTITUTION

From the earliest days, European settlers tended to arrive in the colony without wives, and Chinese labourers flooding on to the island from the mainland usually left their families in their villages. The discrepancy between the numbers of men and women continued as the colony grew. In 1872 there were 78,484 Chinese men and 22,837 women,[15] and 3,264 European men and 699 women.[16] The number of European men does not, however, take account either of merchant seamen or the naval and military presence which was particularly high during and just after the First Opium War (1839-1842), and again at the time of the Second Opium War (1857-1860).

Indigenous women, particularly those from the mobile fishing community, had provided their sexual services from the time that European ships used Hong Kong as a harbour; but from 1841, with the settling of the island by both colonists and Chinese mainland men, immigrant Chinese prostitutes appeared in increasing numbers. According to police magistrates, of the 24,387 Chinese women in the 1876 census, five-sixths were prostitutes;[17] in 1880, the barrister J.J. Francis suggested that there were 18,000 to 20,000 prostitutes, compared with 4,000 to 5,000 respectable women.[18] The latter did not start to arrive until the early 1850s when they sought safety from the Taiping Rebellion in Southern China.

From the beginning, protection of the armed forces from venereal disease was a government priority. In 1857, it instituted a system of registering and inspecting brothels, of licensing and medically examining prostitutes, punishing those who communicated venereal disease and providing a lock hospital. The law and cultural and sociological forces led to the creation of different areas for prostitutes with different clientele.

While, for the government, Chinese women going with Chinese men were segregated from those going with members of the British forces to protect the men, from the Chinese point of view, these latter women were considered beyond the pale; they were below the four levels of women, ranging from high-class entertainers to prostitutes, who were part of traditional Chinese custom transplanted to Hong Kong.[19]

In 1867, Hong Kong was brought into line with new legislation introduced in 1864 in 18 garrison and naval dockyards towns in England and Wales. In reality this meant little change in the colony, except that the police were given wider powers, and licensing was placed under the Registrar General who designated the localities where prostitutes were to live. They were to be inspected weekly at the lock hospital and given a certificate of good health.

In practice, over time, only Chinese prostitutes serving the European forces had to be medically examined. European prostitutes were too expensive for soldiers and sailors, so they were not regulated in the same way, and Chinese prostitutes in the Chinese area were left alone, as happened so often where Chinese custom affecting only the Chinese was concerned.[20] The irony of this will become apparent when Stella Benson and Gladys Forster's research of 1931 is discussed. A Chief Inspector of Brothels was appointed to ensure the licensing and registration of brothels, and the women within had their names up outside. Since a large number was also displayed there, the inmates were known colloquially as 'Big Numbers'.

In the 1870s and 1880s in Britain, a number of groups, drawn together by the Christian feminist Josephine Butler, campaigned for the abolition of the Contagious Diseases Acts. Under these laws, plain-clothes policemen could swear before a magistrate that a particular woman was a common prostitute. The magistrate could then order her to undergo periodic examination; resistance led to imprisonment.

The campaigners argued on moral, political and scientific grounds that the Acts led to the harassment and regulation of women who were more likely to be innocent and that they failed to achieve their aim. Not only was enforced examination 'symbolic rape', but working-class women were obviously more likely to be picked upon and perhaps driven into prostitution by the regulations themselves – which stripped them of their reputation and allowed the police to keep an eye on them. Butler also attacked the double standards applied against women in favour of men: as she put it, 'You cannot hold *us* in honour so long as you drag our sisters in the mire.'[21] But in some ways more convincing was the lack of medical rationale: knowledge was not advanced enough at that time for either adequate diagnosis or treatment of venereal disease.[22]

The campaign was successful and when the Acts were repealed in Britain in 1886, the Colonial Office instructed its colonial dependencies to do the same. The law had already been attacked in Hong Kong. In 1877, soon after Sir John Pope Hennessy arrived as Governor, a case emerged which brought the abuses of the whole system under scrutiny. It became clear that policemen recruited from England to try and create a decent police force, some of them married with their wives in the colony, were encouraged to go with Chinese women who were not licensed as prostitutes to provide evidence that they were breaking the law. On the occasion in question, two women trying to escape the trap fell and were killed. Pope Hennessy set up an inquiry, but his governorship came to an abrupt end before he could act. The colonial authorities continued to believe that it was essential to regulate Chinese prostitutes in order to protect British sailors and soldiers.

Side by side with concern in some quarters during Pope Hennessy's governorship about government treatment of prostitutes, was the first public airing of the problems of the *mui tsai* system. In 1879, the Chief Justice, Sir John Smale, delivered a stern judgement against trafficking in children after several cases had come before him. Thereafter he spoke out strongly against the existence of 10,000 slaves in the colony, emphasising that the system was against the law, the abolition of slavery having been confirmed in Hong Kong law in 1845.[23] Most Europeans criticised Smale's outburst: in attacking Chinese custom, he was liable to undermine the governability of Hong Kong's Chinese citizens. His attempt to provoke reform was effective, therefore, only in so far as it provided a bedrock for later campaigners, both against the *mui tsai* system and licensed prostitution, for the two were, as will become clear, irrevocably linked: girls sold by their families could end up as domestic or brothel 'slaves'.

MISS EYRE'S REFUGE FOR CHINESE WOMEN AND GIRLS

The first relief work on behalf of prostitutes was begun by Lucy Eyre when she set up her Refuge for Chinese Women and Girls in 1901. It was a development of her position as an 'agent in the field' at the Fairlea Mission for the British-based Female Education Society on whose behalf she had arrived in Hong Kong in 1889. Most of the Society's young, unmarried missionary teachers were indentured to it for five years and, indeed, were forbidden from marrying. Miss Eyre, probably the daughter of Colonel C.B. Eyre, a name on one of her donors' lists, was one of those few who came from a background that allowed her financial independence, and thus freedom to act on her own.

Miss Eyre's work is an example of the missionary perception of prostitutes as fallen women to be saved and redeemed, and her refuge, which had 25 inmates by 1905, resembled similar institutions in Britain. Laundry work and prayer pioneered there in the 1880s have been described as 'the standard redemptive regime'.[24] It was a refuge but it resembled a prison, for inmates had to be prevented from leaving or even communicating with former contacts.

The mission felt by Miss Eyre, and Miss Pitts who worked with her, towards the fallen women they rescued seems to have been fuelled by the reservations both women felt towards the Po Leung Kuk, the Chinese committee set up in 1878 to assist in the suppression of kidnapping and traffic in human beings, and the home that went with it. This institution, which is discussed in detail by Elizabeth Sinn in *Women and Chinese Patriarchy: Submission, Servitude and Escape* (1994) was where girls kidnapped and sold into prostitution could find refuge within the Chinese patriarchal system.

The first intimation of the missionaries' feelings is recorded in the diary of Flora Shaw Lugard, the Governor's wife, who arrived in Hong Kong in 1907 and was, within two weeks, approached by Lucy Eyre and Ada Pitts to discuss their financial needs. In seeking to convince her of the importance of their refuge, they emphasised their 'different and better purpose' to that of the Po Leung Kuk.[25]

The strength of their disapproval is further suggested by a confidential report presented to the Colonial Office in London in 1921 by a commission consisting of Mrs C. [Clive] Neville-Rolfe OBE, General Secretary of the National Council for Combating Venereal Diseases in London, and Dr R. Hallam. They visited the Po Leung Kuk, accompanied by Miss Pitts, a regular visitor until two years previously, and from their reaction it is also possible to gain some insight into the difference in attitude towards such matters between European relief workers and the Chinese patriarchs whom Dr Sinn describes.

The commissioners reported that the inmates of the Po Leung Kuk home were unsupervised, and without proper means of recreation. The girls were holding Chinese primers but there were no teachers and no other evidence of either academic education or training in any craft, such as cooking. Girls 'awaiting marriage' were kept separately and they appeared to have no occupation at all. According to the report, Miss Pitts and the missionary Dr Alice Hickling maintained that:

> The Home is largely used as a recruiting ground for cheap supplementary wives by members of the Committee. (Many of these girls become second or third wives, for the welfare of whom the husband can only be held responsible for one year from the date of marriage.) The Committee have luncheon parties there on Sunday and the marriageable girls attend on them. Two members of the Committee are reputed to be owners of the land on which the principal Chinese brothels are situated, but we had not time to verify this from the land register.[26]

The nature of any discussions with Po Leung Kuk directors, based on the unpublished report, is not covered from their side by Dr Sinn's account of the institution in the nineteenth century, but by 1930 the Governor, Sir William Peel, was assuring the home government that 'Several Chinese ladies visit [it] regularly. A recent visit by my wife was much appreciated.'[27] On behalf of the Chinese, he resented any criticism.

The Campaign Against Venereal Disease

The report of the commission on venereal disease and the activity its visit generated in Hong Kong are important precursors to the campaign ten years later against state regulation of prostitution and continue to show the tensions concerning perceived social evils between the home and colonial governments and voluntary organisations and activists. Part of the problem may well have been the involvement of women; indeed, the opening paragraph of the report remarks:

> We had been advised before our departure from England that the Governor of Hong Kong would not welcome a visit … and that he was specially dubious of the advisability of a woman speaking on the subject of venereal disease in the colony.[28]

Stubbs had misread his woman, for two years previously Sybil Neville-Rolfe had disguised herself as a prostitute in order to investigate rumours that police in certain districts of London were conniving at prostitution — and proved they were.[29] In her short visit to the colony, she managed — in spite of official obstacles — to involve all classes of the community, including Chinese women and men, and European women, but excluding the private practitioners who feared a disruption of their lucrative work of examining prostitutes. Following the commission's report, Neville-Rolfe and her council were regularly in touch by visit and letter with the home government concerning Hong Kong. There,

Stubbs, who had refused to countenance a voluntary committee to implement reform, continued to prevaricate. Neville-Rolfe's insistence that the women infected with venereal disease who offered their sexual services from their sampans should be denied access to incoming ships was resisted by Stubbs on the grounds of 'trade rights'.[30]

In 1925, Neville-Rolfe was involved in a broadly-based British government inquiry into the reintroduction of state regulation of prostitution to Singapore to combat venereal disease. The resulting report suggested that,

> State Regulation wherever it has been put to the test has been marked by its failure to provide a remedy for the evils for which it was designed, and has now almost entirely lost the support of expert medical opinion.[31]

THE LEAGUE OF NATIONS INTERVENES

By 1930, not only was there a Labour government in power in Britain which recognised and condemned the illegality of state-regulated prostitution in Hong Kong, but the League of Nations' work on trafficking in women and children was also gathering momentum. Officials in London anxiously awaited the arrival of the League's Travelling Commission in Hong Kong and felt that nothing should be done until it reported.[32] Lord Passfield, formerly Sidney Webb, was of a different mind; he noted that, since prostitutes there came mainly from outside the colony, i.e. China, 'We may expect a very thorough investigation. ... I am far from regretting this.'[33] His successor, continuing his policy and writing in September 1931, following the Commission's January visit, but before the publication of its report in 1932-1933, required action in advance from a still unwilling administration.[34] It was against this background, and unaware of the nature of unpublished government discussions, that Stella Benson and Gladys Forster began their independent research and campaign.

AGAINST THE REGULATION OF PROSTITUTION –
STELLA BENSON AND GLADYS FORSTER

Stella Benson's diaries detail the day-by-day campaign that she and Gladys
Forster waged to persuade the Hong Kong government to abolish the
licensing of prostitution. That story is told in the chapter 'Stella, Gladys,
Phyllis and Brothels' in my book *The Private Life of Old Hong Kong* (1991).
To draw the strands of this chapter together, I will concentrate on three
main areas: Benson's notes from her observation and what was told her
by Mrs Ruby Mow Fung concerning Chinese prostitutes (an area not
elaborated on in my earlier study); the background, attitudes and characters of the two main campaigners; and the relationship between them
and the colonial government.

On 4 March 1931, Stella Benson accompanied Gladys Forster to
the school in Yaumatei run by Ruby Mow Fung. It is not clear when
Forster had met Mow Fung, but it is likely that she was one of three
Chinese women (unnamed in Stella Benson's diary) on the local League
of Nations committee that heard the evidence on trafficking in women
referred to at the beginning of this chapter. During that first afternoon
of research – as they talked to Mow Fung and went to brothels to meet
prostitutes – Stella Benson recorded many pages of notes. But it is from
a later diary entry that the real clue as to what 'made their blood boil' (a
phrase Benson uses more than once) emerges. On 28 November 1931,
almost a year after their first efforts began, she wrote:

> Mrs Forster came down to see me all morning and we drafted
> a letter to the Governor. She was in a weepy mood, being a
> very tenderhearted person; the little girl we found in the
> Tung Wah Hospital last summer who had been used as a
> slave so very drastically and was infected so seriously with
> syphilis that her eyes and nose were almost eaten away (I
> paid for treatment for her) – now seemed so much better
> (though permanently blind, of course) that arrangements
> had been made to send her to a mission home for girls in
> Canton. The child was very happy about this, and is,

according to Mrs Forster, now a merry laughing little thing. She was to be taken to Canton on Monday – but yesterday was taken to a VD specialist for final opinion. He says she is not only incurably diseased – literally rotten with disease, so that the skin breaks at a touch – but she is extremely infectious and will remain so – cannot possibly go to a home or be anything for the rest of her life (she is 17 now). She has all known forms of VD.

All their work – endless research, report writing and rewriting, arguing with unsympathetic committee colleagues, disparagement by government officials, including the Governor – was fuelled by such knowledge and, by it, made worthwhile.

FROM MUI TSAI TO SLY BROTHEL

Much of the extant research material of Benson and Forster comes from general conversations.[35] The case of the girl in the Tung Wah Hospital is, therefore, important as an introduction, for it gives a clear example of how girls might come into prostitution. Following their first meeting with her, Benson wrote in her diary, on 9 June 1931:

The girl lost her parents when she was 7, & the woman next door, out of kindness partly, took her as a mui-tsai. The child was treated well enough, but worked very hard – her owner was in the fish trade, & the child had to catch shell fish etc. While thus engaged she met a young farmer, who told her she would be better off as his concubine than as a hard-worked mui-tsai. He took her to a shed & seduced her, but made no further offer, & she never saw him again. Her owner, though the matter was never discussed between them, evidently guessed she had been seduced, for she sold the child for $200 to a woman who lived next door to an unlicensed brothel. This woman took the child (then 17) to the SCA [Secretariat for Chinese

Affairs] for a license, having first taught her the following questions and answers.

Q Where have you practised prostitution before?

A In Macao (she had never been a prostitute, never been to Macao).

Q Why did you leave Macao?

A Because I heard business was better here.

Q How old are you?

A Twenty one.

The SCA asked exactly these questions, after a bribe had been given, $50 to the pa-an-chang at the door if the license could be granted & $10 to the interpreter whether the licence was granted or not. The child became confused on the last question, & said 20 instead of 21. The SCA cadet ... noticed the confusion & interviewed the procuress separately – she gave the age as 21; the licence was refused on the ground of discrepancy – so the girl was taken back & made to practise prostitution for a year, unlicensed, going in to the brothel next door when sent for – taking usually three or four men a night – beaten if she refused to sleep with a man whom she knew to be diseased. From each customer she took $3 – $1 of this was given to the brothel & the remaining $2 to her owner – nothing for herself. ... After a year the girl became so obviously diseased that men would not use her – her owner then turned her out. She lived by begging for 2 months, until a Chinese preacher noticed her horrible condition & brought her to the Tung Wah. ...

Benson assumes that the seduction of the *mui tsai* and her consequent sale by her mistress came as a result of a 'guess' by the owner. But 'dirty tricks' were very much a feature of luring girls into prostitution, and the seduction may well have been contrived.[36] A prostitute was worth more money than a *mui tsai*.

YAUMATEI – SUPERIOR GIRLS

On 4 March 1931, nine girls attended Ruby Mow Fung's afternoon school in Miu Nam Street. Two of those present said that they had been licensed three years earlier, aged 15. It was a fair assumption that the legal licensing age was 21 – as all the girls had given their age as 22 to the authorities – but A.E. Wood, the Secretary for Chinese Affairs, had already refused to give Benson and Forster any information at all on the subject. The discrepancy in age was easily dealt with: it cost either $30 or $40 in bribes to SCA clerks, inspectors and police, of all races, for it to be overlooked. Whoever paid the bribe, it was always chalked up to the girls' indebtedness to the brothel mistress ('mother') as was any other expenditure. In addition, the girls paid 50 per cent of their earnings to her, and 25 per cent to their personal amah (who washed their clothes and cleaned their cubicles).

On the rare occasions when the inspectors were not corrupt, it was easy to spot them moving from brothel to brothel down the street and to be forewarned to have everything in order. Inspection made the girls more than ever prisoners of their circumstances:

> The brothel mistresses discouraged going out even for an hour, if the inspectors were about, since if an inspector came in & found a brothel empty, or noticed the absence of any special licensed girl, he was likely (unless bribed) to recommend that the brothel be closed as not in sufficient use.

Those girls that Benson and Forster met at the school, and in the nearby brothels, considered themselves a 'superior kind of prostitute' because they went with Chinese clients. They would not associate with Big Number girls who catered for foreigners, particularly soldiers and sailors. These superior girls were less grand than the 'sing song girls of West Point' who catered for high-class Chinese clients and who were not necessarily prostitutes, but singing did often feature in their accomplishments. Learning the complicated songs from male teachers – arranged for and paid for by the brothel 'mother' – involved them in further debt.

Noting that they learned how to write at Ruby Mow Fung's school, Benson asked a girl if she intended to write to her family, particularly her natural mother. This question brought forth answers that encapsulated much of the personal side of the girls' lives as Benson saw it:

> She said rather hesitatingly, yes, she would be able to write letters if she wanted to – her mother was still alive. Another girl said that they would be ashamed to write to their mothers about their present life – but the first girl then said that her mother had sold her to the brothel-mistress eight years before, and would not be in the least interested to hear from her. We asked her whether many of the other girls in her house were in the same position (of having been sold against their will to the brothels and having therefore no family contacts at all) and she said that the girls in her house and in all such houses, lived in their cubicles 'like separate families in separate houses' and did not know or ask for one another's private affairs. This loneliness of each girl struck me as painfully bleak, & I asked whether a girl had any one to turn to, if she should be ill or in trouble – were the 'mothers' attentive; she laughed and said again that each girl lived in her cubicle by herself and her affairs were nobody's business in the house.

This belied the claim made by outside, Western, observers that Chinese prostitutes were part of a family, an impression gained, perhaps, by the use of familial titles, ranging from those of brothel and prostitute owners and brothel mistresses to clients and the prostitutes themselves.[37] Ironically, given their relations with their natural families and, indeed, their own crumbs of education, several girls said that they had been put into prostitution 'in order that their brothers might be educated'. This seems to confirm a change from the nineteenth century; then, girls might be sold direct, and owned entirely by the new buyer. Although Benson does not mention this trend, by the 1930s, 'pawned' girls formed the majority of the prostitutes – that is, a girl was mortgaged by her family to a brothel, so that, as well as receiving a flat sum, they also got a portion of her income. Sue Gronewald's study of prostitution in China, *Beautiful Merchandise* (1985), suggests that filial obligation played a major role in acquiescence by the daughter; increased indebtedness to the brothel mistress further limited her options.[38]

As for how the first girl reacted to the personal questions, Benson noted: 'She did not seem to suggest that she resented *our* questions – she went on most eagerly answering them.' And Benson added:

> Each cubicle where we sat for a time became crowded with visiting girls, really apparently delighted with our visit – though none gave the impression of appealing for sympathy or bidding for rescue. Some very young girls came in, with almost nothing on (a knitted singlet & very short white drawers that showed their thighs). When asked whether they were twenty two too they screamed with laughter at our quaint innocence.

All the time they were there, men water coolies and food hawkers came in and out, 'but women were not allowed in the brothels by the mothers (no Chinese girl friends etc)'.

As for the reaction of these brothel mistresses, Benson noted them standing in doorways 'stout & truculent looking rather, but none made any objection to our going into a house or cubicle.' Benson gives no focus to the involvement of brothel mistresses, amahs and 'pocket mothers' (intermediaries). And there do not seem to have been male pimps living directly off Chinese prostitutes then, as there are today, and as there were then off Western prostitutes. Chinese male entrepreneurs did, however, own the brothels (Chinese and European) and traffic in women. Neither does women's involvement minimise the influence of patriarchy on the whole system; the brutalisation of women exploiters being merely a part of it, as indeed was the acceptance of the system by its direct victims.

THE CORRUPTION OF CHILDREN

Another feature that caught the researchers' attention was the number of children about, not of the prostitutes, but of the amahs. Mrs Mow Fung had already mentioned that there was one at her school aged 11 and added that she was,

> not yet a prostitute, but it is taken for granted by the prostitutes that she is being brought up for this life – this child is turned out on the streets every night, in case an inspector should come & find her in the brothel during its time of business.

The corruption of the young into prostitution is more explicitly spelled out: on 27 December 1931, Benson wrote of how a little girl rescued by a British official was described by him as never being safe because 'she *would offer herself* "all women can give" (aged six) – if there were any indication that there was money to be earned that way! She was bought by her pocket mother to be trained as a prostitute & evidently the beastly woman began early.' And in a letter Gladys Forster wrote to the Colonial Office in 1937, she noted that 'adoption' of daughters, which evaded the 1923 law against the sale of girls as *mui tsai*, was also used to supply brothels via 'pocket mothers'. In addition, prostitutes habitually saved up and 'adopted' a small girl against 'their own weariness and old age'.[39]

Gronewold notes that many prostitutes, mainly as a result of venereal disease, were sterile which is why Benson was probably right about relationships when she noted, continuing her 4 March entry:

> All the amahs – obviously the mothers of the children – said that the children lived somewhere else & only came there to play in the daytime. Almost certainly, in some cases at least, this is not true, but even if it were, the atmosphere for little girls especially, is, one would say, corrupting, even for a few hours … – surely physically dangerous, since the brothel girls mouth & kiss the babies breathing with wet

mouth into their mouths — (they are such affectionate eager little creatures, these girls).

BIG NUMBERS

From the superior girls, the two women were taken further up Nathan Road to visit the Big Numbers; Benson noted the contrast:

> At once one can see that the girls are of a lower class — though also friendly like the superior kind — they are much more brazen, & very obviously *much* dirtier. All were dressed in soiled tawdry satins of a semi-foreign kind — not, like the ones in the Chinese district, in neat natural clean Chinese clothes — these Big Number girls are much older than the others, and at least two I saw were obviously Eurasian ...
>
> The houses had the same kind of gaudy entrance halls, the stairs in these Big Number Houses looked cleaner, newer & lighter, but this was superficial. The mess on the landings of dirty clothes & thrown away filth was indescribable. In all the cubicles we sat in the beds were really filthy & all tumbled just as they had been left the night before. The girls did not seem conscious of this messiness — though the girls in the other district we had been to apologised for the tiniest disorder in cubicles exquisitely neat & clean.
>
> ... All these [Big Number] girls looked as if there was something wrong with their skins, many were pocked, many had pimples & sore places — wherever the skin showed through the paint it looked soft and sallow & unhealthy.

She concluded, somewhat ironically, 'These are the houses to which the soldiers & sailors are recommended to go as being safe.' Indeed, they 'met' one of the clients:

> While we were sitting at the table in the entrance room, with 'mother' and the amahs — an English sailor in uniform

passed, & one of the girls ran to the door and screamed stridently at him – none of your seductive whisperings – but we afterwards found, he turned in two doors down. ...

In the brothel next to the 'cafe' two girls were very drunk, and still drinking – one dark crimson in the face with bulging eyes looked as if she was just going to vomit, and the other was shouting, rolling up the whites of her eyes, waving her glass about quite unaware that we were there.

INTERACTION OF TWO WESTERN FEMINISTS

Stella Benson's conclusion to the above anecdote gives an insight into the two Western women upon which it is possible to build; for their background, relationship with each other and with the objects of their research are useful in analysing their motivations in both feminist and colonial terms. Benson wrote of catching sight of the English sailor sitting beside the prostitutes watching impassively and added:

I was embarrassed at catching his eye & passed on; but Mrs Forster insisted on going back & catching his eye again, so as to make him feel uncomfortable. She brings *morals* much more into this than I do – it is the coercion of a living creature to unnatural courses that hurts me – not the moral side.

Benson and Forster were from rather different backgrounds and were temperamentally dissimilar. When Benson first arrived in Hong Kong in 1920 she was an already-established novelist travelling to broaden her experience still further. Although born into the English landed gentry in 1892, poor health and a keen intelligence guided her away from a conventional existence. She was involved in women's suffrage before World War I, and lived in the East End of London, writing about it in *I Pose* (1915). She had also chosen to work on the land in England and lived in the United States doing menial work. In Hong Kong she taught for a term at the Diocesan Boys School and then continued on to China at a time of feuding and bloodshed. Those two disparate experiences resulted in the autobiographical novel *The Poor Man* (1922). By the time, ten years later, that she came to spend 18 months in Hong Kong – as a result of continuing turbulence in China – she was married to James O'Gorman Anderson of the Chinese Customs Service.

Writing of an exploratory kind, through her experiences, was an integral part of her life and personality. The distinctive style of her diary is revealed in her descriptions of her comrade Gladys Forster; their different approach to prostitution is also highlighted. On 11 April 1931, Benson wrote:

> Mrs Forster lunched with us and we had a good tempered but very incompatible argument about morals. She attacks prostitution as a Christian and a moralist, I as a feminist bone-seeker (there is no bone of nature about the system of prostitution) – and James as a hard-headed practical man. The argument of James and me upholding the idea of less chastity among 'virtuous' women as a counter stimulant to prostitution, dumbfounders Mrs Forster, but she is a brave and just arguer, in spite of her Christian standpoint.

On 8 May, Benson continued her analysis, after Forster, to her surprise, had expressed approval of her, having read her latest novel, *Tobit Transplanted* (1931):

> There is something buoyant and big-dog-like about Mrs Forster. She is fat, she sweats, she is an ardent moralist, and an excellent talker – and she is charmingly honest. Today is the first time I ever heard her express a feeling – mostly she puts opinions most eloquently into words. At least, of course, her morals are founded upon feeling, her feeling against prostitution and in favor of total chastity for all sexes (males, females, and half-&-halfs) amounts to fanaticism. But to hear her express a personal feeling for a person (especially a

disputatious non-moralist like me) was like hearing a dog mew. Both James and I felt rather warmly to her.

The labels of fanatic and Christian moralist, which Benson put on Forster, are disputed by her daughters and by her background.[40] In 1918, aged 24, Forster had arrived in Hong Kong to marry. She came from a family, only one generation away from coal mining, in which women's education and an encouragement to be determined played an important part. Her university education, her marriage to Lancelot Forster, a man from a background of poverty who had nevertheless become a university professor, her own teaching of English at the university and concern about the education of her four daughters, suggest an academic background likely to lead to care in her research and conclusions. And her daughters suggest that her 'horror of unchastity' was more 'social' than 'Christian'. They confirm that she was a feminist – as does her work after she left Hong Kong – and they suggest that it was an important part of her reaction to prostitution, as well as compassion for the young girls who suffered, horror at their condition and a repudiation of slavery.

Her love of and talent for singing provide an important clue to her nature. It was not just that she would have liked to be an opera singer, she even dreamed of going on the music hall stage. Her 'fanaticism' can, therefore, be more usefully seen as a feeling for drama, the open gestures of the performer. Temperamentally, she was quite different from Benson.

Benson talks of her blood boiling. Yet, as a writer whose notes were to form the basis of a report, she was able to be dispassionate. Indeed, she started that long diary entry, 'I want to put down exactly what we saw & heard without comment, since I am trying not to make up my mind on the question until I really have collected all the knowledge I can.'[41] She did end that day, however, with the comment, 'Today's insight into the life of those Yaumati girls makes me feel rather as if I had had a blow on the head.'

Gladys Forster was less able to disengage her emotions, of every sort. That first day when they saw the sailor and Benson avoided his eye, Forster deliberately went back and caught it again to convey her feelings. During one of the setbacks to their report, Benson wrote of her comrade, 'Mrs Forster was too much moved to be as lucid as usual, she spoke in a strangled & halting voice. ...'[42] Of the same meeting Benson wrote of herself, 'My line is anything but eloquence, so I had to be content with asking inconvenient questions, bobbing up like sharp rocks in the flowing tide of [their] words. ...'

Forster's relationship with Ruby Mow Fung and her school was to last long after Benson had left the colony. When in 1937, back in England, she had occasion to write to the Colonial Office, she says that 'for several years a Chinese friend, Mrs Mow Fung, and I had a school for prostitutes – the To Kwong Girls School.'[43] That probably means between 1931 and 1936. It was said of her that she

> made real friends of a number of these prostitutes ... She also used to invite them to her house on the Peak for tea. ... She was criticised by some people for letting them meet her young daughters but I daresay they did not understand who their mother's pupils were (see page 193).[44]

Forster's relationship with Ruby Mow Fung and with the prostitutes seems to have been close and without racial or colonial bias. Benson tended to be an observer rather than an embracer. Because of the loss of some of her diary notes of interviews with prostitutes, when Ruby Mow Fung probably accompanied her, it is impossible to know if she ever described Mow Fung or related to her in anything like the way she did Gladys Forster. She constantly analysed Western women in her diary, yet the only remarks she makes of the Chinese women she encountered and briefly described during her research, and who were not prostitutes, were of the matron at the Tung Wah Hospital and Ruby Mow Fung's sister. The former she called 'a darling Chinese young woman with a face glowing with selfless goodness'; the latter was 'also Christian and altruistic'. Thus we never learn how Ruby Mow Fung came to be involved with prostitutes and know only from newspaper reports that as a Christian activist she later set up a street sleepers' refuge.[45] Benson's regrets about the 'dullness' of the lives of the superior girls and the 'poverty of both their experience & their possessions' have been criticised by Maria Jaschok, author of *Concubines and Bondservants*, as denoting the 'cultural distance between observer and observed'.[46]

On the basis of the foregoing, it is fair to suggest that, while Benson and Forster came at their work from different angles, the feminist component was common; one could be termed a humanist feminist, the other a Christian feminist. There is evidence from the anti-*mui tsai* campaign in Britain that feminism was an issue for both the campaigners and government officials.

The Suffragette Movement had been partly successful by 1918 when votes for women over 30 had been introduced. In 1928, suffrage had been extended so that in the election of 1929 all women over 21 could vote for the first time. It was then, coincidentally, that the anti-*mui tsai* campaign had been resurrected as a result of continuing abuse. Thus an official was prompted, in the margin of a memorandum, to warn against 'the prospect of the Mui-tsai question being made a "test question" by the feminist societies which exploited it to the full last time.'[47]

Benson herself summed up the issue when she heard that the Governor had called their work 'an outcry of hysterical women'. Clara Haslewood had been similarly labelled; indeed, it is a comment still used to denigrate women's activities. 'It seems rash,' Benson coolly observed in her diary, 'to characterise thus any enquiry by women into the treatment of women, now that women are citizens, and can make themselves felt in England.'[48]

The remaining issues left to explore here are the readiness of the campaigning women to oppose the colonial establishment, and their own place within the colonial system.

THE COLONIAL CONNECTION

Clara Haslewood had not only jeopardised her husband's career when she attacked the *mui tsai* system, he himself had willingly sacrificed it and campaigned firmly at her side thereafter. The Haslewoods' attitude seems clear.

They were not anti-colonial; they had just fought a devastating world war to maintain the British Empire, and they were opposed to that empire being besmirched by inhumanity, particularly to innocent children. An acceptance of colonialism, even a pride in it, was part of the political culture of the time.

Mrs Haslewood's stand did not go unnoticed in Hong Kong. In the early days of their campaign, Forster warned Benson that 'few women would support any insistence, since nearly all were wives of govt. servants, and the Governor had men sent home on account of their wives' tactlessness in the colonies.'[49]

Like Haslewood, Benson and Forster were spurred on not only by a perceived evil, and the government's attitude towards it, but also by an order from on high to stop their activities. This is exemplified by what happened in February 1931. The local League of Nations subcommittee of women had served its purpose on the issue of trafficking; it was ready to be dissolved. But the two learned that the Governor, Sir William Peel, felt it had done more than that: 'any enquiry into tolerated brothels here [was] unwarrantable interference';[50] he required that it should stop. Benson asked her diary, 'Why should we drop it? We are citizens, & the enslaved girls are our sex and slaves. There may be no solution of the prostitution difficulty in a place like this ... and yet it is not interference to enquire.'

As their inquiries proceeded, so Benson's disillusion with the administration increased. 'I have always innocently supposed,' she wrote to a friend in March 1931, 'that English officials were straight because they were English.'[51] She was not naive, she had been a suffragette, and she knew the measures taken to stifle protest, but the level of the administration's corruption and insensitivity was a continuing discovery.

Once the two women had prepared the first draft of their report, the administration made efforts to block its further progress by getting at members of the League of Nations Society's committee set up to approve it. In a long account of an acrimonious meeting of 6 October

1931, Benson described what transpired in detail; it can be summed up by her remark that two members in particular were 'very pressing that the matter should be dropped until the League of Nations report comes out two or three years hence.' And she added that her two opponents were 'anxious to make compromises with a government that is really (in principle) *bribed* by the very wealthy "entertainment investors" here not to raise the question of reform. ...'

It was not just the government's connivance at an exploitative industry that bothered Benson; there were at least two other dimensions. As she wrote after that first afternoon's research: '*the Government's toleration of the system actually makes the enslavement of the girls more rigid*, since the corruption that is the rule among government employees adds so much to the indebtedness of the girls.'[52] Not only that, 'Nobody looking at the filthy & neglected condition of the Big Numbers could possibly believe in the only justification of licensing – the protection of men (& secondarily, of local girls) from venereal disease.' Her impression was supported by an army doctor who was an 'ardent abolitionist'; he considered that regulation was 'no protection but on the contrary a danger'.[53] Servicemen were misled by regulation into believing that Big Numbers were safe.

As for the Governor himself, he was, on 9 December, reported by a woman whom Benson described as a 'diehard & entirely featherwitted & uninformed on all subjects' as having pronounced, 'Really, those poor dear ladies, very charming & all that, no doubt, but without any knowledge of what they're talking about.'[54] What incensed Benson even more was that he was prepared to gossip with someone who had no concern in the issue, but not to talk to responsible citizens who wished to discuss it seriously. Taxed about it on 13 November, the informant gave another version of her conversation with the Governor: he had described their report as 'intelligent and interesting and I agree with it almost in its entirety'.

Interestingly, that second morning, he and Lady Peel had visited Ruby Mow Fung's school and, according to Gladys Forster, who was there, he seemed interested in and concerned by what he saw. This is confirmed by his unpublished autobiography in which he wrote that, 'at one time I regarded *maisons tolérés* as the least of several evils, but I came to alter my view.'[55] He suggests that he became convinced that they were, after all, medically unsound. Thus he took a certain pleasure in telling Stella Benson, in private at a dinner party at Government House on 1 December 1931, that he was about to announce the abolition in stages of tolerated brothels, a decision he had been disposed to take for six months. European brothels were then closed at the end of 1931, Chinese ones for Europeans in June 1932 and the last 43 Chinese houses for Chinese clients in June 1934.

The Enthusiasts

In Peel's account of his visit to Ruby Mow Fung's school in November 1931 (which he ascribed to a much later date) he called her 'a philanthropic Chinese lady'. Gladys Forster he mentioned not at all. He did, however, refer to social reformers who passed through Hong Kong; these he called 'enthusiasts' – he did not mean it as a compliment.[56] How valuable, then, was the work of these enthusiasts? And did they have a right to call for social reform as it affected Chinese women?

While Benson and Forster's work is not mentioned in Colonial Office papers, nor in Peel's manuscript, it may be that their persistence was the final determinant in Peel's decision to give way to international and British government and parliamentary pressure. This would be in line with the experience of a modern-day campaign organisation such as Amnesty International – that no one approach should claim success, but that pressure is cumulative.

Indeed, the human rights analogy is entirely apposite in determining whether or not foreign women had, and have, the right to intervene across cultures. The state regulation of prostitution in Hong Kong has been shown in this chapter to have resulted in the loss of human rights to the young Chinese women concerned. In 1931 this was already an issue recognised internationally and is summed up in a departmental memorandum within the Colonial Office of 8 September 1931:

The subject is one that raises some of the most delicate and disputable points in the whole range of human relations. Clearly we ought to be very cautious in assuming that western ideas on such matters are necessarily applicable without qualification to eastern communities, such as Hong Kong. On the other hand, we live in an age of League of Nations Commissions and we are always in danger of being called to order if we fall short ... of Geneva standards.[57]

The fact that slavery was already illegal in China itself confirms that, quite apart from internationally recognised standards, the Chinese were working on their own social reforms. What is more, in retrospect, both footbinding and the *mui tsai* system are seen universally as antipathetic to the human rights of women. Brothel slavery in Asia is an issue of increasing contemporary concern.[58]

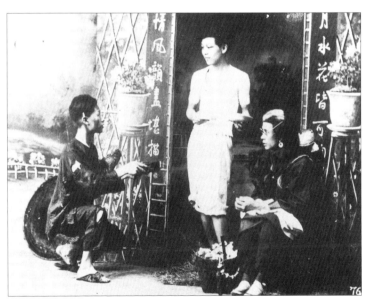

A depiction of a 1930s Hong Kong brothel for Chinese clients

The fact that Western women campaigned for social reform in Hong Kong, and that the government resisted it, has two conflicting rationales. As the nineteenth century progressed, middle-class British women increasingly sought a voice. They had the time, the enthusiasm and the sensitivity to feel the effects of inhumanity. They had no vote; they could not stand for Parliament; social reform was their form of political expression, and campaigning their means of achieving their goals; it became a sisterhood, exemplified by the campaign for the vote.

That tradition moved to Hong Kong, though only very few were involved, for most people went to make money. That was one of the reasons for the pragmatism of the Hong Kong government. Sir Reginald Stubbs wrote to the Colonial Office when his hand was being forced over the abolition of the *mui tsai* system: 'We hold our position in Hong Kong because the Chinese are satisfied to be ruled by us so long as we do not make our yoke heavy.'[59]

And what were the implications of that as far as prostitution was concerned, quite apart from protecting the British services from venereal disease? Dame Rachel Crowdy, Head of the Social Questions and Opium Traffic Section of the League of Nations, who talked to Benson and Forster in Hong Kong in October 1931, agreed that no one who had thoroughly studied the subject could logically advocate state regulation and 'delay could only be accounted for by colonial expediency'.[60] The *South China Morning Post* suggested on 4 December that year that at least 10,000 people were directly or indirectly interested financially in organised prostitution.

The Colonial Office itself had recognised that it was time to change when, in October 1930, it remarked about a dispatch from Peel, that the 'system in Hong Kong may be "more orderly than the state of affairs in London" but that orderliness is purchased at the price of recognising and maintaining large vested interests in vice in the person of brothel owners.'[61] This was entirely in line with the League of Nations' general findings when it published its Report on Trafficking in Women and Children in 1933: 'Efforts should be directed in the first place,' it advised, ' to removing conditions which tend to ensure a market for the trafficker. His surest market is the licensed or recognised brothel.'[62]

The deregulation of prostitution – and thus Benson and Forster's work, as well as that of Josephine Butler – has been criticised for its repercussions, including the rise in venereal disease.[63] The answer to that begins with Benson's diary entry of 7 December 1931 when she talked to Mr Dakers, Assistant Protector of Chinese at Singapore about abolition there:

> All that he said supported our highest hopes. Abolition he says has very definitely strengthened the hands of the government *as protectors* of Chinese girls; As to venereal disease – regulationists say that it has increased since abolition, while abolitionists claim that it has *decreased*.

Sybil Neville-Rolfe had looked at this issue ten years earlier. She wrote in her report:

> His Excellency stated that he considered 'segregation' better than 'scattered clandestine promiscuity', and that none of the Naval and Military infections came from the houses. This, we found subsequently from the Commander-in-Chief was a complete error. Sir Reginald Stubbs stated that the suppression of brothels in Colombo led to 'disastrous results.' When in Colombo we went very fully into the position with the Attorney-General as well as from the medical point of view. … [a government commission] did not even consider any return to the conditions in force before brothels were suppressed … the improvement in health and conditions being so marked.[64]

Moreover, the Colonial Secretary wrote to Peel on 26 September 1931 to confirm their findings:

> I am advised that expert medical opinion no longer views
> such a system as providing any real safeguard against the
> spread of venereal disease and that the abolition of toler-
> ated houses in Ceylon and Malaya has not led to any in-
> crease.[65]

The League of Nations Report added to the benefits when it noted,
'According to the Ceylon authorities, the abolition of the system of
recognised brothels in 1912 had the immediate effect of completely
stopping traffic in foreign women to the island.'[66]

In suggesting reasons for any rise in reported venereal disease cases
in Hong Kong before the Japanese occupation, the effects of Neville-
Rolfe's work in publicising venereal disease, the advances in diagnosis
and treatment, and the expansion of clinics should be borne in mind.

WESTERN FEMINISTS IN HONG KONG TODAY

I believe I have validated the intervention in the past by Western women
in the affairs of Chinese women in Hong Kong, particularly as regards
footbinding, the *mui tsai* system and licensed prostitution. But what
of today?

Following its foundation in 1947, the increasingly Western-domi-
nated Hong Kong Council of Women has campaigned for women's
rights, two of its major successes being the abolition of concubinage in
1970 and the setting up of a refuge for battered wives in 1985. In
1992, Western women, with as little official political status as ever but
still interested in social reform concerning women in Hong Kong,
ask themselves if they have the right to 'interfere' in issues which
affect the majority, who are Chinese. They are less sure of themselves, more introspective about the issue, particularly in organisations
such as AWARE (Association of Women for Action and Research),
than were their earlier sisters in what still seemed like the heyday of
colonial power.

As I was starting to write this chapter, I talked at a reception to a
Chinese woman university lecturer. She told me of the deterioration

over the past two years in her students – their lack of discipline, of motivation.

Instinctively I replied, 'What are you doing about it?' She looked at me witheringly and replied, 'I don't come from the Judaeo-Christian tradition. I don't have to do anything. I wait.'

That non-Chinese tradition, it would appear from this chapter, contributed, through education and example, to the flowering of campaigning for social reform among Chinese women in Hong Kong. The contribution of international standards, increasingly recognised, is also relevant. Is it wrong, then, for Western women, as heirs to the past, to continue to wish to help their sisters? The condition of women now is, after all, as in the past, largely the creation of both the patriarchal coloniser and the patriarchal colonised.

The answer must surely be no, as long as they recognise that Chinese women now have a voice of their own and are part of a region of Asian women – including migrant workers from the Philippines and Vietnamese boatpeople in Hong Kong – developing their own goals and ways of achieving reform.

February 1992 – reworking of a paper given at the 12th International Association of Historians of Asia Conference, Hong Kong, June 1991.

NOTES

1. Stella Benson, unpublished diaries. All quotations, except where stated, are from the same source; references will only be given if the date is unclear from the text. Benson kept her diary from childhood. On her death in 1933, aged 41, the volumes were handed over by her husband to Cambridge University, as she had requested, to remain unopened for 50 years.

2. Maria Jaschok, 'Women and Women's Studies in Hong Kong', paper given at 'Gender and Society' Workshop, March 1991, p. 8.

3. J.B. Jeter, *A Memoir of Henrietta Shuck* (1846), p. 105.

4. Jeter, *A Memoir of Henrietta Shuck*, p. 142.

5. John Morrison to London Missionary Society, 24 July 1837, CWM, China GI Ultra Ganges, Box 3, Folder 3.

6. See *Female Missionary Intelligencer*, vol. 1-3, 1 August 1860, p. 132 (Mrs Smith); FMI, new series, vol. 1, 1881, pp. 146-147 (Miss Johnstone).

7. *Hong Kong Daily Press*, 19 December 1918; *Hong Kong Telegraph*, 27 October 1921.

8. The meeting is described by Alicia Little in *In the Land of the Blue Gown* (1912), p. 216, and in *Hong Kong Weekly Press*, 10 March 1900, p. 164.

9. See Nigel Cameron, *Hong Kong: The Cultured Pearl* (1978), p. 145, and *Barbarians and Mandarins* (1989), p. 366, and Susanna Hoe, *The Private Life of Old Hong Kong* (1991), p. 229.

10. CO129/461 letter of 19 July 1920 from Sir R. Stubbs.

11. Nathan Papers, 351-352, 1 November 1929.

12. Mrs H.L. Haslewood, *Child Slavery in Hong Kong* (1930), p. 20.

13. In fact, *slavery* had been abolished; issues affecting women, such as the *mui tsai* system, were not, in reality, tackled until the 1950 Marriage Law (See Chapter 8, 'The Seventh Gentleman'.)

14. Carl Smith, 'Notes'.

15. Norman Miners, *Hong Kong under Imperial Rule* (1987), p. 191.

16. Miners, *Hong Kong Under Imperial Rule*, p. 191.

17. CO129/522, p. 46, 'Notes on Reprinted Papers from 1880 to 1900'.

18. Parliamentary Papers, vol. 3, 1882-1899, p. 267.

19. Sue Gronewold, *Beautiful Merchandise* (1985), pp. 5-6

20. Miners, *Hong Kong under Imperial Rule*, p. 191.

21. Edward J. Bristow, *Vice and Vigilance* (1977), p. 83.

22. Bristow, *Vice and Vigilance*, p. 81.

23. Elizabeth Andrew, *Heathen Slaves and Christian Rulers* (1907), p. 9.

24. Bristow, *Vice and Vigilance*, p. 237.

25. Flora Lugard, Unpublished Diary, 14 August 1907.

26. Mrs C. Neville-Rolfe, Unpublished Confidential Report, April 1921, p. 5, CO129/472, p. 360.

27. CO129/522, p. 62

28. Neville-Rolfe, Report, p. 1.

29. *The Times*, obituary, 5 August 1955.

30. Neville-Rolfe, Report, p. 6.

31. Advisory Committee on Social Hygiene, Report, 1925, p. 4.

32. CO129/533.

33. CO129/522, p. 71.
34. CO129/533, pp. 25-33.
35. The 'report' which Forster and Benson submitted to the League of Nations Society was embargoed until 1995. It has not yet been possible to identify it in Geneva.
36. Gronewold, *Beautiful Merchandise*, p. 71.
37. Gronewold, *Beautiful Merchandise*, pp. 9 and 74.
38. Gronewold, *Beautiful Merchandise*, p. 70.
39. CO852/23/550 19/37 No. 36, letter from Gladys Forster to W.G. Ormsby Gore, 2 June 1937.
40. I received detailed letters from Helen Clemetson, and talked to Anne Badenoch in person, as well as corresponding.
41. Benson, 6 October 1931.
42. Benson, 4 March 1931.
43. Forster, letter of 2 June 1937.
44. Letter from Beatrice Pope to H.J. Lethbridge, 21 June 1974.
45. St John's Review, vols IV, V and VI; *South China Morning Post*, 2 and 13 November 1936, and 4 May 1960.
46. Letter to me after reading the first draft of this chapter, 17 December 1991.
47. CO129/514, 10 April 1929.
48. Benson, 4 March 1931.
49. Benson, 20 February 1931.
50. Benson, 11 February 1931.
51. R. Ellis Roberts, *Portrait of Stella Benson* (1939), letter to Laura Hutton, 21 March 1931, p. 406.
52. Benson, 4 March 1931.
53. Benson, 5 November 1931.
54. Benson, 9 December 1931.
55. Sir William Peel, Unpublished Autobiographical Manuscript, p. 146.
56. Peel, Manuscript, pp. 147-148.
57. C0129/533, pp. 19-20.
58. See, for example, *Sunday Morning Post*, Hong Kong, 9 February 1992, about Thailand.
59. CO129/478, p. 766, 16 September 1922.
60. Benson, 8 October 1931.
61. CO129/522, including summary of printed correspondence on this question covering the years 1857-1900, p. 16.
62. League of Nations, *Report on the Commission of Enquiry into Traffic in Women and Children in the East* (1933), p. 93.
63. See H.J. Lethbridge, 'Prostitution in Hong Kong: A Legal and Moral Dilemma' (1978); Miners, *Hong Kong under Imperial Rule*, pp. 204-206; James Warren, draft chapter of *Women and Chinese Patriarchy*, p. 22. My paper 'Queen's Women: Western Prostitutes in Hong Kong 1841-1941' at the 12th International Association of Historians of Asia Conference, June 1991, also provoked it.
64. Neville-Rolfe, Report, p. 10.
65. C0129/533, p. 26.
66. League of Nations, *Report*, p. 94.

Bibliography

Unpublished Documents: Private, Missionary and Government

Anti-Slavery Society, Rhodes House, Oxford, Mss Brit. Emp. 225-K25/2.

Benson, Stella, Diaries, Cambridge University Library, Add 6762-6802.

Blake, Edith (Lady), Typescript of 'A Journey in China, Korea and Japan', 1900, Cambridge University Library, Add 8423.

Colonial Office Records, CO129, PRO Hong Kong; otherwise PRO London.

Female Education Society (FES), Catalogue of Papers 1834-1899, Birmingham University Library.

London Missionary Society (LMS/CWM), CWM China 1843-1872, School of Oriental and African Studies (SOAS), GI Ultra Ganges Box 3-7.

Hoe, Susanna, 'Gin and Bridge All Day: Myths About Western Women in Hong Kong 1841-1941', talk given to Royal Asiatic Society, February 1991.

Hoe, Susanna, 'Queen's Women: Western Prostitutes in Hong Kong 1841-1941', paper given at 12th International Association of Historians of Asia Conference, June 1991.

Jaschok, Maria, 'Women and Women's Studies in Hong Kong', paper given at 'Gender and Society' Workshop, March 1991.

Lugard, Flora (Lady), Lugard Papers, Rhodes House, Oxford, MSS Brit. Emp. S.67.

Nathan, Sir Matthew, MS Nathan, Rhodes House, Oxford; 340-342.

Neville-Rolfe, Mrs C. and Hallam, Dr R., National Council for Combating Venereal Diseases, Commissioners' Confidential Report, April 1921, CO129/472, pp. 356-382.

Peel, Sir William, Manuscript of Autobiography, Rhodes House, Oxford, Brit. Emp. S.208.

Smith, Carl T., card index system of Hong Kong ('Notes').

Published Works

Andrew, Elizabeth and Bushnell, Katharine, *Heathen Slaves and Christian Rulers* (Oakland, Cal., Messiah's Advocate, 1907).

Andrew, Kenneth, *Hong Kong Detective* (London, John Lang, 1962).

Benson, Stella, *The Poor Man* (London, Macmillan, 1922).

Benson, Stella, *Tobit Transplanted* (or *The Far Away Bride*) (London, Macmillan, 1931).

Bristow, Edward J., *Vice and Vigilance: Purity Movements in Britain since 1700* (Dublin, Gill & Macmillan, 1977).

British Parliamentary Papers, China 1882-1899 (Shannon, Irish University Press, 1971).

Brooks, Nancy, *Women at Westminster: An Account of Women in the British Parliament 1918-1966* (London, Peter Davies, 1967).

Cameron, Nigel, *Barbarians and Mandarins: Thirteen Centuries of Western Travellers in China* (Hong Kong, Oxford University Press, 1989; 1st published 1970).

Cameron, Nigel, *Hong Kong: The Cultured Pearl* (Hong Kong, Oxford University Press, 1978).

China Mail.

Clarabut, Cecil (ed.), *Some Letters of Stella Benson 1928-1933* (Hong Kong, Libra Press, 1978).

Colonial Office, *First Report of the Advisory Committee on Social Hygiene* (London, HMSO, 1925).

Female Missionary Intelligencer, vols I-XVIII, 1854-1899 (London).

Further correspondence relating to measures adopted for checking the spread of venereal disease in continuation of [c.9253] Straits Settlements; Hong Kong; Gibraltar (HMSO, 1906).

Grant, Joy, *Stella Benson: A Biography* (London, Macmillan, 1987).

Gronewold, Sue, *Beautiful Merchandise: Prostitution in China 1860-1936* (New York, Harrington Park Press, 1985)

Harrop, Phyllis, *Hong Kong Incident* (London, Eyre & Spottiswoode, 1943).

Haslewood, Mrs H.L., *Child Slavery in Hong Kong: The Mui Tsai System* (London, Sheldon Press, 1930).

Hoe, Susanna, 'White Women in the Colonies: Were they Responsible for Setting up Racial Barriers?', *Bikmaus: A Journal of Papua New Guinea Affairs Ideas & Arts*, vol. V, no. 2 (Port Moresby, June 1984).

Hoe, Susanna, *The Private Life of Old Hong Kong: Western Women in the British Colony 1841-1941* (Hong Kong, Oxford University Press, 1991).

Hong Kong Daily Press.

Hong Kong Refuge for Women and Girls, *Annual Report 1904-5* (Hong Kong, 1905).

Hong Kong Telegraph.

Hong Kong Weekly Press.

Hyam, Ronald, 'Empire and Sexual Opportunity', *Journal of Imperial and Commonwealth History*, vol. XIV, no. 2, pp. 34-89 (London, January 1986).

Jaschok, Maria, *Concubines and Bondservants: The Social History of a Chinese Custom* (London, Zed Books, 1988).

Jaschok, Maria and Meirs, Suzanne (eds.) *Women and Chinese Patriarchy: Submission, Servitude and Escape* (Hong Kong, Hong Kong University Press, 1994).

Jeter, J.B., *A Memoir of Henrietta Shuck: The First American Female Missionary to China* (Boston, Gould Kendall & Lincoln, 1846).

Lau Siu-Kai, *Decolonization Without Independence and the Poverty of Political Leaders in Hong Kong* (Hong Kong, Institute of Asia-Pacific, 1991).

League of Nations, *Report on the Commission of Enquiry into Traffic in Women and Children in the East* (New York, 1933).

Lethbridge, H.J., 'Prostitution in Hong Kong: A Legal and Moral Dilemma', *Hong Kong Law Journal* (1978).

Little, Mrs Archibald, *Intimate China: The Chinese as I Have Seen Them* (London, Hutchinson, 1899).

Little, Mrs Archibald, *In the Land of the Blue Gown* (London, 1912).

Loseby, F.H. 'Mui Tsai in Hong Kong', *Hong Kong Legislative Council Sessional Papers*, 1935, pp. 195-282.

Miners, Norman, *Hong Kong under Imperial Rule 1912-1941* (Hong Kong, Oxford University Press, 1987).

Picton-Turbervill, Edith, *Life is Good* (London, Frederick Muller, 1939).

Prochaska, F.K., *Women and Philanthropy in Nineteenth Century England* (Oxford, Clarendon Press, 1980).

Roberts, R. Ellis, *Portrait of Stella Benson* (London, Macmillan, 1939).

Scott, Benjamin, *A State of Iniquity: Its Rise, Extension and Overthrow* (New York, August M. Kelley, 1968; 1st published 1894).

Simon, Lady, *Slavery* (London, Hodder and Stoughton, 1929).

Smith, Carl T., *Chinese Christians: Elites, Middlemen and the Church in Hong Kong* (Hong Kong, Oxford University Press, 1985).

Strachey, Ray, *The Cause: A Short History of the Women's Movement in Great Britain* (London, Virago, 1978; 1st published 1928).

Suter, Edward, *History of the Society for Promoting Female Education in the East* (London, 1847).

Vicinus, Martha (ed.), *A Widening Sphere: Changing Roles of Victorian Women* (London, Methuen, 1980).

Victoria Home and Orphanage, *Annual Report* (Hong Kong, 1903-1906).

Woods, W.W., 'Mui Tsai in Hong Kong and Malaya', *Report of Commission* (London, HMSO, 1937).

CHAPTER 13

MRS MA
A Footnote

Ma Ying-piu, Mrs, née Fok Hing-tong (1872-1957)
Known as the first Chinese woman in Hong Kong with a public position: the only woman on the Anti-*Mui Tsai* Society organising committee, 1922 (see previous chapter).

She was born in the Shuntak district, close to Canton (Guangzhou), second of four daughters of the Reverend Fok Ching-shang who wished them to marry Christians. Christian Chinese men were more readily available in Australia, where many had gone to prospect for gold, but later engaged in fruit marketing (see Chapter 17 'The New Concubines'). One of these, Ma Ying-piu, accepted marriage with Hing-tong; and one of her sisters, Siu-yue, married a relative and business associate of his, Ma Wing-chang.

Upon marriage, the sisters may have gone to Australia, but soon after the turn of the century, Ma Ying-piu and other relatives and friends opened the Sincere Department Store in Hong Kong.

A store selling a multitude of goods under the same roof at a fixed price was an innovation in Chinese marketing; another innovation was the employment of Chinese saleswomen. Mrs Ma Ying-piu took her place in these ranks even though, as her son relates, she had one young child at her right, another at her left (twins), one on her back and one in her belly. She continued working and having children and caring for them, and managing her household with no regular domestic help.

This introduction to a public role began to prepare Mrs Ma for community leadership. She became active in causes to improve the condition of women and girls – for example, the formation of Christian Associations in the girls middle schools under missionary patronage in Hong Kong; her

*Ma Ying-piu (wearing glasses, seated left of centre)
with the Ma family women on the occasion of the
90th birthday of her mother (centre)*

daughter was at school at St Stephen's Girls College. The work developed
into the organisation of the Chinese (as opposed to European) Young
Women's Christian Association (YWCA) in 1920. Mrs Ma served as its
first chair until 1923. Her sister, Mrs Ma Wing-chan, was vice-chair from
1923 to 1927, and chaired it from 1927 to 1932.

Mrs Ma was active in the campaign to abolish the procuring or
buying of young girls to be servants (the *mui tsai* system) which started
in 1921. She was the only woman on the organising committee of the
Anti-*Mui Tsai* Society in 1922 and she also chaired the investigation
committee.

Unusual for Chinese women of her time, Mrs Ma not only involved
herself in public causes, she was also a leading member of many a social
campaign. She cared about women less well off than herself; and she
was not afraid of taking women from her own class to task. As she put
it at a meeting, women too were responsible for the existence of a custom which exploited the vulnerability of young girls.

A draft entry – all that was left of a good proposal put forward by Maria Jaschok in
1991 for a Hong Kong Women's Encyclopaedia; information provided by Carl Smith.

226

CHAPTER 14

IN SEARCH OF PEACE
Hong Kong September 1989

The nostalgia this month for the beginning of World War II is not as great in Hong Kong as it is in Europe. The war did not really impinge on daily life here until 1941. Then, just after Pearl Harbor, on 8 December, the Japanese crossed over from China into Kowloon.

Peggy did not bother to wait for the 50th anniversary; she died a couple of months ago and, in my opinion, she had been more than willing to die for some time.

That was the impression I got when I visited her last November. You may remember I mentioned her when I wrote to you about the contrast in attitudes towards the elderly of Chinese and Western cultures.

The day after I met Peggy, I met Sister L, an Italian nun who was also in Hong Kong before and during the war. It is the contrast between those two women, and how they lived through the war and afterwards, that comes to mind this month.

When I met Peggy she was 69, said she was 79, for reasons of her own, and looked 90. I know she would not mind my telling you that; she was a down-to-earth person. She was also an alcoholic and a chain-smoker. As we talked, she constantly sipped neat gin.

She sat on her bed in a shortie nightie, her legs akimbo – legs like sticks. She had been ill and had not eaten for some time. But her mind was sharp and a bitter sense of humour strong.

I had gone to talk to her about pre-war life in Hong Kong. But whatever my purpose had been, she would have harked back to the war. Someone I talked to about her recently had known her too well, put up with her for too long, to be entirely sympathetic; but to me, as a stranger, what happened then had determined the rest of her life, however she may have behaved in the intervening years.

Six months before the Japanese invasion she married a Dutchman, after waiting the two years that companies then required their young male employees to do before marriage.

When the Japanese overran Kowloon, before Hong Kong Island fell and the Governor surrendered on Christmas Day, Peggy became an auxiliary nurse. Her new husband was a private in the Volunteers.

One night, sheltering in the basement of the hospital from bombs, Peggy thought she heard her husband cry out for her. She never saw him again.

When she was already interned in Stanley Camp, his body was discovered, dug up and reburied in Stanley Cemetery. It was without a head. I don't think Peggy ever got over that. The years in Stanley were hell for her because of that image, as much as for the lack of freedom and food and the illness and anxiety. I think she died with that image stuck fast in her mind.

When I met Sister L, she was dressed in long white robes, her face smooth and pleasant, as only a nun's can be. She was Peggy's age. She talked to me about the world, about the book she had written on one of my historical characters, her life during the war. Then she took me to see the office where she works as her Mission's archivist.

During the war she was frightened, of course, and the nuns lacked sufficient food. She remembers how they would go in twos to the convent farm in the New Territories to pick up fresh produce. She hated to go out because of the bombs.

The convent hospital was bombed, and some nuns died from disease and malnutrition. But the Mission's Chinese school continued, and the nuns who had run the English school managed to do a little private teaching. Today, Sister L stands proud and upright; I saw her a few weeks ago, her face smiley and serene.

It depends a lot on mental reserves how one comes through a War, and on luck. But as long as women like Peggy have experiences like hers, and die welcoming death with such open arms, we must not forget. And we must fight to prevent war.

Printed in *Liverpool Daily Post & Echo*, 'Letter from Hong Kong', 28 September 1989.

CHINA, HONG KONG AND MACAU

CHAPTER 15

WRITING ABOUT CLARA
Clara Ho Tung

There was a time, over 100 years ago, when a certain class of Hong Kong citizen was neither European nor Chinese, and unhappily caught in that divide. Since the turn of the century, however, and the rise and rise of men such as the comprador Ho Tung (later Sir Robert, financier and public benefactor), Eurasian families have formed an increasingly respected, prosperous and homogeneous part of society.

It was, therefore, with some interest that I agreed to write a 3,000-word entry for a five-volume encyclopaedia of Chinese women on Clara Ho Tung, the matriarch. To call her the matriarch, though, is to simplify a rather more complicated story.

Eurasians were usually the product of a union between a European merchant attached to one of the trading houses that were responsible for the colony's birth and its subsequent prosperity, and a Chinese mother.

The father was usually in Hong Kong without a wife; he did not marry the Chinese woman who bore his children, though they might have a comfortable relationship over several years. Historically, such a woman is known as a 'protected' woman, and she might be well-kept and left well-provided for when her protector went home, died or married a European woman.

Both Ho Tung and Clara Cheung were the children of first generation Eurasians, but their marriage and much, though not all, of their subsequent life followed Chinese custom.

Ho Tung married first Clara's cousin Margaret. But she was unable to have children, so he took a concubine, who also appeared childless. Then, in 1895, he married a second wife, Clara, who was, unusually, a 'level' wife, equal in every way, though giving precedence to her cousin.

The reason for Clara's encyclopaedia entry is not as matriarch of the Eurasian community but her legacy as a Buddhist philanthropist. You cannot, however, separate the public from the private. Clara had ten children, several of whom are still alive in their eighties. And the next and subsequent generations are flourishing. It is my communications with Clara's children, survivors of a bygone age, which have prompted me to write this footnote.

Her son Robbie was a Kuomintang general and at 86 writes me precise, helpful and elegant letters. He explains that relations with his natural mother, Clara, led him to move in with his other mother, Margaret, and that he thus became closer to her. He remembers much about her that might otherwise be lost.

Jean Gittins, now 84, who married into another rising Eurasian family, thus uniting two powerful clans, and who was widowed during the war, now lives in Australia. She and I have become friends by post. Her warm, handwritten letters are the opposite of Robbie's impeccably typed ones. (Jean Gittins died in 1995 without us having a chance to meet.)

I met Dr Irene Cheng, number four daughter, yesterday. For some years she has been writing her autobiography, following an earlier biography of her mother. She had arrived in Hong Kong a couple of days earlier from California with suitcases full of computer discs and hard copies of manuscript.

She had come to work with her publisher but she fitted me into her heavy schedule to go over my own little manuscript for a final checking with the doyenne of the family, since her eldest sister Victoria died earlier this year aged 95. My meeting with Victoria's gentle daughter Vera, and instructions received from Vera's powerful brother, T.S. Lo, belong to the story of another generation.

Irene's editor at Hong Kong University Press both preceded and followed me in meetings with her. After her second meeting she left, tactfully saying she would give Irene more time to prepare her manuscript. This was not the first time over the years that such a scene had been played out.

I understand the problem. When I arrived in the bare hostel room at

Robert Black College, my 88-year-old informant was hunched arthritically between two single beds spread with chapters, lading and teeming them from one pile to another.

She broke off to talk to me – not to listen much, for she is rather deaf. She had stayed up late reading and making suggestions for me which neither she nor I could now decipher. But meeting her (and later application to the notes she had made) was worth the effort.

Clara's real life as number two wife, and that of the co-wife who outlived her, may never be written, though I have some inklings about the line it should take. Madame Wellington Koo recorded Clara as saying in 1920, 'I hope in the next generation there won't be any secondary wives. I would hate to have any of my girls live the way I've had to.' (See Chapter 17, 'The New Concubines'.)

I retain a memory of Irene, stately and sprightly still, and rather the Grande Dame, not quite Chinese, though fluent in Cantonese to her amah, not quite English, though fluent in English to me; it adds a warm note to the writing of a biographical entry of her illustrious mother.

Dr Irene Cheng (née Ho Tung), 1993

Written November 1992.

CHAPTER 16

HO TUNG, CLARA (LADY): 1875-1938
An Encyclopaedia Entry

Known also as Ho Cheung Lin-kok (Buddhist name) and Ho Cheung Ching-yung (secular Chinese name). Buddhist philanthropist. Born in Hong Kong, eldest of four children of first-generation Eurasian parents, father Cheung Tak-fai, mother Cheung Yeung-shi. Brought up in China (Shanghai and Kiukiang [Jiujiang]) where her father worked for the Chinese Customs Service. On his death, her mother brought Clara, aged 18, and her brother, Cheung Pui-kai, home to Hong Kong with their father's coffin. Married February 1895 Ho Tung (K'ai Tung), later (1915), Sir Robert (1862-1956), Jardine Matheson comprador; later financier and public benefactor.

In 1881, Ho Tung had married Clara's first cousin, Margaret Mak Sau-ying (1865-1944), who remained childless, as did, for many years, his concubine Chau Yee-man (d. c. 1911). Clara became his *p'ing ts'ai*, or 'level' wife, an unusual arrangement in which she was equal in every way to the principal wife, though giving precedence to her.

Clara had ten children, seven girls and three boys. Between the two marriages, a nephew, Sai-wing, had been adopted, and Chau Yee-man later had a daughter, Mary. Thus Margaret and Clara were in practice co-mothers of 12 Ho Tung children. After 1915 and Ho Tung's knighthood, his two wives were known as Lady Margaret (Lady Mak, Lady M, Lady Ho Tung) and, eventually and unofficially, Lady Clara (Lady Ho Tung).

Clara Ho Tung's life can be divided into five phases: daughter; wife and mother; Buddhist pilgrim; public benefactor; Chinese patriot.

Clara Ho Tung, the daughter of first-generation Eurasian parents, championed education for women

The Ho Tungs were Eurasians who regarded themselves as Chinese, both in observing Chinese customs and concerning themselves with the welfare of China. Nevertheless, because of their wealth and their access, as residents of Hong Kong, to the wider world, they lived a cosmopolitan life which included regular travel to Europe and the United States, as well as to China.

In her early married life, Clara aspired to the ideal for a Chinese married woman: 'to assist her husband and educate her children'; she regarded her husband and children, in that order, as her main responsibility. She had her first child, Victoria, in 1897; there followed: Henry (1898; d. 1900); Daisy (1899); Eddie (1902); Eva (1903); Irene (1904); Robbie (Shai Lai, 1906); Jean (1908); Grace (1910); and Florence (1915). In her day-to-day relations with her children, Clara was passionate – scolding and hugging equally spontaneously. More formally, in bringing up her children to love and revere her co-wife, in observing Buddhist, Confucian and Taoist practices, precepts and rituals, Clara followed Chinese custom, but in other ways, particularly education, Western influences prevailed. Indeed, as her daughter Irene (now Dr Cheng) puts it, 'Mamma wanted us to reap the maximum advantage from our dual heritage.' While Jean (now Gittins) writes, 'She aimed at giving us the cream of the two cultures and taught us to follow in the best traditions of west as well as east.'

It was not customary in China, and therefore in Hong Kong, at the turn of the century to educate daughters – 'it is virtuous for a woman to be uneducated', was the traditional value. Clara did not accept this for her daughters. Her own education had been sketchy. Though she had some schooling in China at nine, she did not like it and was allowed to stop. But during the mourning period for her father, she taught herself to read and write. She could, thereafter, write when necessary; in practice, tutors for her children lived in the house and acted as her secretaries, and later her daughters wrote letters for her. Indeed, Victoria, the eldest, did more than that and often took her mother's responsibilities and anxieties on to her own shoulders.

The younger girls were initially educated by Chinese tutors and English governesses. Later they went to the English-language Diocesan Girls School. This choice was purely educational, for it risked the children of a committed Buddhist coming under Christian influence. Clara had considered sending her daughters abroad to university, then an unprecedented step; but in 1921 the University of Hong Kong (founded in 1912) began to accept women undergraduates. Irene was the first Hong Kong born woman graduate, and Eva the first woman in the medical school.

Western influence was also apparent in the less formal upbringing of Clara's daughters. Under an ordinance of 1904, the Peak area of the colony, where the air in the hot, humid summer was several degrees cooler than below, was, in practical terms, reserved for non-Chinese. Clara, learning that fresh air was essential for the health of her children, did not rest until Ho Tung was exempted under the ordinance and, in

1906, he moved his children and their mother there. (Margaret stayed on in 'Idlewild'; until her death, Chau Yee-man lived in Caine Road). Clara had been told that riding develops 'good posture'; thus, two donkeys were imported from North China. And she considered boots necessary because they 'were good support for our ankles'. At home, the children lived a simple, even frugal life. Clara did not wish them to become accustomed to luxury in case their circumstances changed. Independence was encouraged so that the girls need not necessarily rely on the support of a husband. In these ideas, progressive for their day, it is likely that Clara found little support from her husband.

The independence and profession of Eva, who qualified as a doctor and remained unmarried, may have been Western but her calling was just as easily a manifestation of the family's Chineseness. As Irene put it, 'Mamma set high ideals for us. She wanted us to dedicate our lives to the service of humanity, and at the same time live up to the good Chinese virtues which she herself believed in.'

Clara came from a Buddhist family; and she herself became increasingly devout. She was concerned, too, to fulfil Confucian obligations of filial piety. When her only surviving brother left Hong Kong, she undertook, unusually for a daughter, responsibility for the Cheung family by moving the paternal ancestral tablets to her own home. She exemplified, as Irene explains, 'the non-exclusive nature of the Chinese religious outlook'. Clara espoused the 'Eight Virtues' of Confuciansm and attained, by the time of her death, the 'Five Vows' of Buddhism.

As early as 1896, following the death of her mother-in-law the year after her marriage, Clara travelled with her co-wife to Ting Hu Mountain, Kwangtung Province, to have prayers said in the deceased's memory. But the severe illness of her husband between 1910 and 1913 (when he was bedridden) and the death of her own mother in 1912, strengthened her faith and determination to explore Buddhism more deeply. She became then a vegetarian and started her travels to the Five Buddhist Mountains in China – an achievement which is described in *Travelogue on Famous Mountains* (1935; in Chinese). The work, begun by the first household tutor from her oral testimony in 1920, and revised and brought up to date after her later travels by another, also traces the development of her religious thought. In the latter, she was helped by her two Buddhist 'Masters', high priests from the Putu Monastery in Ningpo (Ningbo) and the Ch'i Hsia Monastery east of Nanking.

Her pilgrimages within China (and in 1929 to India and Burma) and her own development were only part of the manifestations of her Buddhist faith. It was she who was responsible, with the help of Sir Shouson Chow, for obtaining a government permit for the first public Buddhist lecture series in Hong Kong, held in Ming Yuen, a hall in North Point. In the 1920s, there was a revival of Buddhist interest in Hong Kong in which she played a leading, indeed key, role. In 1922 the High Priest of the 'Gold Mountain temple' in Chingkiang, known as the 'Living Buddha', visited the monastery on Lantau Island off Hong Kong. Clara planned to go to hear him preach but because of piracy in local waters and banditry in the hills, her husband dissuaded her, suggesting instead that she invite the priest to stay at 'Idlewild'. Subsequently, many members of the priesthood visited Hong Kong and often stayed at one of the Ho Tung homes. Some of the activities attracted thousands of the faithful.

Clara's Buddhist faith and activism, and views on education, particularly for women, led in the early 1930s to a further development; once again, Chinese and Western influences came together. When her own children were at school, it was not unusual for her to ask a servant, particularly a man, whether he sent his children to school; the answer was usually that the sons did go, but not the daughters. Then she would give a 'little lecture on the importance of women being able to read and write'. In 1927, during a visit to England with her husband and Eva and Irene, she visited Dr Barnardo's Home for orphans. The visit started her thinking and she became convinced that one of the best ways of helping both Buddhism and the poor of Hong Kong was to develop free educational facilities for girls; boys already had some access to free schooling. Educated women would be better able to understand Buddhism and pass on their understanding.

Thus in 1930 she set up two Po Kok primary schools for girls – one in Macau and the other in Hong Kong. In 1932, she established the Po Kok Buddhist Seminary for Women in the New Territories. She dreamed eventually of building a temple to serve as a centre for religious activities. In 1931, to celebrate his and Margaret's golden wedding anniversary, Robert Ho Tung gave his wives HK$100,000 each, thus allowing Clara to begin realising her dream; but finding the right building site took much time and effort. In the end she bought just over 12,000 square feet in Happy Valley and hired an architect. The architecture was to be Chinese; internal features were to be Buddhist, and the deities were always to be smiling rather than ferocious. Backing on to the 'Three Precious Buddhas' was a seated Kuan Yin, the Goddess of Mercy, and her attendants. Supervision was not enough: the wood carvers from China found that their workroom was the garage at 'The Falls' – Clara's home in the late 1920s and 1930s.

The Tung Lin Kok Yuen – a Buddhist temple complex into which the Po Kok School and Seminary were moved, together with a library of Buddhist texts – was opened on 10 May 1935. Clara herself paid for the board and lodging of the seminary students, and on one side of the upstairs hall for ancestors was a small suite of rooms for the superintendent. Until her death, Clara filled this role, visiting the Tung Lin Kok Yuen nearly every day, drafting the rules and regulations, handling the administration of the school and supervising the selection of students. It is said that she always gave preference to the poor, while her staff favoured the brightest. She also travelled most weekends to visit the Po Kok School in Macau and she contributed financially to the largest Buddhist temple there, the Kung Tak Lam, as well as other charitable organisations, Buddhist and non-Buddhist. It should be noted that there was never enough money to pay for Clara's ambitions, which created constant anxiety. She borrowed extra money from her husband and had help, for example, from her daughter Victoria.

Other charitable interests over the years included being a member of the committee of the Hong Kong Society for the Prevention of Cruelty to Animals and building a dogs' home to be run by the Society. Calls for help from hospitals and schools were always responded to with sympathy. Indeed, Clara's interest in medicine was profound; as well as nursing her immediate family, relatives and friends with dedication, she was often invited by doctors to watch and participate in operations.

An example of her commitment to education, to women and to the welfare of China and its people was her response to an appeal from her daughter Irene when she was a lecturer at Lingnan University in Canton (Guangzhou). Irene and her colleagues saw the need there for a junior experimental high school. Clara provided the necessary funds and thereafter invited pupils of the 'Practical Middle School' to visit her in Hong Kong.

The Ho Tungs' involvement with China gathered a momentum outside Clara's Buddhist commitment in the 1920s. As early as 1898, the reformer K'ang Yu-wei had taken refuge at 'Idlewild'. In 1923, Robert Ho Tung proposed a round table conference of war-lords – a project which preoccupied both Clara and her husband during the 1920s. In 1923, for example, the two of them went to Shanghai to try to persuade Marshal Wu Pei Fu to participate, and they went to China on a similar mission in 1929, visiting Marshal Chang Hsueh-liang in Manchuria and Yen Hsi-shan in Shansi (Shanxi) Province.

Early in 1937, with the threat of war between China and Japan, the Ho Tungs' commitment to the welfare of China was further fuelled. During a visit to Nanking, where the National Government was then based, Clara and Robert were received by Chiang Kai-shek. With the outbreak of war later that year, Madame Chiang set up national women's organisations which soon had branches in Hong Kong. Clara was elected vice-president of the Hong Kong Chinese Women's Relief Association. (Mme Sun Fo, daughter-in-law of Sun Yat-sen, was president and Mme T.V. Soong, chair.) Later, Mme Wu Teh-ch'ing, wife of the Governor of Kwangtung Province, came to Hong Kong and organised the New Life Association, of which Clara became vice-chair. Clara had suggested the suspension of classes at the Buddhist Seminary so that students could make padded jackets and trousers, and bandages and dressings for the soldiers at the front, work in which she participated;

now, she and Mme Wu began calling on patriotic members of the Chinese community to solicit funds.

At the end of 1937, 50 wounded soldiers were sent by a relief organisation in Shanghai to be helped to their homes in the adjoining province of Kwangtung by the Hong Kong sister organisation. Clara was in the forefront of visiting the soldiers and raising funds for them. Her last public appearance was for that purpose on 1 January 1938; four days later she was dead.

Her death, from complications arising from asthma at the age of 62, was unexpected, though in retrospect it was obvious that she had taken on too many commitments, including regular visits to Macau to supervise the Po Kok School there. Her health throughout her life seems to have been dominated by a difficulty in walking common amongst Chinese women because of bound feet and being confined to their homes. Both Margaret and Clara's feet were bound, at least until Alicia Little's visit to Hong Kong in 1900 and the meeting of the Natural Foot Society arranged at Government House by Lady Blake. Both Ho Tung wives took an active part in that campaign. Irene mentions family picnics after that when her mother had to be carried part of the way by chair,

Margaret Ho Tung, first wife of Sir Robert Ho Tung

rather than walking with the children, and at 51 Clara, who had a 'nervous heart' and often suffered 'badly from palpitations', was seen as an elderly woman who might slip on the ice in London. It was Margaret, her co-wife for 43 years and conversant with traditional rituals, who arranged the details of Clara's elaborate Chinese funeral.

In preparing her will, Clara's first thought had been for the Tung Lin Kok Yuen, and she left her estate to its benefit in perpetuity, requesting in addition the establishment of a board of directors to guide and direct its external policy.

The board still includes two of Clara's children, Irene and Robbie, and two of Victoria's children, Victoria (later Lady Lo) devoting herself to the project during her life (d. 1992). The board has had to ensure that Clara's creation moved with the times. In the 1930s the land surrounding the Tung Lin Kok Yuen was mostly agricultural; today Happy Valley, apart from the racecourse, is fully urbanised. The Po Kok School was the first Buddhist school in the colony; today there are between 50 and 60 Buddhist educational institutions. Then there was no schooling for poor girls; now there is education for all.

In 1951 and 1954, new premises were opened alongside the primary school, allowing the establishment of a vocational school; that gave way to a secondary school. Between them the two schools now have about 800 pupils, compared with 100 at the beginning. Although girls no longer have to be poor, because the schools are government subsidised, Chinese family values are still instilled. The seminary was phased out, as demand for such education diminished, and a college allowing students a second chance to take exams also outlived its usefulness. But the temple, saved from harm during World War II by Clara's successor and former support, Lam Ling-chun, remains unchanged, still providing inspiration and, more than ever, a haven to Hong Kong's Buddhists. A ceremony is held there each year on the anniversary of Clara Ho Tung's birth (the 22nd day of the 11th lunar month) in her memory and to celebrate her legacy to Buddhism and Chinese culture.

Commissioned entry for Chinese Women's Encyclopaedia still in preparation, written November 1992.

BIBLIOGRAPHY

Cheng, Irene, *Clara Ho Tung: A Hong Kong Lady, her Family and her Times* (Hong Kong, Chinese University Press, 1976).

Gittins, Jean, *Eastern Windows – Western Skies* (Hong Kong, South China Morning Post, 1969).

Ho, Shai Lai, 'Supplementary Notes', published privately in Chinese.

Travelogue of Famous Mountains, published privately in Chinese.

The Tung Lin Kok Yuen and Po Kok Vocational Middle School (brochure, 1954).

OTHER SOURCES

Dr Irene Cheng (née Ho Tung)

Jean Gittins (née Ho Tung)

Peter Hall

General Ho Shai Lai (Robbie)

Vera Hui (née Lo, Victoria's daughter)

Lo Tak-shing (Victoria's son)

Carl T. Smith

Yip Shuk-ping, Principal, Po Kok School for Girls, Tung Lin Kok Yuen

CHINA AND HONG KONG

CHAPTER 17

THE NEW CONCUBINES
What is to be Done?

The girl was 15 when she sold herself as a concubine. Her father had been a hawker, selling his wares from a pole across his shoulders in a village outside Canton (Guangzhou). He and her mother were dead and she had responsibility for her siblings. So the concubine gave the money to a relative and left for her new life in Australia.

Her new husband's wife had come specially to his home area from their fruit farm near Perth. After many years of marriage, she had to accept that she would not have children. Her husband, Lei Yok-lan, must, therefore, take a concubine. The wife had already found a suitable girl but she had a mole on her forehead, and that signified death to a future husband. That girl had to be rejected.

Lei Yok-lan himself had left his village near Canton at the end of the nineteenth century to seek his fortune. Passing by Singapore, he had followed up an introduction and caught the fancy of his future wife's father. Although Lei Yok-lan was impoverished, and the father was rich, he had arranged for the young man to marry his daughter. Soon thereafter, Lei Yok-lan left for Australia.

The wife waited some years in Singapore for Lei Yok-lan to send for her. When he did not, she set out for Australia and found him. He had not been successful, but she was a strong woman and soon they had bought 100 acres of land and started to develop the orchards which, by the time the concubine arrived, were prospering. And the Chinese couple were well-established in their local community.

The wife had forfeited her own education because she was afraid of school. The concubine had started school in her own village; now, known as their niece, she was sent by her new husband and his wife to continue her education.

China was always home, however, so it was natural that a base should be established back in Canton. There, the wife opened a hotel which soon became profitable. And there the concubine had two children who grew up knowing the wife as *Daai-ma* (mother).

In October 1938, the Japanese took Canton. Mary, the daughter of Lei Yok-lan and the concubine, three years old then, remembers the noise of the bombing in the days before the city fell. At about this time, a legal dispute between the concubine and *Daai-ma* came to a head. The concubine was thrown out of the house. But not, of course, her son and daughter; from their birth they had belonged to *Daai-ma*.

As the Japanese closed in around Canton, *Daai-ma* took the concubine's children and left to join her husband in Australia. Mary met her father for the first time. He had cancer and was dead within a year.

The Pacific War indirectly affected the family of *Daai-ma* because of the shortage of labour. The once prosperous orchards fell into decline, though the railway still ran past the farm and the train stopped there every other day to pick up the fruit that *Daai-ma* and her children managed to produce.

Mary went to school, but she also worked while her schoolmates played. She washed the fruit and put it out on racks; and she looked after the poultry and pigs and helped with the housework. *Daai-ma* spoke only pidgin English and brought the children up traditionally, to respect authority. For childish misdemeanours, Mary was beaten. On at least one occasion she was tied in a sack and taken to the water's edge where *Daai-ma* threatened to drown her.

At 21, a university student, but still terrorised by *Daai-ma*, Mary left her for good. Four years later, *Daai-ma* was knocked down and killed by a car while on her way to her solicitor to cut her intransigent daughter out of her will. Overcoming her past, Mary later found fulfilment in her work as a teacher and happiness with a non-Chinese husband

Back in Canton, the concubine, Mary's 'birth mother', had also managed to escape the Japanese in 1938. In Hong Kong, she entered the service of a merchant, part Chinese, part Indian, his wife and three children, as an amah. When the Japanese invaded Hong Kong in

December 1941, they encouraged the Chinese population, many of them refugees from war-torn China, to leave. The concubine's new family went to Macau where they spent the war, returning to Hong Kong after August 1945.

The concubine's position in her new family was more ambiguous than in her last. Early on, the man raped her, and thereafter continued to use her for sex. She had two more children, a son and a daughter, from this union. The wife had no choice but to tolerate the situation.

After the war, the concubine got a job, thanks to her Australian education, as a telephonist. She began to make a little money. Some she gave to the father of her second children for their keep. Most of this money he used for the children of another mistress. Some money the concubine used to invest in property.

There came a time when she was financially secure and then she was sought in marriage by a Shanghainese dance instructor. With him she had a son. She told him that her second daughter was her niece. Her new husband tried to seduce the girl and, later, the Filipina domestic helper; the latter was framed and sacked for refusing to comply.

After the legal marriage in Hong Kong, the concubine discovered that her husband already had a legal wife and family in Shanghai. When he died after more than 30 years of marriage, he willed the concubine's properties to the sons of that earlier union.

Recently, the concubine had a stroke, so that not only has her short-term memory deteriorated with age, but she has also forgotten the details of her past life. That may be as well. As some consolation, her five children, all but one living abroad, return from time to time to her side. She can afford to be looked after by a domestic helper.

———————

The personal story reccounted to me by Mary is by no means an isolated example. Any one of your Chinese women friends can tell you a similar one.

Peggy's grandfather had a wife and two concubines. Between them, the first two women had 18 sons. The third, Peggy's maternal grandmother, had one daughter. She was much loved by everyone, not only because she was the only girl among so many boys but because, as a girl, she posed no threat to anyone's inheritance. This worked against her when the patriarch died. As the mother of a girl, this third woman received no inheritance, and was thus left without support. The child, Peggy's mother, later abandoned her own children; the family never heard from her again following her disappearance.

Elizabeth's father had seven 'wives'. Her mother was number four. She became pregnant at 16. A dream said that she should give the expected child to childless number three wife in order to be well treated. The boy born to her did not know who his birth mother was until he was 17. Meanwhile, as the son and heir, he had treated her with some disdain, a feeling he was unable later to shake off. Ironically, his birth mother's own background was similar: her own mother, about to remarry, had given her to another family who already had seven children.

Anne's father had only one wife for some time, but he had a succession of mistresses, not concubines. Eventually, he took a concubine, who was introduced into the family, and the family home, in the formal way, offering tea on her knees to the wife. She became second mother to the three daughters already born, and to the son and daughter still to be born to the wife. Indeed, the second mother looked after the five children to a greater extent than the wife. She had no surviving children of her own. Now, both wife and concubine are dead; and the 87-year -old man has a relationship with a woman who is neither wife nor concubine, but who was his mistress while the others still lived.

Anne's father did not take a concubine to have a son, although he did not have one then. He described his relationship with women as 'ambitious'. Her mother described her position as one 'without choice'.

Before the war, Daisy's father had a wife and children in China. He came to work in Hong Kong, and took a second wife, Daisy's mother. He spent the war years in Hong Kong with his new family, and it was only after the war that each family learned of the other's existence. In that case, each considered herself the wife; Daisy's mother was not a concubine. Her father certainly saw nothing untoward in having a wife in two places, for in each he needed a woman to look after him. In China, his wife had been chosen for him; he chose his Hong Kong wife.

The friends (late twentieth century Hong Kong women, not feminists) who have told me about their families pity their mothers and have ambivalent feelings about their fathers.

My informants have read and commented upon my original draft, as is my practice. Some names have been changed, but all details are as accurate as family knowledge allows. I thank my friends here rather than by name in the acknowledgements; their discretion is for the sake of their family rather than themselves.

The ethics of re-creating women's history, particularly via oral testimony, has raised its head. At the time they talked to me, some informants did not know that I was mentally recording what they told me; nor was I cold-bloodedly doing it, for it has become second nature to me. What is more, I am constantly trying to persuade informants to make their own record. Some theorists may suggest that I am 'appropriating the narrative' of my informants and their mothers and grandmothers. That is, not just using the details of their lives, but putting my own heavily-laden interpretation on them.

I believe that I am healthily obsessed with the recording of the minutiae of women's past, the raw material, which has formerly been lost or neglected, so that it is less likely to be in the future.

What is more, providing my informants with a draft is no mere formality; in this piece I considerably changed the slant of what is to follow – which is not about her family – based on the input of one informant. And, as the following shows, I am also trying to make my own sense of history in practical terms, as a women's activist.

These stories of woman as commodity are part of the pattern of the history of Hong Kong and the surrounding region. Following the taking of Hong Kong Island by the British in 1841, many mainland men came to find work in the Colony, leaving their families in China. Prostitution flourished (see Chapter 12, 'It Made Their Blood Boil');

those who could afford it had second families in Hong Kong. This was a variant of the tradition of concubinage within China.

Concubinage became illegal in China after the 1950 Marriage Law (see Chapter 8, 'The Seventh Gentleman'), and in Hong Kong in 1971, following a campaign by women's groups. The campaign lasted for at least 20 years and was finally successful because Ellen Li, the first woman Legislative Council member (1966-1972), managed to insinuate the bill through the Council. She persuaded members that it was not for 'our generation but the next'. Even then, a year of grace – time to launch objections – was allowed after the bill was passed before it became law.

Grandmothers, mothers and daughters continue to be dogged by the past but, with the apparent change in family mores, reinforced by law, they have begun to benefit from a new freedom and respect. It may only have been a temporary reprieve, however.

As 1997 approaches and economic ties between Hong Kong and China develop and strengthen, many Hong Kong businessmen travel frequently to China. Increasingly, they are setting up second families there – an ironic reversal of nineteenth century practice. This trend – which is now in the open – has many implications.

Ellen Li (1966), Legislative Council member 1966-1972

Some villages over the border in Mainland China have taken on particular characteristics – a change that is both reported in Hong Kong's press and vehemently denied from China when it is. But a friend, formerly in Hong Kong government service, has written me an account which is irrefutable of his own visit to Sui-foo Chuen. Its local nickname is 'Yi-naai chuen', or 'concubine village' (literally number two wife village).

The new concubines, who are well dressed and take care of their appearance, are much in evidence. The village is well-supplied with hairdressers, beauty salons, clothes shops and, like much of Shenzhen, is generally prosperous. But it also has a VD clinic on almost every street (probably more than 30 or 40 in all); many of the clinics are unregulated and staffed by unqualified people.

He ends his account: 'The friend who took us through the village introduced us to an old school friend of his, who is now a concubine (or a "number three wife" as she jokingly put it). She was completely nonchalant about the whole business.' The visitors 'didn't think it appropriate to ask her any questions about it'.

Not having access to women such as number three wife, I feel it is somewhat invidious for me, too, to probe the situation from her point of view. But from that of Hong Kong's women, it is not enough to stop here, simply to tell a story.

The fact that Hong Kong women are now less biddable than their grandmothers must be positive. But a Hong Kong man who has taken a mistress in China may justify his action – via a radio phone-in – by throwing her 'independent' attitude in the face of his wife. She may be less ready to put up with 'unfaithfulness', more ready for divorce, but that too plays into the hands of the new mistress over the border. Previously, a legal marriage – a piece of paper – was not important; now it is, for it may be the means of emigration to Hong Kong or elsewhere. On the other hand, concubines were previously somewhat protected by culture and law in China, Chinese overseas communities and Hong Kong; that is not so today.

Several factors now put pressure on the first wife to seek a divorce when she finds out about the other liaison; and even when one does not exist, the two-way traffic with China and intense public discussion about the problem breed suspicion. However easy divorce may be legally, and however valid a wife's reasons may be, the implications are hardly happy for society or the individual. Solutions that have been put forward to protect the wives of Hong Kong include rather unrealistic legislation to prohibit men from taking concubines in China.

If Chinese women in Hong Kong today and tomorrow are not to relive the past of their grandmothers, they need to look to their own solutions, within themselves, as well as from society. The importance of the raising of women's consciousness of themselves as women and, thus, the raising of their self-esteem, cannot be overestimated. For some, self-esteem comes automatically from their education and consequent job opportunities. But there are many women who have missed out on these advantages, often because of traditional attitudes towards the education of girls, as well as financial constraints. While recent research shows that slightly more women are today entering tertiary education than men, there is a considerable swathe of women who have missed out almost entirely on formal education. (Six years' compulsory primary education did not come in until 1971; three years of compulsory, universal and free secondary education was not introduced until 1978.) Their requirements need to be more adequately addressed through later education, training, retraining and job opportunities protected from age discrimination.

Nine women in my present English class for Chinese housewives have dreams, even at this stage of their lives, of going to university. How can these aspirations be realised?

At the same time, the community needs to strengthen practical and moral support for single mothers, including divorcees, and provide more adequate child care facilities. It also needs to devise strategies for making the equality of women and men acceptable, indeed sought after, by men.

History is not only about the past; and one woman's story is mirrored around and beyond her.

First draft written November 1994.

CHAPTER 18

INTERNATIONAL WOMEN'S DAY
8 March 1995

Another skirmish won: the women of Sheung Shui – a walled village in Hong Kong's New Territories – are to have the vote. In the elections for village representatives last December, half the 5,000 population were, as usual, excluded. Those elections have now been invalidated, and new ones are to be held.

This move by the government is particularly welcome and appropriate as 8 March approaches, for International Women's Day grew out of demands for votes for women. In 1908, socialist women in New York demonstrated on that day for universal suffrage. (They had been inspired by women garment and textile workers who marched against poor conditions in 1857 – a march brutally broken up by police.)

The state of Wyoming had enfranchised women as early as 1869, but it was not until 1917 that New York State gave women the vote, and 1920 that general female suffrage was secured by the 19th Amendment to the United States' Constitution.

In Britain, the concerted campaign for female suffrage started in 1906, and was unsuccessful until 1918, when women over 30 were allowed to vote. In 1928, all women over 21 were enfranchised.

The earliest country to give women the vote was New Zealand, in 1893; Finnish women were enfranchised, by the Russian Tsar, in 1906, and Norway followed suit in 1907.

The significance of the 1908 demonstrations in New York was their working-class focus; 8 March, therefore, caught the imagination of socialist women leaders.

In 1910, Clara Zetkin, newly established leader of the International Socialist Women's Movement, moved a resolution at their second conference that any kind of limited suffrage campaign was 'a falsification and humiliation of the very principle of political equality for women'. She proposed that 8 March be designated International Women's Day. Its slogan was to be 'Universal Suffrage'.

Starting in 1911, therefore, and continuing up to the beginning of World War I, parades and demonstrations were organised by working women in Europe's major industrial cities.

In Russia, where the first successful socialist revolution was to take place, Women's Day was slower to get off the ground. Alexandra Kollontai, later a minister in the Bolshevik government, recalled that in 1911 'the Party leadership saw no importance in holding a women's day, and my insistence provoked no response'.

But in 1912, several prominent women in Bolshevik and Menshevik circles pressed the issue and Party approval was obtained. On 7 March 1913, *Pravda*, the Party organ, spoke out against feminism, but the following day Kalashnikov Exchange in St Petersburg was packed by women

Alexandra Kollontai — a family archive photograph taken in 1908

for a meeting disguised, for the sake of the authorities, as a 'Scientific Morning Devoted to the Woman Question'.

One participant, A.N. Grigoreva-Alekseeva, movingly described her life as a woman textile worker, and although the police, angered by the 'unscientific' tone of the meeting, tried to disrupt it, a resolution calling for universal suffrage was passed.

The following year, Tsarist authorities reacted by arresting Bolshevik speakers on the evening of 7 March in an effort to disrupt planned events. Konkordia Samoilova recalled that on her way to prison she was asked, 'Why, Madame, did you try to gather all our women together? Are you, like those foreign "suffragettes" as they are called, desirous of throwing bombs at the government?'

The irony of that question became apparent in 1917 when Women's Day in Russia became historically significant and memorable, almost by chance. Meriel Buchanan, daughter of Britain's ambassador to wartime Petrograd, describes what she was told on the drive from the station to the embassy:

> The trouble had begun – even as my father had said it would – by a woman in one of the long food queues throwing a stone at a baker's window. That had been on Thursday, March 8th, and it had been the signal for the long-restrained discontent to flare into open rebellion.

What Ms Buchanan did not realise then or later was the exact confluence of events: on that day, 90,000 Petrograd workers were on strike; 28,000 at the Putilov ironworks were idle because of a wage dispute; and socialists were celebrating International Women's Day. And on that day, Petrograd shops ran short of black bread.

The stone through the baker's window was a spark falling on piles of kindling. Women trying to feed their families, strikers, other disaffected workers, and Socialists, many of them women, got the taste for demonstrations that rumbled on until, five days later, the Russian Tsar was forced to abdicate.

Following the Bolshevik Revolution, Women's Day became a permanent feature of the revolutionary calendar. Anna Louise Strong, the radical American journalist, wrote of 1926:

> While waiting for the trip to the Donetz I visited Kiev, and spoke on March 8th, International Women's Day, to a great throng of women – worn, intent faces under faded shawls. I spoke in very bad French which was probably worse translated. But the band played and the women applauded, thinking me a remarkable person to have come all the way from America. But I knew that every one of those women was more remarkable than I. Every one of them had kept house through sixteen bombardments.

Unfortunately, and perhaps not surprisingly, International Women's Day in the Soviet Union was to evolve into a glorified Mother's Day. A scholarly perception of this, through analysing readers for children, is confirmed by Russian-born, Paris-based journalist George St George who wrote:

> I happened to be in Moscow on March 8, 1969. It was Women's Day, one of the most popular Russian national holidays. It is celebrated along the lines of the old Orthodox carnival which took place before Lent; however the holiday now has no religious connotation. No work is done on this day except, paradoxically, by women who slave in their kitchens cooking Russian *blini* (sour pancakes) and receiving male callers who come to congratulate them. Towards the evening it is hard to find a sober man in the country, or a woman not totally exhausted by the routine.

Much earlier, in 1943, Agnes Smedley, another radical American journalist, was to write, 'I did not fail to tell men in the Soviet Union that I had listened to many men make speeches from the tomb of Lenin in Red Square, but only one woman – and that one on International Women's Day.'

In spite of Smedley and St George's justly cynical view of Women's Day in the Soviet Union, the expression of solidarity that had inspired the day, and still persists worldwide, was also revealed to St George:

> But three chambermaids on the floor of our hotel had to stay on duty, so they organized a little celebration in their service room. They had *blini*, smoked fish, mushroom and dill pickles, and, of course, vodka. They invited me to join them, the only male present, and I accepted with gratitude.

In China, International Women's Day was celebrated for the first time in 1924. Then the Kuomintang Party (KMT) connected the idea of women's liberation with revolution and issued a leaflet calling on women to unite and to organise events in Kwangtung, their base, for 8 March.

The leaflet added, 'Please follow the slogans listed below for making placards and leaflets for the demonstrations on that day … (1) Down with foreign imperialism; (2) Liberate China from its semi-colonial status.'

Vera Vladimirovna Vishnyakova-Akimova, a young Russian interpreter, described International Women's Day in Canton (Guangzhou) in 1926:

> During the day we watched a demonstration in which, the press reported, ten thousand women took part, and we read articles in papers dedicated to the holiday. In the evening at the special invitation of the Kuomintang CEC's Women's Work Department we took part in an amateur night arranged by various Chinese institutions. I also had to perform. … There was a really huge crowd. The thunder of applause greeted us.
>
> Our number consisted of several revolutionary songs, including the 'Internationale', unfortunately without

musical accompaniment because it turned out at the last moment that the piano on the stage was so out of tune that literally not a single note was correct. Special success was enjoyed by a living tableau depicting the countries of the world in the form of women wearing national costumes. They surrounded Soviet Russia – the wife of adviser Rogachev in a sarafan and *kokoshnik* holding a red banner. I was made up as a Chinese woman – dressed in pajamas embroidered with dragons and shod in ancient satin men's slippers on high wooden soles. My head swam in a jet-black wig, parted in the middle, with a bang and long braids, fastened from both sides near the ears; the hairdo was not in the least Chinese. I portrayed awakened China and stretched out my hands towards Soviet Russia. No matter how surprising it may seem, the Chinese recognised themselves in me and applauded deafeningly.

From 1931 and the Japanese invasion of North East China, Women's Day had a more obviously nationalist focus. The civil rights lawyer Shi Liang writes of the day that year:

> When women from all walks of life gathered for a celebration meeting, we raised the slogan: 'Free our people first, or there can be no real emancipation for women.' Our action, which had the strong backing of friends in the Communist Party, infuriated the KMT reactionary clique. As we marched from our meeting hall, we were rounded up by gendarmes armed with clubs and truncheons. Many of us were injured.

Soong Ching Ling, widow of Sun Yat-sen, founder of the Chinese Republic, always made a point of being involved in Women's Day. In 1933, she spoke in Shanghai at the inauguration of an anti-Japanese united front organisation. On 7 March 1938, as a refugee in Hong

Soong Ching Ling (left) at the 50th International Working Women's Day in Shanghai, 8 March 1960

Kong, she reiterated her view that 'the liberation of women and of all the oppressed are one'.

In the interior of China during the Sino-Japanese war, women were mindful of Soong Ching Ling's calls. Twenty-five-year-old Tang Cheng-kuo, director of a 1,500-strong Women's Defence Corps, described how:

> Every year, usually around March 8th – International Women's Day – we hold general maneuvers. The girls gather from all the hsien villages, bringing their weapons and enough food for ten days. The meeting place is secret, of course, and is changed from year to year. The last meeting over which I presided before coming to Yenan [Yan'an] was held within four miles of the nearest enemy strong point and only ten miles from the Peiping–Hankow Railway.
>
> We try usually to work out some practical problem. On this occasion our problem was to destroy communications between the Jap strong points at Peilu and Ankuo, about two miles apart. And, if need be, we were to be prepared to fight, too.

The irony of the enthusiasm with which women rallied to the war effort and the revolution was revealed by China's best-known woman writer, Ting Ling, in her 1942 essay, 'Thoughts on March 8', the last occasion on which she was able to write frankly for four decades. Responding to various criticisms of the women at the Communist Party headquarters at Yan'an, she wrote:

> I am a woman myself, and I understand women's shortcomings better than anyone. But I also understand their sufferings. Women cannot transcend their times, they are not ideal, they are not made of steel. They are unable to resist all of society's temptations and silent oppressions, they have all had a history of blood and tears, they have all felt grand emotions (no matter whether they have been elated or depressed, whether they are lucky or unlucky, whether they are still struggling on their own or have entered the stream of ordinary life), and this is all the truer for the woman comrades who have managed to reach Yan'an. How I sympathize with all those women who have been cast down and called criminals! I wish that men, especially those in positions of power, as well as women themselves, would see women's shortcomings in the context of social reality.

The story goes that a couple of months later Mao Tse-tung gave his place in a group photograph up to Ting Ling saying, 'We don't want to be rebuked again on 8 March.'

Another irony attends Soong Ching Ling's words at a Women's Day rally in Hong Kong in 1939 attended mostly by Western women:

> We Chinese are fighting ... at the same time for peace for you. ... If China had surrendered, did not fight but turned into a source of material and manpower reinforcements for Japan, just think, would we be sitting here like this in Hong Kong?

Soong Ching Ling managed to catch the last plane out when the Japanese invaded Hong Kong two and a half years later.

Using International Women's Day to call for peace was a natural evolution and after World War II it became a central issue. The British pacifist Dora Russell describes 8 March 1946, when there were such calls in many towns in Britain. A conference held in London was attended by newly-founded women's organisations from France and Italy. There, too, among general women's rights discussed, those of women in the workplace were specially emphasised.

In Hong Kong, Women's Day has been celebrated since at least 1939. Now the position of working women is as topical as ever. In the anti-discrimination legislation being considered by the Bills Committee of the Legislative Council (Legco), working women are being offered some protection in areas such as equal pay.

This legislation comes as a result of campaigning by a women's coalition which gathered renewed energy and strength at a rally on Women's Day in 1992. But not every point raised on behalf of women at work has been included in the legislation. The government refuses to accept that age discrimination applies particularly to women.

Discrimination against women on the grounds of age is rife in the service industry here. And that industry is the main source of work for many women now that Hong Kong's manufacturing has transferred to Southern China (where labour and land are cheaper).

Recently an investigative journalist confirmed what women's groups have been saying for some time: she claimed to be 40 years old and was refused work in one cake shop not only because she was over 25-30 but also because she was not 'good-looking'. In another she was told that women over 25 were likely to get married or become pregnant. A furniture shop told her that '"over-aged" people did not fit well with the style of their furniture'.

This International Women's Day, the omission from the proposed legislation of age discrimination in the workplace will again be highlighted, harking back to the working women in New York in 1857. And we have come full circle from that 1908 demonstration for voting rights.

The government has issued guidelines to villages in the New Territories in the hopes of persuading them to allow women to vote. But so far only 280 villages out of 690 have accepted the need to change.

Women's groups, including women in the New Territories, and legislators want voting rights, too, to be incorporated into the anti-discrimination legislation.

To this end, a private member's bill has been introduced to ensure that village representatives not elected by universal suffrage become disqualified. The government is considering ... and, meanwhile, taking action piecemeal.

But lest Hong Kong women get too excited by such examples of progress, this is how it was reported in one newspaper: 'The Government has promised to consider legislating for one-*man* one vote rural elections. ...'

Meanwhile, in the village of Sheung Shui, the men and women say *almost* the same thing. Leader Lim Kam-choi, more than anyone responsible for the exclusion of women over the past 20 years, explains: 'The women here want to remain low-profile. They do not want to take part in men's affairs. It is our tradition.'

New Territories women sing for their rights, 1994

While a village woman, preferring to be unnamed through fear of retribution, suggested:

> We were told the election was the men's business, so women were not qualified to vote. None of us dared say a word … because it is our walled villages tradition. It would be best if the Government could intervene and help us.

When the elections are re-held, with women on the electoral roll for the first time, we'll see …

As Women's Day approaches this year, there are other elections to consider – Urban and Regional Council elections on 5 March; then there are Legislative Council elections in September. Our sisters across the world sacrificed themselves for many years to gain the vote for women. The least we can do is make sure we use it.

Alternative ending commissioned by Women's Feature Service:
[Leave out from 'In Hong Kong, Women's Day …' (on p. 268) and replace with:]

What started as a Western celebration of women's demands for change and spread throughout the socialist world, has now been taken up truly internationally.

In India on 8 March 1980, a country-wide anti-rape campaign was launched. This was partly in response to a controversial Supreme Court ruling regarding a 15-year-old girl raped by policemen following a family disagreement over her future.

In Thailand, the issue of prostitution and sex tourism is the most significant exploitation of women, many of them children. In 1984, the bodies of five young girls were found after a fire in a brothel. Thus the 'Anti-Trafficking Women Week Campaign' became part of International Women's Day observance.

On 8 March 1986 in Manila, a huge slogan was painted on a backdrop in Luneta Park. It proclaimed to the thousands of Filipino women representing a coalition of 70 women's groups, 'A nation is not free unless its women are free.'

It echoed Soong Ching Ling's words in China nearly 50 years earlier. And she, in turn, echoed the 1920 words of Margaret Sanger, the birth control pioneer, in New York, the cradle of International Women's Day: 'We are interested in the freedom of women, not in the power of the state.'

First draft written November 1994.

CHAPTER 19

IN THE FOOTSTEPS OF
XIAO HONG

It's 53 years since the death of Xiao Hong (Hsiao Hung). She died in Hong Kong on 22 January 1942, aged 30. There may be some of you who remember that time, a few weeks after the fall of Hong Kong, and the 18 months leading up to it as well. I'm rather counting on that. It's my reason for writing. If I jog your memory, I hope you will let me know.

You may reply, but who was Xiao Hong? I'm sorry you don't know of her. But it's not too late. That's another reason for this letter. If you love reading read Xiao Hong's *Tales of Hulan River*. She finished it here in Hong Kong and the English translation, at least, is still in print.

Xiao Hong was born in 1911 near Harbin in what is now the province of Heilongjiang (Heilungkiang). *Tales of Hulan River* is an autobiographical novel about her childhood. It evokes a world of icy winters and small-town China just after the 1911 Revolution which, as you might imagine, had little impact on that far-off region. Xiao Hong then takes you into the traditional courtyard where families interact.

Her account is vivid and subtle; she wasn't as obviously revolutionary in her writing as her friend Agnes Smedley, the radical American journalist and activist. Because Smedley also wrote a fine autobiographical novel, *Daughter of Earth*, I'm researching a comparative study of the two of them. That's why I need more background material.

Xiao Hong and Agnes Smedley met in Shanghai in the early 1930s. Xiao Hong had fled there from the Japanese invasion of the North East and become a protégée of the greatest of all modern Chinese writers, Lu Xun (Lu Hsun). Agnes Smedley was a friend of his, too. I have not yet come across an account that mentions Xiao Hong and Agnes Smedley together in that context; have you?

In Hong Kong, in 1940-1941, the two caught up with each other. Agnes Smedley's stay in Hong Kong is quite well documented. Xiao Hong's is less clear, though much has been written about her, particularly in Chinese. Accounts tend to contradict each other because contemporaries had or have their own agenda.

I'm not suggesting that no effort has been made to separate fact from fiction. There's a good English-language biography covering her writing in depth, and I'm in frequent touch with the Hong Kong writer and literary researcher Xiao Si. Without her work and commitment over many years, I would have been able to make little headway.

But for my own work, several gaps need still to be filled. So I'm going to sketch for you some areas where I would be glad of your help. And perhaps I can best do that by going with you through Hong Kong in Xiao Hong's footsteps. For me, the places where she lived, moved, died and was buried here are an essential part of exploring her experience and expression.

Xiao Hong arrived here from the Chinese wartime capital Chongqing, probably in the spring of 1940. She was accompanied by her second husband, another well-known North Eastern writer, Duanmu Hongliang (Tuan-mu Hung-liang). He is still alive and lives in Beijing where I've talked to him.

Their home was No. 8 Lock Road, off Nathan Road, behind today's Hyatt Hotel. It was the first place I visited. But both the Balwin Linen & Arts Co. and the Paradise Restaurant are on the ground floor of No. 8 now, and the building is obviously post-war. What was it like then? I can use my imagination, of course; but it would make a difference to know the reality. Even then, The Peninsula hotel was just round the corner.

Duanmu says that their room was adequate, but when Agnes Smedley discovered Xiao Hong there she was shocked. She found her living in poverty and ill health and, being Agnes, she took her off – to Shatin.

Looking at Shatin today, you may wonder how that would have helped. But 52 years ago, the Bishop of Hong Kong, Ronald Hall, had a country cottage, Lin Yin Tai, on top of Tao Fung Shan (Hill). Agnes Smedley had spent some months there following an operation in 1940;

now, in the following spring, she took Xiao Hong there to recover.

I had assumed that the cottage would have long since been pulled down but it's still there, in the same grounds, five minutes' drive from the railway station. Of course, in those days, the sea almost reached the foot of the hill, a river cut through the valley, and market gardens filled the plain where phalanxes of high-rise blocks now march.

The owner for many years of Lin Yin Tai understood my whim to visit the house to try and recapture Xiao Hong's experience. It is very easy, as you stand on a terrace smothered in bougainvillea and giant golden bamboo surrounded by unspoilt woodland. The air is fresh and you cannot quite hear the throb of the traffic.

Company at the house was more mixed than was usual in pre-war Hong Kong. Any memories of the Bishop's unpretentious hospitality would be welcome; or of his radical activities. His biographer does not mention Agnes Smedley or Xiao Hong, nor does he give the whereabouts of the diaries of Hall's secretary, Amy Corney.

Either before or after her sojourn at Bishop Hall's house, Xiao Hong introduced Agnes to her circle of intellectual Chinese friends, most of them refugees from war-ravaged China. Or perhaps Agnes knew them already from Shanghai and elsewhere. It would be useful to know the sequence of events and to have more details about Agnes and Xiao Hong's involvement with this group. Among them was the literary editor Zhou Jingwen (Chou Chingwen), who was also from Manchuria and who befriended Xiao Hong. In a 1975 article he mentions meeting Agnes Smedley at a tea party.

I need more information about Zhou. There seem to be no biographical details in English. What exactly were the 'Human Rights' he talks about having advocated then? Another brief mention talks of him in connection with the North Eastern Democratic League, or People's Movement in the North East. Where did this circle of writers and activists meet? Where was the tea party Agnes attended? Was it in the Gloucester Hotel, or at Gripps in the Hong Kong Hotel? The two used to be side by side where the Landmark building now stands, and both were meeting places within and across racial boundaries.

The office of Zhou's literary journal, the *Shidai Piping*, was said to be at 10 Icehouse Street. I walked down it the other day looking for the number; it turned out to be New Henry House. I faxed a distinguished QC who has chambers there and who might remember the days before the new building. He rang a friend whose father bought the two buildings that stood there before. One was the Stock Exchange, the other a bank. Where in either of those would be the office of a literary journal? What was the street like then? My informant remembers that one of the buildings, perhaps that on Icehouse Street, was rather ugly. Balconies on every floor made it look like a chest of drawers with its drawers open. I'm searching for photographs and memories.

Unfortunately, the air of Shatin did not help Xiao Hong's health. And Agnes Smedley, before she left for the United States in May 1941, managed to get her into Queen Mary Hospital to be treated for tuberculosis. At least Agnes says she did. Chinese friends who have written about Xiao Hong's last year have their own story of who made the arrangements and footed the bill, and of how long she was there.

Hospital records might help, but either the Japanese destroyed them, along with most of Hong Kong's written records, or they have been disposed of in the natural course of administration.

The vegetable garden at Lin Yin Tai, 1995; Xiao Hong and Agnes Smedley lived briefly at Lin Yin Tai in the early 1940s

I went to Queen Mary Hospital to make sure and to get a feel of Xiao Hong's stay there. I had no time to lose because I had heard that major renovation work was in progress. Florence from public relations showed me round the new facilities because there was nothing left of the past. But when she took me to the office of the medical social worker to see if there was a view from the back, I struck lucky. Agnes Wong explained that the block under reconstruction was, beneath the shell, just as it had been. What was more, her father had been treated there for tuberculosis in the 1950s and she would bring in some photographs to show me what the private rooms had looked like.

So I was taken over the piles of rubble and cement and I peered into crevices that Xiao Hong might have known. Later I watched the sun set across the sea, almost as she would have seen it. But she was unhappy there and stories vary as to who helped her to leave and return to Lock Road, and when that was.

If Xiao Hong had remained at Queen Mary Hospital, as her medical needs probably dictated, she would not have been in Lock Road when the bombs started falling at dawn on 8 December 1941. Her movements thereafter are almost as confused, in the memory of contemporaries and in the written accounts, as everything else was. At some stage she and Duanmu made their way over to Hong Kong Island.

From then on, Xiao Hong became increasingly ill. They had to move often and every move became more difficult.

At first they stayed with the Zhous in Alliance Road. Where is or was that? Later they moved to the Si Ho Hotel in Icehouse Street – Alexander House is now on the site. But it was not a long-term proposition, so Zhou lent them quarters in Stanley Street, backing on to 88 Queen's Road Central. That is the Regent Centre today, occupying the double site. But two doors along in Stanley Street is a building that could have been there then. I climbed the 40 narrow concrete stairs that rise almost perpendicularly to a locked door. It was not difficult to think backwards in time. But perhaps you remember the reality?

Then Xiao Hong became so ill that on about 13 January 1942 she was taken to the Hong Kong Sanatorium, Yeung Wo Yuen, in Happy

Valley, founded by Dr Li Shu-fan. There she was operated on for a suspected throat tumour. By this time, Hong Kong had surrendered and transport was almost impossible, but for some reason she was taken all the way from Happy Valley to Pokfulam, back to the government-run Queen Mary Hospital.

The Japanese commandeered that on 21 January and Xiao Hong, after a second operation resulting in failure and infection, was moved to St Stephen's Girls School in Lyttelton Road, a temporary hospital. I need to know more about that. Much has been written about St Stephen's College in Stanley, where a massacre took place on Christmas Day, but not of the other St Stephen's. I have talked to Chan Tse who served there for 37 years, from 1940 to 1977. But she left to return to China on about 1 January 1942. Was it a Red Cross hospital? What happened there from 25 December? The school records no longer exist, though the former headmistress, Kay Barker, is working on a history. Twenty-four hours after Xiao Hong's arrival at St Stephen's, she died there.

Duanmu Hongliang tells of how he then arranged for her body to be separated from the others. She was cremated at the Japanese facilities behind the racetrack in Happy Valley, and her ashes were halved and taken by Duanmu to two locations: the grounds of St Stephen's Girls College and Lido Gardens in Repulse Bay. Do you remember the Japanese crematorium? Most war accounts talk of the mass burial of bodies. How could Duanmu have managed the enterprise logistically? I must talk to him again; I know more and have more detailed questions to ask than previously.

The Repulse Bay ashes were moved to the Star Cemetery in Canton in 1957 because of plans for development of Beach Road. No one quite knows whereabouts in the grounds of St Stephen's Girls School the second half was buried. All Duanmu can remember is that it was on a hill under a tree. But the school grounds and the post-war public gardens separated by a wall are all hills and trees!

A former teacher remembers reading somewhere that a swing was erected on the spot (knowingly or unknowingly) after the war. Since then, a low concrete maze — a game for smaller children — has been built

Xiao Hong's formal grave in the Star Cemetery, Canton

there on a large concrete platform.

To prepare for the anniversary of Xiao Hong's death, Xiao Si and a group of 14 other writers went to Repulse Bay a week or so ago, and then wrote about it in the Chinese newspapers in the days that followed. One of them had been there when the ashes were exhumed in 1957. He walked around, looking up and down, and looking sad, tried unsuccessfully to locate where the site was before the development. Can you identify the exact spot of the Lido Gardens? Have you, perhaps, got a pre-1957 map? The mapping office has not been able to help.

On 20 January, I went to St Stephen's accompanied by the friend, Simon Che Wai-kwan, who has been translating material about Xiao Hong for me. It was my first visit there since I heard that the maze might cover her ashes. This strange structure does not invite you to appreciate her or her writing. It badly needs doing up, or pulling down; and the gardener keeps his brooms there. I laid a flower on a black plastic rubbish bag in a gesture of defiance on Xiao Hong's behalf.

On the anniversary of her death, I went to Repulse Bay to look for where the Lido Gardens used to be. Along the front, there was a

McDonald's, a Kentucky Fried Chicken, a Pizza Hut and all the tackiness of seaside resorts. There is also a giant statue of the Goddess of Mercy, Kuan Yin. Gazing up at her outlined against a bright blue sky I felt, in spite of the surroundings so different from when Xiao Hong was buried there, that the visit had not been a complete waste of time.

Please help me to reconstruct details of Xiao Hong's life and death in Hong Kong. If you can't, please read *Tales of Hulan River*. If you have already read it, I'd like to know what you thought of it. I believe it is an inspired celebration of Xiao Hong's life; it transcends her death.

'Letter From Hong Kong' broadcast, 29 January 1995.

CHAPTER 20

POSTCRIPT TO A BROADCAST

My broadcast was productive to some extent and in roundabout ways. Its text was particularly useful to send to people from whom I was asking help. Some of the results of further research can be seen in the conference paper that follows, such as the extent of Xiao Hong and Agnes Smedley's acquaintance in Shanghai. Other results I shall detail here.

As regards Lock Road, where Xiao Hong and Duanmu Hongliang lived in Hong Kong, Carl Smith drew my attention to the 25th anniversary report of the Wing On Company, which owned it. Photographs taken in 1932 reveal a street quite different from the typical Chinese one I had imagined. Rather elegant four-storey, identical townhouses lined both sides. But by 1940 some of the exterior façades must have been deceptive.

Just before Xiao Hong went into hospital for the last time, on about 13 January 1942, she was living in a flat lent to her by Zhou Jingwen in Stanley Street on Hong Kong Island. What was the street like then? I asked. Emily Hahn, who by subterfuge managed to stay out of Stanley Internment Camp, wrote vividly about wartime Hong Kong in her ironically titled *Hong Kong Holiday* (1946). Stanley Street was soon one of her haunts and that of her Eurasian housemates; she introduces it to her readers on her first visit:

> Before Pearl Harbor I hadn't been aware that Stanley Street existed. It was a small street running along behind the big shops and movie houses that lined Queen's Road, the main business thoroughfare. Just after the surrender, when none

of the shops could open because they didn't have permission from the Japanese authorities, a few Chinese peddlers started to sell things along the curbstone in Stanley Street, which wasn't very public and yet was near the shopping center. Little by little other people set up tables, and you saw where a lot of the town's looted stuff had gone to if you walked down Stanley Street every day. Then the big shop-keepers caught on to it and set up their own booths. After a few weeks Stanley Street was the fashionable place to go shopping, and the rows of tables and booths overflowed into neighboring streets. (pp. 135-136)

Xiao Hong probably heard the hustle and bustle of the early days of this trade from her window; and she must have passed it when she left to go to the Hong Kong Sanatorium in Happy Valley.

The Hong Kong home of Xiao Hong and Duanmu Hongliang (1940- 1941), Lock Road, Kowloon (c1932)

By the time she arrived there, Dr Li Shu-fan had been joined by his family, including his brother Dr Li Shu-pui and the latter's wife, Ellen Li, later well known as Hong Kong's first woman Legislative Councillor. Both Li Shu-fan's book, *Hong Kong Surgeon* (1964), and Ellen Li's autobiography, privately printed in 1993, tell of that period but, not surprisingly, do not give a hint of Xiao Hong, nor can Ellen Li recall her. Ellen left at about this time for the relative safety of Macau, but her husband remained at the hospital and cannot add anything. Nor is it possible with complete accuracy to reconstruct the state of the hospital during the few days that Xiao Hong was there. But, given that she had an operation there which led ultimately to her death, some idea of the difficulties of diagnosing and operating are given by Dr Li; unfortunately, it is not possible accurately to date his account:

> Difficulties multiplied when the city's gas and electric supply was cut. We were then unable to X-ray a single fracture or bullet wound, and had to operate by the light of kerosene lamps. For the sterilization of instruments, gowns, and dressings we had to use firewood and coal, in spite of the resultant ash and smoke. Moreover, as the elevator stopped working, we had trouble enlisting enough stretcher-bearers for the six floors.
>
> In these days of aseptic surgery, it was strange to have to revert to the crude methods of early Listerian times, when surgery was performed with the use of antiseptics. Since we had run out of rubber gloves, the surgical staff had to sterilize their hands and arms by dipping them into an antiseptic solution of biniodide of mercury in crude alcohol, which was effective and available. Wounds were bathed in a solution of carbolic acid or euflavine, since sulfa drugs were scarce and penicillin unobtainable. Despite these crude methods, I had the impression that the wounds healed satisfactorily on the whole. (p. 99)

Emily Hahn suggests that the public services were reconnected towards the end of January.

Xiao Hong moved from Queen Mary Hospital to St Stephen's Girls College, in its guise as an auxiliary hospital, on about 21 January. That led me to speculate about the Girls College during the war, in the hopes of finding someone who remembered Xiao Hong. It was a vain hope; she was there barely 24 hours. But two sources have given conflicting pictures of St Stephen's long-term wartime function, emphasising the pitfalls of historical research, even using primary sources.

One story comes from Miss Baxter, a teacher there before the war, who was interned in Stanley in mid-January. She had her information from Miss Lucy Goodridge, St Stephen's matron, who was allowed to remain at the college throughout the Japanese occupation because she had a Japanese mother. The brief College History suggests that it became a Japanese school and, indeed, after the war the inscription *School of East Asia* remained up outside. Miss Baxter was repatriated two weeks after coming out of Stanley. During that time she had a chance to talk to Miss Goodridge and 50 years later she has written to me to say that the Japanese 'wasted no time in transforming the College from an auxiliary hospital back into a Girls' College "equipped for Japanese teachers to live in"'.

A persistent rumour has suggested that that was a front and that really the college was used as a 'spy school'. But Joseph Tam who, as a male nurse, was transferred from Queen Mary Hospital and stayed at St Stephen's until early 1943, denies this in a letter to the former headmistress Kay Barker. He says that St Stephen's was a relief hospital and 'acted as such for a period of close on five years'. It took in only Chinese Hong Kong citizens. He names three doctors there following the internments of mid-January who could, if contactable, still help: the Irish surgeon Dr G.E. Griffiths, Dr K.D. Ling, a physician, and another surgeon from Hong Kong University, Dr Raymond Lee. (6 March 1995)

Both Miss Baxter and Joseph Tam were right, but their accounts need to be supplemented. Other sources, including the *Hong Kong News* of 25 December 1943, make clear that St Stephen's became the 'School of East Asia' (*Tao Gakuin*) on 1 April 1943. The educationalist Anthony Sweeting describes it as a co-educational institution staffed by Japanese lecturers, and catering for teachers, government employees, and a few other students seeking vocational training and family life education at hardly more than high school level.

I now know more about what happened after Xiao Hong's death. Information comes from a long letter Duanmu wrote in reply to my further questions to him, and from an article he sent me. My letter to him and the text of my broadcast were translated for him by Yu Jing, the law student at Peking University who acted as interpreter for us on my earlier visit. His reply to me, and several accompanying articles, were translated by Simon Che Wai-kwan.

The relevant article is 'Xiao Hong and Some Circumstances After Her Death' by Sha Xunze and Sun Kai, Hulan Teacher Education Special Journal (*Hulan-shifan-zhuanbao*) (1980s?). It draws on a 1949 article in Week End Newspaper (*Zhoumo Bao*) by Ma Chaodong which has not proved possible to find because it does not give a precise date.

In 1942, Ma Chaodong was a health inspector in the Japanese administration with responsibility for collecting corpses and arranging for their disposal. In late January, he and his crew arrived at the Park Road Hospital (St Stephen's Girls College) to collect bodies from the mortuary there. He was accosted by a Chinese man with a North Eastern accent, Duanmu Hongliang, who asked him for help in burying his wife. Duanmu had managed to accumulate $200 towards the burial but had been robbed of it on his way to the hospital. He had no way to prove this and the use of graveyards was restricted. But Ma Chaodong was an admirer of Xiao Hong's writing and he therefore ignored regulations. He did not put her corpse among the others he was taking to be buried in the sportsground off the High Street in Sai Ying Pin.

Duanmu managed, with the help of a Japanese acquaintance, to obtain death and cremation certificates and a permit to claim the dead body. To show respect for Xiao Hong, she was wrapped in a hospital blanket and put separately in the truck with the pile of naked unclaimed corpses. Her body was taken to the Japanese crematorium.

In English-language sources this crematorium – without the above story – was said to be in Happy Valley, but Carl Smith has information in his files about a site acquired by the Japanese community in 1911 in So Kon Po, the next valley along to the east. There, in 1912, they built a crematorium. The *Hong Kong Telegraph* reported that 'A portion of the hillside has been levelled and a handsome wall with ornamental iron work gate has been erected on the north side of the piece of land set aside for the crematorium.' It is now clear that this is where Xiao Hong was cremated.

Cremation was not common among the Chinese, though it had existed in Hong Kong since 1893 when Matilda Sharp (to be commemorated by the foundation of the Matilda Hospital) was cremated. Emily Hahn gives a clue as to why Duanmu, with the right contacts, was likely to persuade the Japanese to help. In her wartime account she reports a conversation with a Japanese officer about cremation and the sending home of ashes: 'That is one reason we sometimes respect the Chinese. They care for their dead bodies just as we do.' (p. 176)

Today the site of the former Japanese crematorium is hard by the Buddhist Association School, just near the Tung Wah Eastern Hospital. I went to see exactly where it had been and if there is any vestige of it left. It seems likely that an Urban Council playground, set back and into the side of the hill, has taken its place. On a winter's day, the place was deserted – just a few gaily painted wooden animals on springs giving any hint of life. The tropical vegetation of the hillside is kept at bay only by a fence. It is easy to use one's imagination.

Duanmu collected Xiao Hong's ashes from there and divided them in two. He has written to me about the half that he took to St Stephen's, after I sent him a contemporary map of the grounds and asked him if he could mark the spot. His letter must surely still any doubts about the story he has consistently told to anyone who would listen:

> I have studied again and again the map enclosed in your letter of Hong Kong in the 1930s showing the grounds of St Stephen's Girls College. However, I cannot remember

through which gate I entered the grounds with the Hong Kong University undergraduate. I can only remember that at the back of the school garden I purposely chose a tree of medium size located on a slope at the northeast. [I believe he means south, a common mistake on Hong Kong Island.] The student found a pick and dug a hole. As I was about to put the jar containing the ashes into it, I found that the hole was not deep enough. So I put the jar aside and continued to dig for a while, removing the soil with my bare hands. Then I put the jar right into the hole.

At that moment, my heart was aching. I originally intended to take that half of her ashes back to Shanghai to be buried beside the grave of Lu Xun, as she had wanted. However, I realised that was an occupation zone and anything could happen. It would be better to bury them somewhere for the time being. Since half her ashes had been buried at Repulse Bay, no one would guess that the other half was here. In this way I could carry out her wishes. Besides, St Stephen's Girls College was now a hospital, the place where she died, and thus a suitable place for her ashes.

I was by then completely exhausted, sitting on the slope watching the student levelling the hole. When he used his feet to press down the soil, I shouted out, startling him. I then told him gently, 'Don't tread. Use your hands.' He seemed to realise what I meant and used his hands to pat for a while. I then levelled the loose soil on top and replaced the patch of turf. It seemed that it could escape notice. I then took a good look around, making sure I could identify that medium sized tree. It was so tranquil there, no people, no sound. I stood in silence for some time. The student attracted my attention and we left together. I was not conscious of how far we walked. I only recall that the student said goodbye at the doorstep of the room which Ma Jianming had prepared for me.

I do wish your broadcast could help find the student.
For I can't even remember his name. (6 April 1995)

I shall try to track down the student. I owe that to both Xiao Hong
and Duanmu.

CHAPTER 21

AFTER READING XIAO HONG

The Experience and Expression of Xiao Hong and Agnes Smedley

INTRODUCTION

I do not read Chinese, so to be asked to present a paper on a Chinese writer is to feel surprised, flattered and ill-equipped. What is more, I do not come from a literary background but from a historical one. I did not ask Tao Jie (Professor of English, Peking University) why she invited me; an answer might have stifled the creative process.

She knew that I had written about Western women in Hong Kong; she knew that I was researching progressive Western women in China between 1919 and 1949; she knew that, to do so, I was beginning to look at Chinese women writers of the period, at their lives where they touched those Western women, and at their writing for what it might reveal about that. She knew that I lived in Hong Kong and that Xiao Hong spent the last 18 months of her life there.

When I received the invitation, I knew that I would have to look at Xiao Hong and present her from a point of view relevant to my own research and experience, and to turn my lack of Chinese into an advantage. I knew that Xiao Hong had been acquainted with Agnes Smedley in Shanghai and Hong Kong; indeed, I had already written two lines about that relationship. I had written even more about Agnes Smedley.

She, I decided, would be my entrée to a distinctively Western, Hong Kong-oriented and personal look at Xiao Hong.

Xiao Hong and Agnes Smedley came from entirely different backgrounds. The former was born into a landlord family in North East China in 1911, the year of the fall of the Qing dynasty, a time when the old feudal and patriarchal ways might be starting to crumble in Guangzhou, but when they were still firmly entrenched in the small town of Hulan River near Harbin.

Agnes Smedley, on the other hand, was born in 1892 into the labouring class of mid-West America at a time of burgeoning capitalism, and her family declined further into poverty during her childhood. And yet, there is more of a link to explore than the fact that they knew each other. Both were highly autobiographical writers. Agnes Smedley was best known in the 1930s for the autobiographical novel *Daughter of Earth* (1929); Xiao Hong's greatest work is the autobiographical novel *Tales of Hulan River* (1941).

Two questions then arose. What could the researcher learn about their lives from comparing their writing? And, what might emerge for more general application from comparing the experience and expression of two women from opposite ends of the earth?

Luckily for me, most of Xiao Hong's work is translated, almost all by Howard Goldblatt (excluding, as yet, her last completed work *Ma Bo-le*). Translations include her first novel, *The Field of Life and Death* (first published 1935), the autobiographical novel *Market Street* (1936), the autobiographical stories 'Hands' and 'The Family Outsider' (a precursor to *Hulan River*), 'Vague Expectations', and her last writing, the story 'Spring in a Small Town'. Goldblatt has also written a literary biography of her (1974). Agnes Smedley's work is all accessible, including the autobiographical *Battle Hymn of China* (1943) (later published as *China Correspondent*, 1984), and there is a biography by Janice R. Mackinnon and Stephen R. Mackinnon (1988).

It was not until I had almost finished my research that I came across an untranslated article by Xiao Hong called 'After Reading *Daughter of Earth* ...' (1938); hence the title of this paper.

Agnes Smedley (centre, back) photographed with her family in 1899

DAUGHTER OF EARTH

Agnes Smedley's *Daughter of Earth* was widely read in revolutionary circles in the Shanghai of the 1930s. She had met Soong Ching Ling in Moscow in 1928 when she had just finished the book, written to get over a period of depression caused by her personal life. Meeting again in Shanghai in September 1929, Smedley wrote on the flyleaf of a presentation copy, 'To Mme Sun Yat-sen, whom I respect and love without reserve as a revolutionary who keeps faith.'[1]

Soon after her arrival in Shanghai, following travels in Manchuria for her newspaper the *Frankfurter Zeitung*, Smedley met writers such as Mao Dun (Mao Tun) with whom she started working on literary translations. It was through Mao Dun that she met Lu Xun in December 1929. China's most revered writer had been reading the German edition of her book and, finding they could communicate in German, they quickly became friends. Now Lu Xun set about finding a Chinese translator and publisher for her.

He was Yang Quan (Yang Chien) who was to become secretary of the China League for the Protection of Civil Rights set up by Soong Ching Ling in 1932 (see Chapter 8). Smedley was one of only two

Westerners to be involved in the League which was forced to disband when her colleague, friend and translator was shot dead by Chiang Kaishek's Blue Shirts in 1933. Nevertheless, *Daughter of Earth* was published in Chinese in 1935, and is still kept in print.

Edgar Snow encouraged his students to read it and some, such as Xiao Qian (Hsiao Chien), did so in English. He wrote in March 1995, 'I agree it is a great book with much influence here.'[2] Li Min was secretary of the Discussion Group of Women's Problems, and another of those students influenced at Yanjing (Yenching) University (now Peking University) in the 1930s by Edgar and Helen Snow. Of Li Min it has been said that she was 'moved by human suffering and injustice', and she recalled *Daughter of Earth* as 'a landmark' in her thinking.[3]

By 1935, Xiao Hong was also a friend and protégée of Lu Xun, and through him she met Agnes Smedley and read her book. Xiao Hong waited to write about her reaction to it until she had read an autobiography by another Western woman – Lilo Linke's *Restless Flags* (1935). Before she had a chance to do so, the Japanese air attacks on Shanghai of August 1937 started and, what with those and the sight of dead bodies in the streets, Xiao Hong felt unable to write at all, or even to discuss what she read or thought with others. Indeed, she found her thoughts led down paths of morbidity and pacifism.[4]

In spite of this, one scene in Smedley's book made a strong impression on her and Xiao Hong's recollection of the passage, and her reaction to it, make a useful start to an exercise in comparison.

Xiao Hong, probably writing in the temporary capital of Wuhan in 1937,[5] noted of Smedley:

> She knew what was meant by a patriarchal society through her father's treatment of her mother. I seem to recall her father coming home in a wagon, bringing with him a piece of flowered cloth, obviously for her mother, to whom he gave it. Because she did not say thank you, her husband said sharply, 'Can't you ever say anything nice?'

This was the life of a woman in a patriarchal society. She then began to cry, her tears falling onto the piece of cloth. A woman cannot receive something for nothing. Even though it is not what she wants, favourable words or tears are necessary. Such tears are useless to the man, but they are still necessary. Shedding tears brings discomfort to the eyes and the face, but the sacrifice must still be made.[6]

Smedley herself had written of how her father returned home having abandoned his family for seven months in order to go off and make money. For the only time that Smedley recorded, he had temporarily made good and arrived unexpectedly well-dressed in a carriage with a doctor companion:

My father brought my mother black silk for a dress and she stood in her loose calico wrapper and bare feet, with her hands folded, gazing at it sadly.

'Now you can't say any more that I ain't done nothin' fer you!' he said to her.

'Ain't you even got a kind word?' he continued bitterly, when she made no answer.

'It's awful purty,' she answered, and her tears began to fall on the gleaming silk.

He turned and tramped into the kitchen and sat down with the white-haired doctor. They passed the whisky bottle to each other.

The next day I heard the sound of angry voices and weeping from the kitchen. With dread I crept in at the door, drawn to something that I knew would torture me. My father stood near the door, accusing my mother of having drunk whisky with the doctor. He accused her of other mysterious things. She was first angry and then wept. He kept shouting at her. Small as I was, I knew instinctively by some loose expression about his mouth that he was lying.

He was making a deliberate effort to keep his voice con-
vincingly angry, and I felt ashamed … as if I myself had
done something.[7]

The scene continues, then the father turns to leave, exhorting his
wife to say goodbye politely to the doctor; and it ends, 'My mother fell
on her knees and cried in uncontrolled anguish: 'Don't go, John! Don't
go! Think of me an' the children.'

Xiao Hong was later to perpetuate her mistaken detail about the
cloth and embroider an aspect of that scene; or did she especially remember Smedley's story because a bolt of cloth was a common present
in China? In the poignant story 'Vague Expectations' (written in October 1938 and published in Chongqing a year after her review of Smedley's
book), a young serving woman expects a soldier to confirm their relationship before leaving for the war front; he does not do so. Earlier, he
had given her 'a bolt of cotton print material, the mere sight of which
brought her to tears afterwards.'[8]

Smedley never mentions that scene of her childhood again, though
her book is full of often violent railing against marriage and the humiliation of women by men – something which she will never put herself in
a position to suffer. Later, too, her own sexuality, as a burden which she
tries to reject, becomes a constant theme, making sense of the words, 'I
felt ashamed … as if I myself had done something.'

Xiao Hong, quite rightly, sees that passage as a key scene in the
Smedley drama. What makes her remember it some time later, is not
only perspicacity, however. Her own father and mother had a similar
relationship. In her piece *At Grandfather's Death*,[9] she wrote of their relationship:

He would laugh and talk with her when he was high spir-
ited, but simply scolded her when he was crossed. Eventually, mother developed a kind of fear towards father. Mother
was neither poor nor old, nor was she a child. Why was she

afraid of father? When I looked at my neighbours, the women were afraid of their men. When I called at my uncle's home, I also found that my aunt was afraid of him.[10]

What is more, Smedley's story struck even closer to home: when Xiao Hong wrote the review, her own relationship with her first husband, Xiao Jun (Hsiao Chun), had reached a nadir from which it never recovered; she was finally to rebel against the physical and mental abuse to which he subjected her and go off with Duanmu Hongliang, their neighbour in the writers' hostel.[11]

What is equally interesting, that review of Smedley's book appears to be one of the few times that Xiao Hong spells out what much of the rest of her writing only infers – the inferior position of women in a patriarchal society, and her disgust with it. Thus, a rather wooden, untypical piece of writing by Xiao Hong, lacking the usual poetry and subtlety, is, nevertheless, crucial.

Any influence by Smedley on Xiao Hong's writing, other than what Xiao Hong herself suggests, is pure speculation. Nevertheless, much of Xiao Hong's work was written after she had read *Daughter of Earth*. What is more, although the style and temperament of the two writers were dissimilar, their experience and, at times, their expression, have some remarkable similarities.

A feature of both childhoods was the experience and observation of physical abuse; both women vividly remembered and recorded it in adult life. How they reacted to it, however, suggests their different background (class, as well as ethnicity) and personality.

Agnes Smedley was physically attacked by her mother as a child, though, before her mother died when Smedley was 16, her sympathy towards her mother as a suffering woman had given some warmth to the relationship. Smedley's mother used to tap her hard with her steel thimble which 'aroused all my hatred'; but she also often whipped her with 'a tough little switch that cut like a knife in the flesh'.[12] Smedley elaborates on her reaction to this punishment:

She developed a method in her whippings: standing with her switch in her hand, she would order me to come before her. I would plead or cry or run away. But at last I had to come. Without taking hold of me, she forced me to stand in one spot of my own will, while she whipped me on all sides. Afterwards, when I continued to sob as children do, she would order me to stop or she would 'stomp me into the ground.' I remember once that I could not and with one swoop she was upon me – over the head, down the back, on my bare legs, until in agony and terror I ran from the house screaming for my father. Yet what could I say to my father – I was little and could not explain. And he would not believe me.[13]

Xiao Hong, in a piece of straight reporting about her childhood, simply observed, 'Whenever my father beat me I would go to Grandad's room and stare out of the window from dusk to late into the night.'[14] She wrote also of her father:

When I was nine my mother died. My father changed even more; when someone would on occasion break a glass, he would shout and carry on until the person was shaking in his boots. Later on, even my father's eyes underwent a change, and each time I passed by him I felt as though there were thorns stuck all over my body; he would cast an oblique glance at you, and that arrogant glance of his would shift from the bridge of his nose, down past the corner of his mouth, and continue moving down. [15]

Xiao Hong's mother was as cruel: not only was she a woman of 'mean words and nasty looks', but she 'often hit and even threw stones at her.'[16] Xiao Hong reports one of her mother's beatings in conversation with 'The Family Outsider', an uncle: "'Look, I was crouching up in the tree, and she came at me with a poker. Look here, she broke the skin on my arm." I dropped the firewood and rolled up my sleeve to show him.'[17]

Both girls were also present at physical violence, or attempts at it. Attempts, in Smedley's case, because in both incidents she records she comes between the protagonists. She tells how she (as her fictional character Marie) hears the angry voices of her parents and hurries to the kitchen door:

> 'Marie, he's goin to hit me with that rope!' Her voice was lifeless.
>
> It was as if she had turned to me for help against him. I saw him standing there, broad-shouldered, twice her size, the tobacco juice showing at the corners of his mouth. He was going to beat her ... he had of late spoken admiringly of men who beat their wives. Still he had not carried out the hidden threat. Something held him back; he had had to curse and accuse much to whip himself up to this point. As I stood watching him I felt that I knew everything he had ever done or would do — he and I knew each other so well. And I hated him ... hated him for his cowardice in attacking someone weaker than himself ... hated him for attacking a woman because she was his wife and the law gave him the right ... hated him so deeply, so elementally, that I wanted to kill ... why hadn't I brought my revolver from my trunk![18]

Marie stands in front of her mother and outfaces her father, and she ends the account, 'Turning without a word, he walked heavily through the alley-gate, his big shoulders round and stooped ... so stooped ... his shirt ragged and dirty ... he stumbled along the railway track. That I should ever have been born!'

The second time, her father returns home drunk and goes for her younger brother Dan with a horsewhip: 'He reached for Dan, who rushed behind me and threw his arms round my waist, keeping me between him and my father. I held the little hands tightly about me.' Again she outfaces him: 'I watched like an animal, ready to spring, for he should never use [the whip]!'[19]

Smedley's character, as is clear from reading accounts of her uncompromising activities in revolutionary and war-torn China, was moulded by these events, so that she writes in the novel words which could equally well have been written when she was 50. 'I was always a person who felt and acted first and thought afterwards';[20] and, 'I do not write mere words. I write of human flesh and blood. There is a hatred and bitterness with roots in experience and convictions.'[21]

Xiao Hong's experiences of second-hand violence were similar, but her reaction was quite different. In *Tales of Hulan River*, an extended section describes the short life and brutal death of 'The Child-Bride'. Because of traditional superstition, the mother-in-law has to tame the twelve-year-old who arrives in her new home full of bounce and vigour. After months of torture, described in ethnographical detail by Xiao Hong remembering when she was about six, the climax nears:

> The young child-bride was quickly carried over and placed inside the vat, which was brim full of hot water – scalding hot water. Once inside, she began to scream and thrash around as though her very life depended upon it, while several people stood around the vat scooping up the hot water and pouring it over her head. Before long her face had turned beet-red, and she ceased her struggles;...
>
> I watched for the longest time, and eventually she stopped moving altogether; she neither cried nor smiled. Her sweat-covered face was flushed – the colour of a sheet of red paper. I turned and commented to Grandad: 'The young child-bride isn't yelling any more.' Then I looked back toward the big vat to discover that the young child-bride had vanished. ...[22]

The next occasion was the beating by her father of his brother You Erbo, 'The Family Outsider'. Xiao Hong continues, after her eccentric uncle has already been knocked to the ground several times:

Father was as efficient as a machine. He still had his reading glasses on, standing with his legs apart, and each time You Erbo came over to him, I saw the corner of the sleeve of his white satin gown move gracefully. ... [23]

The neighbours from the compound gather round to watch as this ghastly performance continues. And adult Xiao Hong later records the end in horribly poetic detail:

Eventually You Erbo's head was pillowed in his own blood, and he got up no more; the hempen wrapping from around his toes was lying beside him, and there was nothing left of the little round gourd from his tobacco pouch but a clutter of shreds to his left. A rooster crowed, but then scrambled off into the distance; only some ducks came over to peck at the blood on the ground. I could see one with a green head and another with a spotted neck.[24]

FEMINIST AND REVOLUTIONARY?

Agnes rails and acts; Xiao Hong (ten years younger) internalises and records. This difference is crucial to two questions that have dogged Xiao Hong over the years. Was she a feminist? And was she a bona fide revolutionary at a time when critical approval depended upon it?

The former question was debated at a 1982 conference in Berlin which resulted in the publication *Women and Literature in China* (1985), edited by Anna Gerstlacher et al. In 'Women and Sexuality in Xiao Hong's *Sheng Sichang*' (*The Field of Life and Death*), Simone Cros-Morea writes, using the revolutionary Qiu Jin (Chiu Chin) as a contrast:

Xiao Hong has been presented as a feminist, which can lead to confusion if the word is understood in the contemporary western sense, and one would be disappointed if one expected to find her as ardent a feminist fighter as Qiu Jin, who devoted her life to undermining male dominance of society. Qiu Jin described explicitly male exploitation and oppression, inciting women to revolt and reject their lot, never losing hope in the crusade that led to her execution.[25]

Another participant, Ruth Keen, in her paper 'Xiao Hong's *Vague Expectations* – a Study in Feminine Writing', declares:

> In the case of Xiao Hong, participants at the conference were not willing to agree whether she could be categorized as a feminist or not. I do not intend to go into this discussion, for one, because I do not believe in putting labels on people, and secondly because feminism is too complex an issue to be adequately analyzed within the limits of this paper. And thirdly, feminism in China of the 1930s was quite a different matter to what it had become in the China of the 1980s, let alone to Berlin of 1982.[26]

The second is a common sense approach, and yet, one would like to be clear, was she, or wasn't she? The same applies to her revolutionary credentials. Mao Dun, for example, writes of this as kindly as he can from his lofty heights as a revered revolutionary writer. Ending his preface to *Tales of Hulan River*, completed when Xiao Hong was a refugee in Hong Kong – poor, sickly and unhappy – he says that these factors 'cut her off completely from the tremendous life and death struggle being waged outside'. And he concludes:

> As a result, although her high principles made her frown on the activities of the intellectuals of her class and regard them as futile talk, she would not plunge into the laboring masses of workers and peasants or change her life radically. Inevitably then, she was frustrated and lonely. This has cast a shadow over *Tales of Hulan River*, evident not only in the mood of the whole work but in its ideological content as well. This is to be regretted.[27]

Ideology has become too muddied a pool to plunge into, but there does seem to be something to be gained from contrasting Xiao Hong with Agnes Smedley. Smedley has always been accepted as a good feminist, socialist and revolutionary. And yet, reading these accounts, one senses not only a difference in temperament (and of culture) but also a difference in style, such that Xiao Hong, read casually or from a set perspective, may mislead.

Note how Xiao Hong ends the scalding of the child-bride (there is still another session before she finally dies):

> A few moments earlier, when the young child-bride was clearly still alive and begging for help, not a single person had gone to rescue her from the hot water. But now that she was oblivious to everything and no longer seeking help, a few people decided to come to her aid. She was dragged out of the big vat and doused with cold water. ...
>
> Someone said that the water had been too hot, while someone else said that they shouldn't have poured it over her head, that anyone would lose consciousness in such scalding water.
>
> While this was going on, the mother-in-law rushed over and covered the girl with the tattered coat exclaiming: 'Doesn't this girl have any modesty at all, laying here without a stitch of clothing on!'[28]

Xiao Hong's laconic style, with a hint of satire, to this reader at least, is quite deliberate; by highlighting the devastations of superstition, patriarchy and feudalism in this fashion, she intends the *reader* to judge, to react; and, in doing so, she suits her tactics to her literary gift and her personality. By that ploy she plays her role as a feminist and a revolutionary. Agnes Smedley demands that her reader share her judgement; she was a polemicist and a revolutionary activist. Xiao Hong had it in her to fire the imagination of revolutionary activists; that was her contribution to the cause. There is more than one way of raising consciousness, feminist or revolutionary, as a necessary precursor to action.

What is more, while Smedley has become a historical character, essentially lovable, and essential reading, Xiao Hong had insights which continue to be relevant to women in the 1990s. There is one in *The Field of Life and Death* which contradicts a criticism made of it by Simone Cros-Morea in her study:

> Since publication coincided with the Japanese invasion of China, one must raise the question of Xiao Hong's motives in including this event in her novel, and ask if it came from a need merely to stay in line with the intellectuals of her time, rather than to make a personal protest.[29]

For the reader coming fresh to the novel in 1995, the 50th anniversary of the end of World War II, and when contemporary concerns include the so-called comfort women or sex slaves, Xiao Hong's marker is prescient. The thousands of Asian women whose life was ruined by the Japanese military were forgotten by the world for half a century; but Xiao Hong pointed the finger at the time and thus set up a lasting monument to them.

It is said, disparagingly, that Xiao Hong had no first-hand experience of the Japanese military in the Manchurian countryside, that she merely borrowed. For once her writing was not autobiographical but she was able to transform information given to her by a male informant (probably her first husband, Xiao Jun, a former guerrilla) and the result decisively contradicts the male critic who suggested that her style prevents the (male) 'reader from experiencing the tension he should feel'.[30]

Two women are talking in the village in which the novel is set; one mentions chickens, 'Then, dropping her voice, she confided to Mother Wang: "Those Japs are vicious and mean! All the young girls of the village have fled. Even the young married women. I heard that a thirteen-year-old girl in the Wang Village was taken away by the Japs in the middle of the night."'[31] Later, Japanese soldiers, accompanied by Chinese policemen, arrive to search Mother Wang's house:

'Who do I have? Nobody.'

With their hands covering their noses, they took a turn through the house and went out, the flashlights in their hands sending out crisscrossing blue rays. As they stepped over the threshold on their way out, a helmeted Japanese soldier said in Chinese: 'Bring her along too.'

Mother Wang heard every word he said. 'Why are they taking away the women too?' She thought. 'Are they going to shoot us?'

'Who wants an old hag like her?' the Chinese policeman asked. The Chinese guffawed at this and so did the Japanese, even though they didn't understand what the words meant. Since others were laughing, they laughed right along with them.

They did, however, take one of the other women and led her away, bent over like a pig. In the faint glow of the flashlights Mother Wang could not tell who the woman was. Before they had even gone past the fence they began having fun with the woman. Mother Wang saw the hand of the helmeted Japanese soldier give the woman's buttocks a swift pat.[32]

As is so often the case, Xiao Hong puts the enormity of what she is describing in the reader's mind through a misleadingly laconic style. It is given an added twist, in today's terms, by the 'swift pat'; there are still too many men who assume that the gesture is inoffensive. We now have some idea of what the sex slaves went through, what that pat presaged.

Xiao Hong was decades ahead of her time on sexual harassment at the most basic level, using words that you might see behind any institutional guidelines today. One of her characters, Golden Bough, leaves the village, following the Japanese incursion, to look for work in Harbin. She falls in with other women workers who swap experiences. 'After a while,' Xiao Hong writes, 'someone said she had been pinched on the cheeks by a messenger at her residence [where she worked]. She said she was so upset over this that she had taken sick.'[33]

Mao Dun refers to Xiao Hong's background which is, of course, crucial in putting together the jigsaw pieces. And, in contrasting it with Smedley's, the 'burden' of class acquires a certain irony, for what could be more sophisticated than that line about Xiao Hong's father as he raised his hand to exercise his feudal rights, 'I saw the corner of the sleeve of his white satin gown move gracefully. ....'?[34] While the emotional Smedley writes of her father, as he retreats from trying to beat her mother, or Smedley would have killed him, 'his big shoulders round and stooped ... so stooped ... his shirt ragged and dirty ... he stumbled along the railway track.'[35] Xiao Hong points to the privileges of feudalism and rejects her father; Smedley bows to the suffering imposed by capitalism and forgives her father.

In the light of the foregoing, Mao Dun's elaboration of his criticism elsewhere in his Preface to *Tales of Hulan River* jars; he writes, 'We are shown no trace of feudal oppression and exploitation, no trace of the savage invasion of Japanese imperialism. But these must surely have weighed more heavily on the people of Hulan River than their own stupidity and conservatism.'[36] The Japanese had not yet arrived in Manchuria when Xiao Hong was a child; and she convinces this reader, at least, that she had a clear perception of ordinary women's concerns of her time.

There is at least one other major example of the difference in the style of Xiao Hong and Agnes Smedley caused by the difference in temperament and background; it is less obviously central to the exploitation of women by men, but it certainly touches on more general revolutionary ideology.

It is impossible not to suspect that in writing her story 'Hands', Xiao Hong was influenced by two separate aspects of *Daughter of Earth*. And yet Xiao Hong probably wrote 'Hands' before reading Smedley. Without knowing the exact months of events, it is impossible to be certain.

'Hands' was part of a collection of short stories by Xiao Hong published under the title *The Bridge*; the stories were written between 1933 and 1936 and published in mid (?) 1936. Xiao Hong seems to have met Smedley in Shanghai in 1936[37] but may not have read *Daughter of Earth* until 1937.[38] Added to which, as I shall show, the two did little more than 'meet' in Shanghai.

'Hands' is based on the time when Xiao Hong attended a girls' school in Harbin, the major city near her home town of Hulan River. Wang Yaming is a peasant girl who, somehow, attends this academy for young ladies. There, she is an intensely motivated scholar but her country background, including lack of nourishment, renders her slow, awkward and different. She is the butt of the bullying and ostracism that only middle-class girls and their teachers can inflict. The motif of the story is Wang Yaming's hands; she comes from a family of dyers and they are therefore 'black' from being perpetually dipped in dye.

By horrible coincidence, Agnes Smedley's mother at various stages of her wretched and impoverished life takes in laundry. At least three times Smedley mentions her hands: 'hands so big-veined and worn that they were almost black';[39] 'her hands, big-veined and almost black from heavy work';[40] and, on her death bed, 'rough, big-veined hands almost black from work, clasped across the thin breast.'[41] While Xiao Hong starts her story, 'Never had any of us in the school seen hands the likes of hers before: blue, black, and even showing a touch of purple, the discolouring ran from her finger tips all the way to her wrists.'[42] And later, 'finally the black-handed girl had to sleep on the bench in the corridor.'[43]

Wang Yaming is sleeping in the corridor because, as Xiao Hong describes, the boarders refuse to have her sleeping next to them; and their attitude is reinforced by the housemother:

> 'As far as I'm concerned,' she said, 'this won't do at all. It's unsanitary. Who wants to be with her, with those vermin all over her body? ... Take a look at that bedding! Have a sniff at it! You can smell the odor two feet away.[44]

Then there is Agnes Smedley herself – a poor girl obsessed by the need to educate herself – at least twice in her childhood and girlhood finding herself at a middle-class education establishment and having similar experiences to those of Wang Yaming. The first time, a doctor's pretty daughter invites the clever little Smedley home to her party, but everything about Smedley is out of place:

> Here I was in a gorgeous party where I wasn't wanted. I had brought three bananas at a great sacrifice only to find that no other child would have dreamed of such a cheap present. My dress, that seemed so elegant when I left home, was shamefully shabby here . . . I was seated next to a little boy at the table.
>
> 'What street do you live on?' he asked, trying to start a polite conversation.
>
> 'Beyond th' tracks.'
>
> He looked at me in surprise. 'Beyond the tracks! Only tough kids live there!'[45]

Smedley leaves miserably before the party ends. Years later, she finds herself in a similar position:

> Those months of study were among the most miserable I have ever endured. The girls in the school often smiled and said things to each other as I passed. I was awkward and crude. I spoke badly – perhaps they smiled at that. Or perhaps it was my clothing.[46]

Again, Xiao Hong is the observer from the background of the oppressor (though she does, as far as is possible, befriend Wang Yaming); again Smedley's reaction grows directly from her background of the oppressed and leads to her future activism. And, if Xiao Hong had not read *Daughter of Earth* when she wrote 'Hands', what can one make of this coincidence?

EXPERIENCE AND EXPRESSION

It is probably not coincidence that both women stamped the major autobiographical works about their youth with the same seal; this time it is possible to suggest, chronologically, that Xiao Hong was influenced by the older woman's writing. She started *Tales of Hulan River* in Chongqing in 1939, and completed it in Hong Kong in 1940. By then she had read Smedley's book. The same running introduction to several sections of their lives is surely a recognition of their inescapable sisterhood.

Smedley, on the first page, describes her book as 'the story of a life, written in desperation, in unhappiness'.[47] She starts part two, looking at the grey sea (of Denmark): 'So was my life in those long years that followed: grey, colourless, groping, unachieving.'[48] And part three: 'To us beyond the tracks the spring brought defeat.'[49]

And Xiao Hong, once she starts the intensely personal part of her book, writes at the beginning of a chapter, 'My home was a dreary one.'[50] And the next one, 'The compound in which we lived was a dreary one';[51] the same words start the next chapter.[52] And then, 'My home was a dreary one.'[53]

In spite of that 'dreariness', there were aspects of Xiao Hong's young life that were happy, including her relationship with her grandfather and her love of nature; the book is by no means as gloomy as the foregoing suggests; on the contrary, the light and shade is one of its attractions. The bright moments are recorded as lyrically as the horrors are recorded without sentiment.

Howard Goldblatt, Xiao Hong's English-language biographer, has compared *Tales of Hulan River* to Turgenev's *Sketches of a Hunter's Album*, which she may well have read.[54] But, in those parts which may be compared with Turgenev, there is, too, scope for suggesting a relationship with *Daughter of Earth*. Agnes Smedley wrote of one of her many childhood home towns:

> The church stood on Commercial Street, the main thoroughfare that twisted its way like a snake through the city. It

was also a part of the ancient Santa Fe Trail. The church and
the saloon were the two landmarks on Commercial Street.
The saloon was across the street from the church and a little
way up the hill. There I could find my father at all times
when he was not at work. It was a small, one-story building
with swinging doors and behind these doors men gambled,
drank and 'swopped yarns'. Next to it stood the cigar store
in front of which men lounged, smoked and spat all day
long, exchanging obscenities and blasphemies.

Across the bridge at the foot of Commercial Street, beyond the railway station that was the boast of the city, stood
the boarding house where I now worked. ...[55]

Xiao Hong's bird's-eye description of Hulan River is very much
longer, but an extract from the beginning gives an idea of the similarity:

Hulan River is one of these small towns, not a very prosperous place at all. It has two major streets, one running north
and south and one running east and west, but the best-known
place in town is The Crossroads, for it is the heart of the
whole town. At The Crossroads there is a jewelry store, a
yardage shop, an oil store, a salt store, a teashop, a phar-
macy, and the office of a foreign dentist. Above this dentist's door hangs a single shingle about the size of a rice-
measuring basket, on which is painted a row of oversized
teeth. ...[56]

Xiao Hong went from Hulan River to school in Harbin when she
was 18, in 1929. This was a relatively happy time for her. With her
grandfather she had studied the Chinese classics; now, she had the chance
to read modern Chinese writers – including the woman writer Bing Xin
(Ping Hsin) – and Western literature, including Upton Sinclair and
Russian novelists. She was caught up in the still-pervasive spirit of the
May 4 Movement of 1919, and particularly with the issue of women's

rights.[57] She had the chance to develop her painting skills too and these made use of the childhood love for nature that was also to imbue her future writing.

But then her beloved grandfather died and her father arranged a marriage for her. It was time to take action unheard of a generation before but increasingly common among her contemporaries. She wrote later, 'The year I reached the age of twenty, I fled from the home of my father, and ever since I have lived the life of a drifter.'[58] Agnes Smedley took the same decision in 1908. She wrote in the autobiographical *Battle Hymn of China* (1943) of her life of 'semi-vagabondage'.[59]

Xiao Hong was to have a lover and two husbands, whom some call 'common law' husbands, before her death aged 30. She was to have a child which she could not keep (through poverty) and one born dead.[60] Smedley was to have a husband from whom she was divorced, a long-term lover and at least one pregnancy termination before she reached China aged 36 in 1928. The private life of both is so shrouded in myth and prurience that it is fruitless to pursue it in detail here. For Xiao Hong, in particular, the discussions in print in Chinese have taken on an almost Byzantine partisanship. One aspect of their sexuality does, however, provide a useful area of comparison because of what it suggests about attitudes to them. An age-old means of marginalising women, perhaps because they do not conform, has been to attack their virtue.[61]

When Xiao Hong ran away from home and an arranged marriage, she had a relationship first in Harbin and then in Beijing with a married man. In Beijing she had a chance to study but it was there that she was abandoned. Destitute and pregnant, she made her way back to Harbin. From this situation she was to be saved by her first husband, later the novelist Xiao Jun. The following description of this time from a Chinese source is typical of how Xiao Hong is viewed: 'The innkeeper [where she took refuge], seeing she couldn't pay, made up his mind to sell her to a brothel'.[62] A contemporary of Xiao Hong in a telephone conversation of November 1994, described her as 'something like a prostitute.'[63] At that time she also, apparently, became addicted to opium.[64]

From this period, too, emerges Xiao Hong as victim. These two images — prostitute, or loose woman, and victim — were to dog Xiao Hong until long after her death. Xiao Hong wrote about the period, alone in Harbin until her rescue by Xiao Jun[65] but not overtly, it appears, of being or nearly being a prostitute. That she understood a young woman, alone and lost in Harbin, forced into that position is, however, apparent from *The Field of Life and Death*; and there is some suggestion that Xiao Hong identified with her character Golden Bough.[66]

Golden Bough is raped by one of the men for whom she does sewing in Harbin and returns to the group of women of which she has recently become a member; they notice something is amiss:

> 'What happened? Why are you so troubled?' Chou Ta-niang was the first to broach the subject.
>
> 'She must have cashed in!' The second one to speak was the fat bald woman.
>
> Chou Ta-niang, too, must have sensed that Golden Bough had earned some money, because every time a newcomer 'earned money' for the first time, she felt ashamed, and shame was devouring her now. She felt as if she had contracted a contagious disease.
>
> 'You'll get used to it. It's nothing. Money is the only thing that's real. I even got these golden earrings for myself.'
>
> The fat bald woman tried to console her by showing off her ears with her hands. But the others upbraided her: 'You shameless hussy. You have no shame at all!'
>
> The women around Golden Bough were witness to her distress, for her suffering was also their suffering. Gradually they dispersed and went to bed, showing no more sign of surprise or interest in the incident.[67]

Xiao Hong has created a real scene, but the point of raising the prostitute/victim issue is that it has been used to define her and, from there, to marginalise her. Everything, every flaw in her writing or character, or in the behaviour towards her of her 'husbands', stems from her as irredeemable victim.

There is evidence to suggest that male contemporaries, acquaintances and critics, found it hard to accept the reconciliation of contradictions in her writing. She is able effortlessly to combine lyricism and muscularity, lack of sentiment and concentration on women's concerns. Contradictions also apply to her life. She was able to continue single-mindedly writing under conditions of poverty, ill health and war, and she needed both to seek love and to break free of the patriarchal constraints that were the result. Both Xiao Hong and Agnes Smedley were beset by the double standards that continued to determine how a man might live his life, and how a woman should.

In an Epilogue to *The Field of Life and Death*, Hu Feng, the well-known critic and contemporary of Xiao Hong means to compliment her when he writes of the novel, 'In it we can discern subtle, feminine sensibilities as well as a vigorous manly mentality.'[68] Instead, he suggests that women have feminine sensibilities and men have vigorous mentality. Xiao Hong's Hong Kong patron, the North Eastern editor Zhou Jingwen, makes a similar point, while at least, unusually, dismissing the impression of victim, when he writes of her, 'Although Xiao Hong was a woman, she was a strong character with the air of a man.'[69]

The strength of Xiao Hong's writing is that she was able to reconcile the feminine and the masculine within herself. She did not live long enough, or under the right conditions, to have the chance similarly to straighten out her life. And this obviously confused Hu Feng. At the time he wrote his epilogue (1935), Xiao Hong was deceptive as a person. Lu Xun wrote man to man to Xiao Jun (in a way that was probably not helpful to Xiao Hong),

> She seems to have grown a bit since she came to Shanghai, and her two pigtails are a little longer; but still she keeps her childish ways ... what can we do about her?[70]

Ironically, Lu Xun's wife, Xu Guang-ping (Hsu Kuang-ping), noted when they first met Xiao Hong's pallid face and greying hair (she was 24).[71] And, a few years earlier, in a photograph taken soon after she first married Xiao Jun, she has the air of a Hollywood vamp of that era, pigtails and all.[72] In another photograph, she holds a pipe.[73]

Hu Feng's inability to accept the contradictions in Xiao Hong, which contributed towards what I do not hesitate to call her genius, extended even to the memorial meeting held in China when news of her death reached the literary community. One biographer reports that 'Hsiao Hong's fondness for nice clothes was criticised by her close friend Hu Feng.'[74] Another contemporary to have missed the point, and thus dismissed her, has said that, 'she didn't impress me with her physical beauty or brilliance', and he was prepared to ascribe to her only the 'competent writing of articles'.[75]

Agnes Smedley has been similarly marginalised. In her case it was initially the sexual double standards of her society; later it was the

Xiao Hong and Xiao Jun, early 1930s

political ambiguities of her time. At least twice in *Daughter of Earth*, Marie/ Smedley is taken for a prostitute because she is making her way in a man's world. The first time was when she was at her weakest, acting as a travelling saleswoman when it was uncommon and hitting such a lean patch that she came near to starvation in a hotel room; she evaded rape because another room was mistaken for hers. The second time she was propositioned when she was strong. She was living temporarily apart from her husband and had become a stenographer in a hotel frequented by businessmen – 'vultures', as she calls them. She writes:

> 'What's yer price?' he asked finally … 'but you needn't pitch it too high just because you've got the monopoly. I never pay more'n five dollars a night. My room's number nine. If the price suits you, I'll be waiting for you.'[76]

What is more, Smedley's Aunt Helen was a prostitute, driven to it by her need to help her poverty-stricken sister, Smedley's mother, and her own need not to live a similar life of degradation. And Smedley admired her aunt; her lifestyle was a badge of courage. Smedley sums up her feelings on the whole subject when she writes, at a moment when she is battling against falling in love:

> In my hatred of marriage, I thought that I would rather be a prostitute than a married woman. I could then protect, feed, and respect myself, and maintain some right over my own body. Prostitutes did not have children, I contemplated; men did not dare beat them; they did not have to obey. The 're- spectability' of married women seemed to rest in their ac- ceptance of servitude and inferiority. Men don't like free, intelligent women. I considered that before marriage men have relations with women, and nobody thought it was wrong – but they were 'sowing their wild oats.' Nobody spoke of 'fallen men' or men who had 'gone wrong' or been 'ruined'. Then why did they speak so of women? I found the reason!

Women had to depend upon men for a living; a woman who made her own living, and would always do so, could be as independent as men. That was why people did not condemn men.[77]

After this period in her life, Smedley became involved in politics, particularly that of Indian nationalism. For this she was imprisoned in New York by the United States' authorities acting hand in glove with the British. And from then on she became *persona non grata* in any British territory. When she came to China and espoused the cause of Chinese nationalism, and worked with the Communist Party among other revolutionaries, she compounded this reputation. Her sexuality was the weapon used to marginalise her for her political activities and, instead of being seen as a victim, she was a threat.

Freda Utley, an English journalist who met and briefly worked with Smedley in Hankou in 1938, told the story in *China at War* (1939) of how most journalists stayed at the Lutheran Hospital there; but the 'elderly women whose writ ran at the Lutheran Mission considered [Smedley] to be either too dangerous a Red or too Scarlet a woman, we never quite knew which.'[78]

Then, when in 1940 Smedley arrived in Hong Kong because of her health, after being with the Chinese guerrilla army, she was taken from the plane into custody by the British colonial authorities. The following morning she was taken to court and accused not only of supporting Indian nationalism but also of being a woman of questionable moral character.[79] (Although the case was dismissed, she was prohibited from public activities.)

Lu Xun

For both Xiao Hong and Smedley, there was one haven in their adult life from the bitterness of parental relations in childhood, and the later problems associated with their sexuality. By a strange coincidence, that person was the same – the revered Chinese writer Lu Xun.

Xiao Hong had enjoyed a loving relationship with her grandfather until his death; Smedley had found similar non-sexual consolation with the Indian nationalist La Lai Pat Raj (in *Daughter of Earth*, Saradar Ranjit Singh). Smedley recognised her need when she first met her Indian 'teacher':

> Perhaps my need for affection, for someone to love, for someone to take the place of a father was strong, and when I found a person who seemed to promise this, I did not lightly release my grip.[80]

She met Lu Xun through Mao Dun in 1930; until his death in 1936 he was to be her political mentor. Xiao Hong arrived in Shanghai with Xiao Jun at the end of 1934. They had already written to Lu Xun and sent him some of their work, including the manuscript of *The Field of Life and Death*. He was to become their literary patron, enabling their first novels to be published. That catapulted them to the forefront of a literary scene where their patriotic evocations of North East China under Japanese domination struck the right note.

Lu Xun on his 53rd birthday with his wife Xu Guangping and son Zhou Haiying

But for both Xiao Hong and Agnes Smedley, Lu Xun was more than a mentor; he was a surrogate father and Xiao Hong, at least, was a surrogate daughter. She makes that clear in 'A Remembrance of Lu Xun' (written c. October 1939). It opens with this slightly unwieldy but charming domestic scene:

Lu Xun's laugh was bright and cheerful – it came from his heart. Whenever someone said something funny, he laughed so hard he couldn't even hold a cigarette. Sometimes his laughing ended in a fit of coughing.

Lu Xun walked with a light, nimble step, and my clearest memory is of seeing him put on his hat and walk out the door, left foot first, without a thought for anything else.

Lu Xun didn't pay much attention to styles of attire; he would say: 'I don't even notice other people's clothes. ...'

Once when he was recovering from an illness, Lu Xun was having a smoke in a reclining chair next to an open window. I was there in an outlandish bright red blouse with puffy sleeves.

Lu Xun said: 'This muggy weather is typical for the rainy season.' He pushed the cigarette farther into his ivory cigarette holder and changed the subject. Xu Xiansheng [his wife] was busy with her housework, running back and forth, and she, too, took no notice of my clothes.

'Zhou Xiansheng [Lu Xun],' I asked, 'how do you like what I'm wearing?'

He glanced at me. 'I don't. ...' After a moment he added: 'You're wearing the wrong colour skirt. It's not that the blouse isn't attractive – all colours are attractive – but with a red blouse you should wear either a red or a black skirt. Brown's no good. The colors clash. Have you ever seen a foreign woman wearing a green skirt with a purple blouse, or a white blouse over a red skirt? ...' He looked at me from his reclining chair then said: 'Now, your skirt is brown, and it's a plaid design, which makes the blouse look unattractive.[81]

Xiao Hong identifies there both his physicality and her own, as well as their relationship. Smedley writes in retrospect of her first sight of their mutual friend, and evokes more the master and disciple relationship than the father and daughter one that Xiao Hong enjoyed. She has been invited to the 55th birthday party given by the League of Left Wing Writers in September 1930 and Lu Xun walks down the road towards her:

> He was short and frail, and wore a cream-coloured silk gown and soft Chinese shoes. He was bareheaded and his close-cropped hair stood up like a brush. In structure his face was like that of an average Chinese, yet it remains in my memory as the most eloquent face I have ever seen. A kind of living intelligence and awareness streamed from it. His manner, speech, and his every gesture radiated the indefinable of a perfectly integrated personality. I suddenly felt as awkward and ungracious as a clod.[82]

By the saddest coincidence, both Xiao Hong and Agnes Smedley were absent from Shanghai, and Lu Xun's side, when he died in October 1936. His influence was to remain with both of them. Xiao Hong not only remembered him as a father but as the embodiment of Justice – 'with your death I feel as though justice has gone with you.'[83] He was to inspire her writing, not only in what she wrote about him, but also in future subject matter and style.[84]

In spite of the close relations both women enjoyed with Lu Xun, I do not believe they knew each other well in Shanghai, although both biographers imply a continuing acquaintance that was renewed in Hong Kong. They undoubtedly knew each other by repute through Lu Xun. Smedley wrote in *Battle Hymn of China* that he had spoken of *The Field of Life and Death* as 'one of the most powerful modern novels written by a Chinese woman'.[85] Xiao Hong wrote in 'A Remembrance of Lu Xun', 'He also spoke of Smedley, an American woman who first lent her support to the independence movement in India and is now helping China.'[86]

But I believe the two women only met once in Shanghai, for Xiao Hong writes in 'After Reading *Daughter of Earth* …':

> I've met Smedley. It was in Shanghai last year. She wore a leather jerkin and was a bit plump, not really fat but just rather bulky. She laughed so much that she was close to tears. She is an American.'[87]

It was probably after that meeting, in 1936, that Xiao Hong read *Daughter of Earth*; and they were not, it seems, to meet again until Hong Kong, though they undoubtedly overlapped in Wuhan and Chongqing.

It may seem strange that they did not meet more when they were both so close to Lu Xun, but Xiao Hong's description suggests that there was not an immediate rapport. Although their work has shown so many points of affinity, the two women were also very different. Xiao Hong obviously found Smedley a little overwhelming; Smedley may have overlooked Xiao Hong. They may even have been a little jealous of each other, and Lu Xun had probably oversold each of them.

And there was more to life in Shanghai than personalities; Agnes Smedley was scrupulous about security at a time of political uncertainty and danger. When I asked Ruth Weiss, who also knew Lu Xun (and has written a personal biography of him), why she did not even know of Xiao Hong, she replied:

> In those days of Chiang Kai-shek terror, you just did not try to meet too many progressive people, or it would have been dangerous for them. If you knew Agnes Smedley, she did not propose to have you meet anybody else unless there was some political need. … You had to be aware of the danger you put others into – a foreigner didn't visit a Chinese, and a Chinese visited a foreigner only if he (she) had a good reason: to teach or pretend to teach or something. (27 February 1995) [87]

As George Hatem, a friend of Smedley in Shanghai, writes, 'Of course, there were many Chinese friends and comrades involved with her activities but these were of a separate and of an "underground" nature.'[88] In Shanghai, Xiao Hong was not of political interest to Smedley, and the younger Chinese woman did not need her help; in Hong Kong the situation was to be rather different.

HONG KONG

Xiao Hong arrived in Hong Kong with her second husband, Duanmu Hongliang, in the spring of 1940. She had parted from Xiao Jun and taken up with Duanmu in 1938. What drove her to the British colony was the Japanese bombing of the wartime capital of Chongqing which began in May the previous year. The Japanese, who had invaded Manchuria in 1931, had driven Xiao Hong from Harbin in May 1934; Japanese bombing, which started on 13 August 1937, had driven her from Shanghai in early October that year. In Wuhan she wrote soon afterwards in 'After Reading *Daughter of Earth*...', 'During that period, I

Xiao Hong and Duanmu Hongliang in Sian, 1938

could only watch the traces of anti-aircraft guns or read. It was impossible to discuss or exchange views and all publication came to a standstill. Even reading was done in a state of perplexity.'[89] Now Xiao Hong hoped for peace and quiet in Hong Kong to continue her writing.

Xiao Hong's aversion to bombing, both the noise and the death and destruction, have been seen as yet another weakness, because she allowed it to cut her off from the struggle.[90] But she had her own views on this; she did not believe you had to be deliberately involved in struggle to write. Her ability to observe, internalise and describe is given support by her comment:

> As I see it, we aren't cut off from life at all. For example, taking refuge during an air-raid alert, that is part of wartime living conditions. The problem is that we haven't grasped its significance. Even if we were at the front line where people were being killed by Japanese soldiers, if we haven't grasped its significance, then we still couldn't write of it.[91]

What is more, few writers had to uproot themselves so many times because of the approach of war, and Xiao Hong needed a degree of peace to write. And she needed to write. It was her haven and means of identity and self-expression. In the 18 months left of her writing life, she was to complete two major novels, as well as several short stories and other pieces.

Agnes Smedley did not need to write to survive: she needed to be part of any earth-shaking human activity within her grasp. Since the previous meeting between the two women, Smedley had been involved in and reported on the Xian Incident of December 1936; she visited the Communist leaders in Yenan at the end of the Long March, and interviewed them at length; she had nursed wounded Chinese soldiers, and fought the foreign establishment that hindered that effort; and she had marched with the New Fourth Army. As her friend Rewi Alley put it, 'Agnes lived every battle through in the telling; though she would never admit it, it was the romance of the thing that caught her then.'[92]

Her intensity was, however, one of her worst enemies, and she was encouraged to leave her commitments in China. Her health made the ideal excuse for everyone and she arrived in Hong Kong in October 1940 ill and depressed. The British colonial authorities tried to prevent her staying and, when they failed, prohibited her from making any public utterances.

She was fortunate in her friends. Hilda Selwyn-Clarke arranged for her immediate admittance to Queen Mary Hospital. Hilda was the wife of the Colony's Director of Medical Services, known simply as Selwyn-Clarke; she was also an activist in her own right. She was Honorary Secretary of the China Defence League, founded by Soong Ching Ling, and she had met Smedley in Hankou in 1938 when Hilda was on a Red Cross mission from Hong Kong.

When Smedley was well enough to leave hospital, she was invited to recuperate at the country cottage – Lin Yin Tai, at Shatin – of Ronald Hall, the Bishop of Hong Kong. While Agnes was known, not always affectionately, as a Red, and Hilda Selwyn-Clarke as 'Red Hilda', not only because of her hair, Bishop Hall was known as the 'Pink Bishop'. In India on his way to China for a short visit in 1922 he wrote home, 'Go on putting your money on Mr Gandhi.'[93] He spent a year in Shanghai in 1925 and arrived in Hong Kong as Bishop in 1932. At his inauguration, he pronounced, 'Foreigners have exercised too much authority over the years. If ever there should be a difference of opinion between a European and a Chinese, I shall back the Chinese.'[94]

It is not clear how Agnes Smedley and Xiao Hong met up again in Hong Kong. One Chinese source suggests that on hearing of the arrival of Smedley in Hong Kong, Xiao Hong and Duanmu Hongliang immediately made arrangements to meet her.[95] Smedley's biographer writes of Xiao Hong, 'By early 1941, she was living in a hovel in Kowloon with two genuine scoundrels. When Smedley found her in March of that year, she was seriously ill with tuberculosis.'[96]

Xiao Hong and Duanmu were living at No. 8 Lock Road in Tsim Sha Tsui, just behind the colony's premier hotel, the Peninsula. Photographs of the time show a road of rather gracious houses, some of which, seemingly, were divided into 'bedsits'.[97] Zhou Jingwen, who be-friended Xiao Hong in Hong Kong, described their accommodation as 200 square feet with a big bed in the middle, a desk, things strewn about, and a little stove for boiling water.[98] Asked to comment, Duanmu replied that in Chinese eyes their accommodation was 'comfortable'; in those of foreigners it was (no doubt) 'poor'.[99]

As for the genuine scoundrels, one of them was obviously Duanmu. In this paper I have decided not to explore Xiao Hong's relationships with her husbands; the relevant material – of great bulk – is mostly in Chinese and shows a quite startling partisanship. It should be said, however, that I have met and interviewed Duanmu, now in his eighties, and have since corresponded with him. His charm and helpfulness to me, and his expressions of undying love (in some poignant detail) for Xiao Hong will doubtless be treated by some with scepticism. I can only thank Duanmu for his efforts to further my research.

Whatever the conditions under which Xiao Hong was living, she was obviously ill and Agnes Smedley, at her best when someone needed help and she could take positive action, acted. She took Xiao Hong off with her to Bishop Hall's cottage in Shatin. Had Xiao Hong been less ill, she might have benefited from such enchanting physical surroundings.

The two women stayed in the main, rather small house while Bishop Hall, if he came at the weekend, or commuted during the week while they were there, stayed in St Francis House (the lodge).[100] Because of this, there may have been little social activity at Lin Ying Tai; normally it lent itself to 'profound, unpretentious hospitality'.[101] And the company was 'more mixed than was customary at social occasions in Hong Kong'.[102]

Smedley and Xiao Hong could not have spent more than a month together at Lin Yin Tai, probably less. Smedley had already been based there for some time and by the late spring she was staying for three weeks with the American writer Emily Hahn – a member of the progressive circle that included the Selwyn-Clarkes, Bishop Hall and Margaret Watson, almoner (social worker) at Queen Mary Hospital.

Hong Kong, 1940, (left to right) Agnes Smedley,
Emily Hahn, Hilda Selwyn-Clarke,
Hilda's daughter Mary and Margaret Watson

The shortlived friendship, as opposed to acquaintance in Shanghai, between Xiao Hong and Agnes Smedley dates from this time. The two women shared a great deal, in spite of differences in temperament, background and culture. They also shared bad habits which are likely to have provided an initial bond. It is clear from several sources that Xiao Hong drank and smoked quite heavily – neither of which can have helped her health.[103] The same applies to Agnes Smedley.

They were also part of a pattern of relationships for each other. Xiao Hong had earlier been looked after by Lu Xun's wife, Xu Guangping, by the writer Ding Ling – six years her senior – and by two Japanese women friends in Chongqing.[104] The American woman enjoyed the friendship of Chinese women writers. She had been close to Ding Ling since they met through the civil rights movement in Shanghai, and Yang Gang through the Union of Left-Wing Writers; that latter friendship was later renewed in New York.[105]

Although Smedley's Chinese was not fluent, and Xiao Hong's English was 'rather poor', they certainly would have been able to talk at a certain level of profundity.[106] By now, though unable to read Xiao Hong's

317

work, Smedley was obviously impressed by her.[107] In *Battle Hymn of China* (1943), she commented on the famous Soong sisters but suggested it was a mistake to think of them as representative. 'A new Chinese woman,' she insisted, 'in many ways far in advance of American womanhood, was being forged on the fierce anvil of war.'[108] Her example was Xiao Hong.

Smedley adds that her Chinese friend wrote a war novel (*Ma Bo-le*) 'which she completed while living in my house'.[109] By chance, this novel, rather different from Xiao Hong's previous work, owed much to Lu Xun, providing the two with specific scope for discussion.[110] But the stay had more important implications for Xiao Hong: what Smedley gave her was not her health, unfortunately, but briefly the 'luxury of privacy', even, perhaps, 'A Room of Her Own', something the Chinese writer had never known before.[111] When asked what Xiao Hong had given Agnes Smedley (in return), Duanmu replied, 'She couldn't do much because of her lack of money and power. But she could give her her heart, because Xiao Hong was a pure person.'[112]

Probably during their time together, Smedley tried to persuade Xiao Hong (and Mao Dun and his wife) to leave for Singapore. Hong Kong, she felt, would quickly fall to the Japanese; Singapore was 'impregnable'.[113] Xiao Hong demurred, because she was too ill, according to Duanmu. Mao Dun says, in retrospect, that she wanted to leave to escape from 'fearful loneliness'. But work kept Mao Dun in Hong Kong and he tried, at the time, to reassure Xiao Hong about the war situation.

Smedley had known Mao Dun for some years, and many of the other Chinese intellectuals who flocked to Hong Kong after the Anhui (Anhwei) incident of January 1941. Now Xiao Hong introduced her to Zhou Jingwen, leader in Hong Kong of the North Eastern Democratic League. He had already helped Xiao Hong and was to help her further after the fall of Hong Kong. He writes of meeting Smedley at a 'tea party'. This was probably held either at the Gloucester Hotel, a common interracial meeting place, or the Luk Kwok Restaurant frequented by Chinese intellectuals. They talked of human rights in China – a subject to which all progressive intellectuals and political parties represented in Hong Kong were committed. Smedley promised that on her return to the United States she would raise the matter with senators there.[114]

The friendship between Smedley and Xiao Hong in Hong Kong was quite unusual and, therefore, of interest to researchers of the period. First, friendships across race were rare in pre-war colonial Hong Kong; second, Smedley was very much *persona non grata* in the eyes of the authorities. Duanmu explains that Xiao Hong and Mao Dun were close to her, but they were warned not to be because of Smedley's communist connections which could count against them (as refugees in the colony).[115]

In April, Smedley arranged for Xiao Hong to be admitted to Queen Mary Hospital to be treated for tuberculosis. She left money to pay for bills, and later sent more;[116] then she left for the United States. She took with her a present from Xiao Hong to Upton Sinclair. Xiao Hong had read *The Jungle* in 1929 and she had introduced it into a touching moment of her best-loved short story 'Hands'. Sinclair wrote to thank her (and to send her another book and some pamphlets), and a copy of his letter remains in his papers.[117] Her last known story, 'Spring in a Small Town', was written the month of his letter, June 1941.

In this deceptively understated story of unrequited love, it is difficult, as it is in *Tales of Hulan River* and, apparently, in the untranslated *Ma Bo-le*, to sense what Xiao Hong was going through and was now to go through until her death. Her English-language biographer observes, 'Everyone has characterised her as a desperately lonely, frightened and gravely ill woman who no longer seemed to have any control over her own destiny.'[118] It is this disparity between her life and her contemporary writing that makes her last 18 months so poignant and her skill so impressive. The volume and quality of her writing contradicts, in my view, the contention that she was weak and a victim. Since she gave everything to her writing, and her writing was strong and effective, so was she.

Xiao Hong's next six months of illness and hospital treatment are a shocking tale of bungling, bad luck and disaster, not helped by her own hostility to hospital treatment. She should have been in Queen Mary Hospital when the Japanese invaded Hong Kong on 8 December 1941 and her life may well have been saved. But she was at Lock Road. After two unsuccessful operations in two hospitals, she died in a third, the temporary one of St Stephen's Girls College, on 22 January 1942.

There are many avenues of exploration regarding Xiao Hong's death and the disposal of her ashes and I have touched on some of them elsewhere; the one that is of concern here is why she was not helped in her last months by Smedley's progressive Western friends.

Bishop Hall left Hong Kong for a sabbatical in the United States in September 1941, but the Selwyn-Clarkes, Margaret Watson and Emily Hahn remained. What is more, at the crucial time when Xiao Hong was moved from the Hong Kong Sanatorium (Yeung Wo Yuen) in Happy Valley to Queen Mary Hospital on 18 January (following the surrender of 25 December) all four were living within the environs of that hospital. They, too, had to leave Queen Mary Hospital at about the time when all patients left – 21 January 1942 – and Xiao Hong was taken to St Stephen's Girls College.[119]

I have read Emily Hahn and Dr Selwyn-Clarke's writing of the period; and I have talked to Emily Hahn, Margaret Watson and the Selwyn-Clarkes' daughter. There is no mention of Xiao Hong, and no memory of her. And yet, in her last days in Hong Kong, Xiao Hong was obviously very much on Smedley's mind and at least one (Chinese) source suggests that she approached Selwyn-Clarke to get Xiao Hong into Queen Mary – a connection which one would expect to be used.[120] Why then did Smedley not ask Hilda Selwyn-Clarke to keep an eye on the Chinese woman; more important, why was she not mentioned to the almoner, Margaret Watson?

That Smedley did not mention Xiao Hong to Emily Hahn during the three weeks Hahn and Smedley shared accommodation is strange in view of Hahn's other connections with Chinese women – not only the Soong sisters whose biography she had written – and her ability to speak Mandarin. But it is only partly strange. Hahn was progressive in an eccentric way; she was certainly without any taint of racism. But she had Kuomintang connections at a time when the Communists, whom Smedley supported, and the GMT were in an uneasy wartime alliance. What is more, Hahn was pregnant by Charles Boxer, an intelligence officer in the British Army. For all that Smedley enjoyed Hahn's company, Hahn was not discreet, as her writing shows, and Smedley's security antennae would have been alert.

As far as Margaret Watson is concerned, is it simply that she cannot remember Xiao Hong after more than 50 years? This is possible and illustrates one of the ambiguities of historical reconstruction. Conditions at the time, following the fall of Hong Kong, were traumatic in the extreme; Xiao Hong, on that occasion, was only three days in Queen Mary's and, about the time that Xiao Hong left for St Stephen's Girls College, there to die, Margaret Watson was taken into internment in Stanley Camp. There she spent the war, another experience to test the memory. Hilda Selwyn-Clarke, in fear from her political activities and with a young daughter to look after, was free for a bit longer because of her husband's duties, but by then Xiao Hong was dead, and Hilda was later also interned. Selwyn-Clarke himself was badly tortured because of the help he had given many people before being interned.

At one time in my research, I was tempted to explore the possibility that Smedley was 'jealous' of her Chinese connections and, therefore, kept the various strands of her life apart. But I now doubt this. Throughout her time in China, within the confines of her obsession with security, Smedley ruthlessly used her Western contacts to help her Chinese ones in trouble. It is certainly true that it is of this period that her friend Rewi Alley wrote, 'She had grown very sensitive on the point of Western attitudes towards the Chinese people, even when well meant, of arrogance and condescension.'[121] But, given what she wrote of her Hong Kong friends in *Battle Hymn of China*, this cannot refer to them.[122]

The answer lies perhaps in turning the question on its head. It is unlikely that Agnes was sensitive to her intrusion into Xiao Hong's life, but the Chinese woman's husband and friends may well have been. They undoubtedly felt able to look after her and might well have discouraged cross-racial help. Zhou Jingwen writes how he had meetings with friends who agreed about the necessary cure and that Xiao Hong should be in Queen Mary Hospital with the best doctors and equipment. He adds that he was responsible for all medical expenses when Xiao Hong was admitted there again in November.[123] Xiao Hong did not die alone; she died needlessly. If Smedley's friends – particularly Dr Selwyn-Clarke and Margaret Watson – had known of her circumstances, I believe that it would have made a difference.

Agnes Smedley's death had some strangely similar connections. Hounded in the early days of McCarthyism in the United States, she heard of the Liberation of 1949 and set out for China. In transit in Britain, she was helped and looked after first by Hilda Selwyn-Clarke in London, and then by Margaret Watson in Oxford. Following an apparently straightforward, though major, stomach operation there, she died on 6 May 1950, with Margaret Watson at her side. Her ashes are buried in Beijing; half of Xiao Hong's are finally buried in Guangzhou.

CONCLUSION

What, then, is the result of my comparing the life and writing, the experience and expression, of Xiao Hong and Agnes Smedley? I have four answers to suggest. Though I make no claim to have contributed to literary criticism, the comparison may add something to the growing appreciation of women's autobiograhy. Also, I have enjoyed crossing disciplinary boundaries and my historical understanding of their lives and times has been much enhanced.

A more general gain is that from such a comparison in any discipline: both women are brought into sharper focus. This works particularly well because of their differences – of age (generation), culture, race, class and temperament, and because of their similarities – of experience and expression.

This leads to the vexed question of 'universality'. The only defining attribute the two had in common was their sex. I am of the school which has for some years been increasingly unpopular: the one that believes that gender is of itself unifying – that there is an essential 'womanness'. This is said to be a bias in white middle-class feminist thought.[124] I cannot avoid that label, but Xiao Hong and Agnes Smedley can. And yet they shared much, almost uncannily, in their lives and how they wrote about it.

Lastly, it seems that this symposium itself, and the UN Women's Conference which follows it, are intended as unifying agents. Xiao Hong and Agnes Smedley set us a good example.

Women and Literature Symposium, Peking Univeristy, 20-23 June 1995.

NOTES

1. Janice R. Mackinnon and Stephen R. Mackinnon, *Agnes Smedley* (1988), p. 154.
2. Letter to the author, 9 March 1995.
3. John Israel and Donald W. Klein, *Rebels and Bureaucrats* (1976), p. 39.
4. Xiao Hong's review is called in full 'After Reading *Daughter of Earth* and *Restless Days*'. Lilo Linke was a refugee from Nazi Germany who was befriended by the English writer Storm Jameson. Jameson helped Linke with her English and then to get her books, including her autobiography *Restless Flags*, published in England. The Chinese translation was probably made from the United States' edition, *Restless Days*.
5. Howard Goldblatt, *A Literary Biography of Hsiao Hung* (1974), p. 163, fn. 1.
6. Xiao Hong, 'After Reading *Daughter of Earth* ...' (1938). All translations for this paper have been done for me by Simon Che Wai-kwan who, in doing them, has become 'a friend of Xiao Hong'. His help has allowed me a much deeper understanding, and thanks here can only be inadequate.
7. Agnes Smedley, *Daughter of Earth* (1977), pp. 22-23.
8. Xiao Hong, *Selected Stories* (1982), p. 152.
9. It is not clear when this piece was written. Goldblatt gives a meticulous list of Xiao Hong's works at the end of his biography; but this is not included.
10. Tifeng, 'The Image of Women in the Studies of Xiao Hong', nd.
11. Goldblatt, *A Literary Biography*, pp. 153, 162 and 182.
12. Smedley, *Daughter of Earth*, p. 4.
13. Smedley, *Daughter of Earth*, p. 4.
14. Xiao Hong, *The Field of Life and Death* (1979), p. xvi.
15. Xiao Hong, *The Field of Life and Death*, p. xvi.
16. Goldblatt, *A Literary Biography*, p. 13.
17. Goldblatt, *A Literary Biography*, p. 14.
18. Smedley, *Daughter of Earth*, p. 72.
19. Smedley, *Daughter of Earth*, p. 90.
20. Smedley, *Daughter of Earth*, p. 124.
21. Smedley, *Daughter of Earth*, p. 168.
22. Xiao Hong, *Tales of Hulan River* (1988), p. 170.
23. Xiao Hong, *Selected Stories*, p. 124.
24. Xiao Hong, *Selected Stories*, p. 125.
25. Anna Gerstlacher, *Women and Literature in China* (1985), p. 342.
26. Gerstlacher, *Women and Literature in China*, p. 364.
27. Xiao Hong, *The Field of Life and Death*, p. 290. The volume has useful appendices, such as Mao Dun's preface. Goldblatt discusses other criticisms in his biography, p. 220.
28. Xiao Hong, *Tales of Hulan River*, pp. 170-171.
29. Gerstlacher, *Women and Literature in China*, p. 334.
30. Xiao Hong, *The Field of Life and Death*, p. 281.
31. Xiao Hong, *The Field of Life and Death*, p. 74.
32. Xiao Hong, *The Field of Life and Death*, pp. 75-76.
33. Xiao Hong, *The Field of Life and Death*, p. 93.
34. Xiao Hong, *Selected Stories*, p. 124.

35. Smedley, *Daughter of Earth*, p. 72.
36. Xiao Hong, *The Field of Life and Death*, p. 220.
37. Goldblatt, *Literary Biography*, p. 134.
38. She did not write the review of the book until the end of 1937.
39. Smedley, *Daughter of Earth*, p. 30.
40. Smedley, *Daughter of Earth*, p. 54.
41. Smedley, *Daughter of Earth*, p. 93.
42. Xiao Hong, *Selected Stories*, p. 46.
43. Xiao Hong, *Selected Stories*, p. 58.
44. Xiao Hong, *Selected Stories*, p. 56.
45. Smedley, *Daughter of Earth*, p. 33.
46. Smedley, *Daughter of Earth*, p. 93.
47. Smedley, *Daughter of Earth*, p. 1.
48. Smedley, *Daughter of Earth*, p. 27.
49. Smedley, *Daughter of Earth*, p. 59.
50. Xiao Hong, *Tales of Hulan River*, p. 109.
51. Xiao Hong, *Tales of Hulan River*, p. 118.
52. Xiao Hong, *Tales of Hulan River*, p. 119.
53. Xiao Hong, *Tales of Hulan River*, p. 124.
54. Goldblatt, *Literary Biography*, p. 217.
55. Smedley, *Daughter of Earth*, p. 46.
56. Xiao Hong, *Tales of Hulan River*, p. 4.
57. Xiao Feng, 'The Story of Xiao Hong' (1980).
58. Xiao Hong, *The Field of Life and Death*, p. xvi.
59. Smedley, *China Correspondent* (1984), p. 12.
60. Xiao Hong, *The Field of Life and Death*, p. xix.
61. Susanna Hoe, 'Gin and Bridge all Day' (1991).
62. Xiao Feng, 'The Story of Xiao Hong'.
63. Xiao Qian in telephone conversation with the author, 22 October 1994.
64. Goldblatt, *Literary Biography*, p. 38.
65. Goldblatt, *Literary Biography*, p. 37.
66. Xiao Hong, *The Field of Life and Death*, p. xxi.
67. Xiao Hong, *The Field of Life and Death*, p. 99.
68. Xiao Hong, *The Field of Life and Death*, p. 281.
69. Zhou Jingwen, 'In memory of Xiao Hong' (1975).
70. Goldblatt, *Literary Biography*, p. 88.
71. Goldblatt, *Literary Biography*, p. 112.
72. Joseph Lau, *Modern Chinese Stories and Novellas* (1981).
73. Leo Lee Ou-fan, *The Romantic Generation of Modern Chinese Writers* (1973).
74. Goldblatt, *Literary Biography*, p. 239, fn. 3.
75. Xiao Qian, in telephone conversation with the author, 22 October 1994.
76. Smedley, *Daughter of Earth*, p. 133.
77. Smedley, *Daughter of Earth*, pp. 123-124.
78. Freda Utley, *China at War* (1939), p. 41.
79. Mackinnon, *Agnes Smedley*, p. 225.
80. Smedley, *Daughter of Earth*, p. 174.
81. Xiao Hong, 'A Remembrance of Lu Xun' (1981), p. 169.

82. Smedley, *China Correspondent*, p. 60.

83. Goldblatt, *Literary Biography*, p. 156.

84. Gerstlacher, *Women and Literature in China*, pp. 330-331.

85. Smedley, *Portraits of Chinese Women in Revolution* (1976), p. 102.

86. Xiao Hong, 'A Remembrance of Lu Xun', p. 173.

87. Xiao Hong, 'After Reading *Daughter of Earth* ...'.

88. George Hatem, 'A Woman Made by History', p. 141.

89. Xiao Hong, 'After Reading *Daughter of Earth* ...'.

90. Goldblatt, *Literary Biography*, pp. 199-200; Xiao Hong, *The Field of Life and Death*, pp. 289-290.

91. Goldblatt, *Literary Biography*, p. 164; from *July*, 16 January 1938.

92. Rewi Alley, *Six Americans in China* (1985), p. 147.

93. D.M. Paton, *RO* (1985), p. 35.

94. Paton, *RO*, p. 79.

95. Cao Gecheng, 'Romance Between Chinese and American Writers' (1993).

96. Mackinnon, *Agnes Smedley*, p. 231.

97. Wing On, 'Commemoration' (1932).

98. Zhou Jingwen, 'In Memory of Xiao Hong'.

99. In conversation with the author, 23 October 1994.

100. Letter from Bishop Hall's daughter, Judith Richardson, 22 April 1995.

101. Paton, *RO*, p. 90.

102. Paton, *RO*, p. 91.

103. Goldblatt, *Literary Biography*, pp. 143, 154 and 180; Xiao Feng.

104. Goldblatt, *Literary Biography*, p. 166; Ikeda Yukio 'loved Hsiao Hung almost like a young sister, and often scolded her', p. 180; p. 231.

105. Smedley, *China Correspondent*, pp. 109-118; Mackinnon, *Agnes Smedley*, p. 311. The Mackinnons write of Smedley and Yang Gang that in New York 'the writings of the two women about conditions in the United States and China in the 1940s are strikingly similar in point of view.'

106. Goldblatt, *Literary Biography*, p. 28, fn. 2; throughout Smedley's journalistic career in China she travelled with an interpreter and tended to type her interview notes directly on to her typewriter (Hatem p. 145). But by 1941 she had lived in China for 13 years and had conversational Mandarin.

107. Smedley was conversant with Chinese literature and was involved with translating it into English, including the writing of Lu Xun (Hatem, p. 144).

108. Smedley, *Portraits of Chinese Women in Revolution*, p. 101.

109. Smedley, *Portraits of Chinese Women in Revolution*, p. 102. The first part of Ma Bole was published in January 1941; the second part started to be serialised in Zhou Jingwen's journal, *Shidai Piping*, beginning February 1941; the third part remained incomplete.

110. Xiao Hong's increasing use of satire, particularly overt in *Ma Bo-le*, has a direct link to Lu Xun and his appreciation of, for example, Gogol.

111. Jean Kennard, *Vera Brittain and Winifred Holtby* (1989), p. 13; see also Virginia Woolf.

112. Interview with Duanmu, 23 October 1994; a small overt literary mark of their friendship is Smedley's use of 'Fields of Life and Death' as a chapter heading in *The Battle Hymn of China*.

113. Xiao Hong, *The Field of Life and Death*, p. 285.
114. Zhou Jingwen, 'In Memory of Xiao Hong'.
115. Interview with Duanmu, 23 October 1994.
116. Smedley, *Portraits of Chinese Women in Revolution*, p. 102.
117. Letter provided by Howard Goldblatt.
118. Goldblatt, *Literary Biography*, p. 202.
119. Goldblatt, *Literary Biography*, p. 237; Xiao Si, 'Loneliness Among Mountain Flowers' (1988), p. 181; Sha Xunze, 'Xiao Hong and Some Circumstances After Her Death'; interview with Duanmu, 23 October 1994. Emily Hahn, *China To Me* (1987), pp. 307-308; Emily Hahn, *Hong Kong Holiday* (1946), pp. 80 and 84-85, discusses in some detail the evacuation of Queen Mary Hospital. Hahn also talks of roaming round the hospital visiting patients; she was a patient under somewhat false pretences.
120. Cao Gecheng, 'Romance Between Chinese and American Writers'.
121. Alley, *Six Americans in China*, p. 153.
122. Smedley, *China Correspondent*, pp. 354-356.
123. Zhou Jingwen, 'In Memory of Xiao Hong'.
124. Elizabeth Spelman, *Inessential Woman* (1990), p. ix.

BIBLIOGRAPHY

Alley, Rewi, *Six Americans in China* (Beijing, Intercul, 1985).

Benstock, Shari, *Feminist Issues in Literary Scholarship* (Bloomingdale, Indiana University Press, 1987).

Cao Gecheng, 'Romance Between Chinese and American Writers: A Note of Friendship Between Duanmu Hongliang, Xiao Hong and Agnes Smedley' (*Zhong mei zhuo jia yi duan qing-ji … di you yi*) in *Literary Journal* (*Wen yi bao*) (Beijing, 9 October 1993).

Cao Gecheng, 'The Agony of Farewell in Death in Hong Kong (*Feng yu xiang gan si bie ai*) *Literary Journal* (*Wen yi bao*) (Beijing, 22 October 1994).

Cros-Morea, Simone, 'Women and Sexuality in Xiao Hong's *Sheng Sichang*', in Gerstlacher.

Duke, Michael (ed.), *Modern Chinese Women Writers: Critical Appraisals* (New York, M.E. Sharpe, 1989).

Epstein, Israel, *Woman in World History: The Life and Times of Soong Ching Ling (Mme Sun Yat-sen)* (Beijing, New World Press, 1993).

Feuerwerker, Yi-tsi, 'Women as Writers in the 1920s and 1930s', in Wolf and Witke.

Fokkema, Dowe W., 'Lu Xun: The Impact of Russian Literature', in Goldman.

Gerstlacher, Anna et al., *Women and Literature in China* (Berlin, Buchum, 1985).

Goldblatt, Howard, *A Literary Biography of Hsiao Hung (1911-1942)* (Ann Arbor, Michigan, Indiana University PhD 1974, Xerox University Microfilms).

Goldblatt, Howard, 'Life as Art: Xiao Hong and Autobiography', in Gerstlacher.

Goldman, Merle, *Modern Chinese Literature in the May Fourth Era* (Cambridge, Mass., Harvard University Press, 1977).

Hahn, Emily, *China To Me* (London, Virago, 1987; 1st published 1944).

Hahn, Emily, *Hong Kong Holiday* (New York, Doubleday, 1946)

Hartem, Charles, 'Han Yu and TS Elliot: A Sinological Essay in Comparative Literature' in, *Renditions*, No. 8, pp. 59-76 (Hong Kong).

Hatem, George, 'A Woman Made by History, and in Turn Made History'. (No reference: could be the same as 'On Agnes Smedley', *Voice of Friendship* No. 12 (August 1985): pp. 11-12).

Hoe, Susanna, 'Gin and Bridge All Day: Myths About Western Women in Hong Kong 1841-1941' (Hong Kong, Unpublished talk to Royal Asiatic Society, 22 February 1991).

Hoe, Susanna, *The Private Life of Old Hong Kong: Western Women in the British Colony 1841-1941* (Hong Kong, Oxford University Press, 1991).

Hsia, C.T., *A History of Modern Chinese Fiction 1917-1957* (New Haven, Yale University Press, 1961).

Hsia, Tsi-an, *The Gate of Darkness: Studies on the Leftist Literacy Movement in China* (Seattle, University of Washington Press, 1968).

Israel, John and Klein, Donald W., *Rebels and Bureaucrats: China's December 9ers* (Berkeley, University of California Press, 1976).

Jameson, Storm, *Journey From the North* (London, Virago, 1984; 1st published 1934).

Jelinek, Estelle C., *The Tradition of Women's Autobiography: From Antiquity to the Present* (Boston, Twayne, 1986).

Keen, Ruth, 'Xiao Hong's *Vague Expectations* – A Study in Feminine Writing', in Gerstlacher.

Kennard, Jean E., *Vera Brittain and Winifred Holtby: A Working Partnership* (New England, University Press, 1989).

Lau, Joseph S.M. et al., *Modern Chinese Stories and Novellas 1918-1948* (New York, Columbia University Press, 1981).

Lee, Leo Ou-fan, *The Romantic Generation of Modern Chinese Writers* (Cambridge, Mass., Harvard University Press, 1973).

Linke, Lilo, *Restless Flags: A German Girl's Story* (London, Constable, 1935).

Mackinnon, Janice R. and Mackinnon, Stephen R., *Agnes Smedley: The Life and Times of an American Radical* (London, Virago, 1988).

Mason, Mary G., 'The Other Voice: Autobiographies of Women Writers', in Olney.

Paton, D.M., *RO: The Life and Times of Bishop Ronald Owen Hall of Hong Kong* (Diocese of Hong Kong and Macau, 1985).

Schyns, Jos et al., *1500 Modern Chinese Novels and Plays* (Beijing, 1948).

Sha Xunze and Sun Kai, 'Xiao Hong and Some Circumstances After Her Death', in *Hulan Education Special Journal* (Hulan – Shiyan Zhuanboa).

Smedley, Agnes, *Chinese Destinies: Sketches of Present-Day China* (New York, Vanguard Press, 1933).

Smedley, Agnes, *Daughter of Earth* (London, Virago, 1977; 1st published 1929).

Smedley, Agnes, *China Correspondent* (London, Pandora, 1984; 1st published as *Battle Hymn of China*, 1943).

Smedley, Agnes, *Portraits of Chinese Women in Revolution*, ed. Jan Mackinnon and Steve Mackinnon (New York, Feminist Press, 1976).

Snow, Edgar (ed.), *Living China: Modern Chinese Short Stories* (London, Harrap, 1936) (see Wales).

Snow, Helen Foster, *Women in Modern China* (Hague, Mouton, 1967).

Snow, Helen Foster, *My China Years* (London, Harrap, 1984).

Spelman, Elizabeth V., *Inessential Women: Problems of Exclusion in Feminist Thought* (London, Women's Press, 1990).

Tiefeng, 'The Image of Women in the Works of Xiao Hong' (*Xiao Hong xiao shuo zhong di fu nu xing xiang*) in *Studies Of Xiao Hong* (*Xiao Hong yan jiu*) (Harbin University of Teacher Education, 1992).

Tien Chun, *Village in August* (London, Collins, 1943).

Tsau Shuying, 'Xiao Hong and Her Novel Tales of Hulan River', in Gerstlacher.

Utley, Freda, *China at War* (London, Faber and Faber, 1939)

Wales, Nym, 'The Modern Chinese Literary Movement', in *Living China* (see Snow).

Wing On, 'In Commemoration of 25th Anniversary 1907-1932' (Hong Kong, Wing On Co. Ltd, 1932).

Wolf, Margery and Witke, Roxane, *Women in Chinese Society* (Stanford, Stanford University Press, 1978; 1st published 1975).

Woolf, Virginia, *A Room of One's Own* (London, Grafton, 1977; 1st published 1929).

Wu, Xiaozhou, 'Tom Jones and Ju-lin Wai-Shih as Novels of Manners: A Parallel Study of Genre', in *Journal of Oriental Studies,* vol. XXXI, 1993, No. 1 (Hong Kong, Centre of Asian Studies).

Xiao Feng 'The Story of Xiao Hong' (Xiao Hong chuan) in *Prose* (*San wen*) (Hundred Flowers Literary Publisher (*Bai hua wen yichu ban she*), January/February 1980).

Xiao Hong, *Market Street: A Chinese Woman in Harbin*, trans. Howard Goldblatt (Seattle, University of Washington Press, 1986; 1st published in Chinese, 1936).

Xiao Hong, 'After Reading *Daughter of Earth* and *Restless Days*' (*Da di di er nu yu dong luan shi dai*) in *July*, No. 7, Chungking, 16 January 1938).

Xiao Hong, *Tales of Hulan River*, trans. Howard Goldblatt (Hong Kong, Joint Publishing Co. 1988; 1st published in Chinese, 1941).

Xiao Hong, *The Field of Life and Death*, trans. Howard Goldblatt (Bloomington, Indiana University Press, 1979; 1st published in Chinese, 1935)

Xiao Hong, 'A Remembrance of Lu Xun' in *Renditions,* trans. Howard Goldblatt, pp. 169-190 (Hong Kong, Spring 1981).

Xiao Hong, *Selected Stories*, trans. Howard Goldblatt (Beijing, Panda Books, 1982).

Xiao Hong Studies, Harbin, University of Teacher Education (in Chinese) (Heilongjiang, c. 1983).

Xiao Si, 'Loneliness Among the Mountain Flowers – Xiao Hong in Hong Kong', trans. Janice Wickeri in *Renditions,* Nos. 29 and 30, pp. 177-181 (Hong Kong, 1988).

Xiao Si, 'Shame' (in Chinese), in *Sing Tao Daily* (Hong Kong, 1 November 1994).

Yang, Winston L.Y. and Mao, Nathan K., *Modern Chinese Fiction: A Guide to Its Study and Appreciation* (Boston, Hall, 1981).

Zhou Jingwen, 'In Memory of Xiao Hong' (in Chinese) *The Times Critique*, vol. 33, issue No. 12 (December 1975), also in *Da Ren Weekly*, No. 2, pp. 39-42 (26 February 1976).

CHAPTER 22

FINDING XIAO HONG

'Having seen the copy of your broadcast, I realise you are deeply in love with my late wife Xiao Hong and her works,' wrote Duanmu Hongliang to me on 6 April 1995. And he joked, 'I am so happy about this. If you were not a woman, I would have felt jealous.'

What, then, of the relationship between the historian and her characters?

In the last chapter, the conference paper, I explored the relationship between Xiao Hong and Agnes Smedley – one across space, China and the United States. The fact that the two knew each other is only part of the equation. A comparison of their experience and expression stood without that.

Here, in looking at my relationship with Xiao Hong, time is as relevant a dimension as space. But I will start with space – that is, Xiao Hong as Chinese and myself as English; and, to do so, I shall look first at my relations with the Hong Kong-based Chinese researcher on Xiao Hong, Xiao Si (Lo Wai-luen).

I went to see Xiao Si not long after I was asked to write about Xiao Hong. I met her at her university with a colleague of hers, an acquaintance of mine, as interpreter. Although the interpreter was helpful, she was not essential. Our mutual interest in Xiao Hong, body language and Xiao Si's better English than she had confidence in would have sufficed.

I wanted particularly to explore a remark of Xiao Si's in her article 'Loneliness Among the Mountain Flowers – Xiao Hong in Hong Kong' (*Rendition*, 1988). Xiao Si had met Duanmu in Beijing some years before I did and heard from him the story about burying half Xiao Hong's ashes in the grounds of St Stephen's Girls College. She agreed to try and track them down. In her article, she speculated about building works and changes over the post-war years that might have disturbed them, and she concluded with the words: 'On my return to Hong Kong, I went several times to St Stephen's and stood outside, feeling wretched, trying to figure out what to do. But my finding those ashes would depend on the will of heaven.' (p. 181)

Sitting beside Xiao Si, I asked her if that is how it had really been; she admitted that it was. I therefore developed a theory with her that this was the Chinese way – to palely loiter, to dream, to imagine, not to press the issue. She seemed to agree. On a later occasion, on the telephone, I speculated with her that Duanmu's own search for the ashes of his wife was similar: he did not really want to see that jar of her remains dug up from the ground; the memory of the burial, the dream of the finding was more important. Indeed, when I sent Duanmu a 1930s map of the grounds I told him of my conversations with Xiao Si, adding, 'So I realise that I'm intruding when I send you this map and ask you to mark the place. I will understand if you are unable to do so, quite apart from the fact that it was 53 years ago.'

Earlier I had planned the piece that I would write about Xiao Si and Duanmu and my theory of the difference between their Chinese approach and my practical, persistent, heavy-handed, English one. But Xiao Xi pre-empted me. On 1 November 1994, she published her own piece, entitled 'Shame', in the *Tsing Tao Daily* where she writes a regular column. She wrote:

'So you just looked from outside the garden, and didn't go inside? Have you had any contact with the school authorities about the matter? Is that so? Really?'

The Western lady scholar kept on asking me questions, her sparkling blue eyes staring at me with incredulity. When I shook my head to give a negative reply, she shook hers as well. 'Oh! No! How could it be!' Suddenly I seemed to have a great fall. In hardly more than a murmur I told her that all I had done was to ask one of the teachers to pass on a message; and I had never followed that up. She then shook her head again and surprised me by saying that she had arranged an appointment with the school authorities, and would enter the school garden in a few days to clear the matter up.

The story is about half of the ashes of Xiao Hong buried inside the grounds of St Stephen's Girls College. Moreoever, she was going to check the records of Queen Mary Hospital, and those of the Red Cross. She wondered what the flats in Lock Road, Kowloon, had looked like, and how difficult it would have been to move about during the wartime chaos. In the face of her serious enquiries, I turned out to be a lazy student, caught totally unprepared; what is more, a student not using her brain.

She ascribed our different attitudes to our different cultural backgrounds.

Yet, upon reflection, I have to ask, why have I not followed up the story of Xiao Hong's ashes? Is it just a different cultural background? With years of research behind me, I consider that I have a serious attitude towards the checking of data. When compared with her, however, my deficiency stands out. I am afraid it is not a result of a difference in culture. It is my lack of patience; I give up too easily when my pursuit seems futile. For example, when the Luk Kwok Restaurant was about to be demolished, I wrote to the people in charge asking for access to the records; I told them of the significant role the restaurant had played in the history of Hong Kong's literary activities. When I received no reply, I simply gave up.

Two foreign scholars have been to Hong Kong one after the other, searching for references to the story of Xiao Hong. With Hong Kong as my field of study, I could do nothing but drop my head before them. What shame!

When I read that piece, my anguish at apparently showing Xiao Si up in that way knew no bounds. I consoled myself with the thought that her self-deprecation was cultural too. It had some similarities to English self-deprecation, though it had essentially Chinese characteristics. What is more, without Xiao Si's work, mine could not have started; she was my entrée. The point about scholarship is not only the building on the work that has gone before, but also the sharing, as Xiao Si has, without reserve, shared with me.

It seems to me, in trying to look objectively at the difference in style between Xiao Si and me, that I can better understand the differences between Xiao Hong and Agnes Smedley. And, in doing that, I can better understand each of them in isolation.

As for Duanmu, he really wants to find the ashes!

Now I come to my relationship with Xiao Hong. When I was first asked to write about her, I put off reading any of her writing for quite some time. I busied myself with reading everything about her that I could lay my hands on. I wrote to countless people who might have known her in Hong Kong, or Shanghai, or might have known the places she knew. I followed in her physical footsteps in Hong Kong. I became immersed in her life. And the more I became committed to her as a person, the more I put off reading what she had written, anxious that I might find myself disappointed by her writing. I might be left producing a conference paper about a body of literature that I could not wholeheartedly support.

Finally, on a trip to Beijing, I carried with me a copy of *Tales of Hulan River*. I had the morning to myself in our hotel room. I picked up the book and started to open it. Then I looked outside. It was a beautiful early November day, blue sky, golden sunlight sifting through the gently rustling leaves. I put the book down. I would go for a walk first.

When I got back an hour or so later, I immediately wrote an account of what I had seen. I described walking along a lane, or *hutong*, that could have existed since time immemorial. I described the hawkers peddling their wares, and the customers coming out of their courtyards to buy. I had been much taken by the experience.

Having got the duty of recording out of the way, I picked up *Tales of Hulan River*. The first two pages are about a hawker peddling his wares along a *hutong* in far off Harbin. Across 50 years, and all that space, Xiao Hong and I met, and linked arms.

*Susanna Hoe with Duanmu Hongliang,
Beijing, 1995*

Written June 1995.

INDEX

Wolf, M. (and R. Witke), 15, 17
Women, Asian, 219, 296; and bobbed
  hair, 99-101, 120; British, 142,
  185, 216; chastity of, 101; Chinese,
  3-4, 8; Chinese and Western, 3-4,
  11, 81, 187, 189, 214, 218, 227,
  283, 320; as domestic servants, 23;
  demonstrations, 105; economic
  status, 12-6, 118-9, 195, 237;
  education of 95-6, 188-90, 209,
  236, 239, 242, 247, 249, 254;
  emancipation of, 99, 105, 110,
  117, 189; equal pay for, 263 (see
  also factory workers); and their
  families, 99; as fighters, 99-100,
  110, 261; fighting for rights, 3, 14,
  99; health, 111; as lawyers, 97;
  freedom for, 261, 266; inheritance,
  249; independence of, 253 (see also
  International Women's Day);
  liberation and revolution, 259;
  literacy, 15, 106, 109, 114;
  marginalisation of, 97, 101, 209; in
  Northern Expedition, 99-101;
  Philippine, 219, 249, 265-6;
  politicisation, 106, 109; 'protected',
  231; as protesters, 94-6; provision
  of facilities for, 254; public office,
  9-10, 106; raising consciousness of,
  254, 295-6; rape, 249, 265; rights,
  302-3; in their own right, 124,
  302-3; Russian, 142-4; saleswomen
  (Chinese), 225; sexuality, 11;
  suffrage of, 6, 96, 105, 207, 211,
  255, 257, 263-4; Third World,
  186; traditional role of, 79, 119,
  235, 252, 264; travellers, 139–52;
  travelling with men, 3, 154-82;
  violence towards, 101, 103, 105;
  Western, 3-5, 47, 121, 145, 152;
  working, 263
Women of China, 106
Women and Chinese Patriarchy, 16, 195
Women in Chinese Society, 15
Women, Hong Kong, Encyclopaedia of,
  225-6
Women and Literature in China, 293

Women and Literature Symposium,
  Beijing, 283, 293, 322-3
Women, Marriage and Politics 1860-1914,
  35
Women's department (Wuhan), 101
Women's Feature Service, 5-6
Women's studies (see History)
Wong, Agnes, 271
Woolf, Virginia, 6
Wu Pei Fu, Marshal, 240
Wu San-kei (Wu Sangui), General 85-
  8, 89
Wu The-ch'ing, Mme, 240-1
Wuchang Women's Union, 99
Wuhan (Hankow [Hankou], Wuchang,
  Hanyang), 100, 261, 286, 308,
  312, 315
Wujin, 94
Wusih (Wuxi), 21, 94

Xiao Hong (Hsiao Hung), 4, 6, 25-6,
  127, 134, 267-74, 275-82, 283-
  323, 331-35; and Agnes Smedley,
  267-8, 275, 283, 286, 289, 295,
  298-300, 308-13, 315 17, 323-4,
  326, 331; on Agnes Smedley, 286-
  8, 311-2; appearance, 306, 308;
  attitude to war, 286, 313;
  background and childhood, 267,
  284, 289-91, 298, 301-3; in
  Beijing, 304; as drifter, 303; death
  and burial, 272-4, 279-81, 331;
  and Duanmu Hongliang, 268, 271,
  275, 313, 315-6, 331; English
  translations of, 284, 301; as
  feminist, 293-5, 297-8, 320-3,
  305; on gender relations, 289; and
  grandfather, 302-3, 308; habits,
  303, 317; Harbin and Hulan River,
  267, 295, 297, 299, 302-4, 313;
  health and hospitals, 268-70, 275,
  277, 315, 317-22; in Hong Kong,
  267-74, 275-82, 294, 313-21;
  language, 317; and Lu Xun, 267,
  305, 308-12; at Lin Yin Tai, 269,
  316-7; marginalisation and
  sexuality, 303-6; and marriage/